POET-SAINTS OF INDIA

This volume is a collection of papers presented at a two-day seminar organised in 1991 in Hyderabad by Samvad, the Centre for Creative Dialogue. Samvad is concerned with the complex of dialogue in which implicit responses interact reflectively with social structures. To identify these responses in different areas is to discover the usable past in cultural streams like literature and religion.

A study of the Indian poet-saints is an attempt in this direction. These poet-saints were great integrators responding to experience from the most earthy angle and yet catching a glimpse of divinity in it. They wrestled with words only to discover the resultant distortion. In their awareness of the profanity masking the ultimate reality they sound a poignantly modern note.

The aim has been to cover as many linguistic groups as possible so that a concerted, comprehensive picture emerges. There have been poet-saints in all parts of the country. When diverse forces are dividing the people in the name of religion, caste or region, the poet-saints continue to serve as a powerful integrating force. This is possibly their greatest contribution. Therefore, apart from providing intellectual stimulus, it is hoped that the essays in this volume will illumine and enrich our lives.

M. Sivaramkrishna, former Head, Dept. of English, is the founder of Samvad, the Centre for Creative Dialogue. He has also been actively participating in the activities of the Ramakrishna Math for the last four decades. He has spoken and written extensively on literature, philosophy, religion and psychology. He has published widely; some of his recent books are: *Contemplating Swami Vivekananda* (1995), *Ramakrishna Gathaprana: Musings on Holy Mother* (1995), *Radiant Eternity* (1995), *Ramakrishna: The Unique Phenomenon* (1993) and *Gadia Katha* (Telugu, 1994). He is on the advisory board (Telugu) of the National Book Trust, New Delhi and a Panel Member of the UGC Panel for English and Western Languages. Presently he is engaged in a UGC Major Research Project on "Indian Theories of Interpretation".

Sumita Roy teaches English at Osmania University. She is closely associated with Samvad and actively involved in the various programmes of the Ramakrishna Math. She has presented papers and published articles. Her published works include the volumes *Consciousness and Creativity: A Study of Sri Aurobindo, T.S. Eliot and Aldous Huxley* (1991) and an abridged version of *Twenty Thousand Leagues Under the Sea*. She is working on a UGC Major Research Project on "Indian Philosophic Prose in English".

Prof. Sivaramkrishna and Dr. Sumita Roy have jointly authored/edited a number of volumes some of which are: *Perspectives on Ramakrishna Vivekananda Vedanta Tradition* (1991), *Never Say No to Life: A Biography of O.P. Ghai* (1993), *Reflections of Swami Vivekananda: Hundred Years After Chicago* (1993), *Art of Writing a Biography: Structures and Strategies* (1995). They have completed a work on the biography of an eminent freedom fighter and journalist of Hind Samachar fame, Lala Jagat Narain, entitled *Punjab's Pride: Lala Jagat Narain*. They have plans to bring out a five-volume encyclopedia on Ramakrishna-Vivekananda Vedanta.

Published by
Sterling Publishers Private Limited

POET-SAINTS OF INDIA

Edited by
M. SIVARAMKRISHNA
&
SUMITA ROY

A Sterling Paperback

STERLING PAPERBACKS
An imprint of
Sterling Publishers Private Limited
L-10, Green Park Extension, New Delhi-110016

Poet-Saints of India
© 1996, M. Sivaramkrishna and Sumita Roy
ISBN 81 207 1883 6

All rights are reserved. No part of this publication may be reproduced, stored in a retrieval system or transmitted, in any form or by any means, mechanical, photocopying, recording or otherwise, without prior written permission of the publisher.

Published by Sterling Publishers Pvt. Ltd., New Delhi-110016.
Laserset at Vikas Compographics, New Delhi-110029.
Printed at Ram Printograph (India), New Delhi-110020.
Cover design by: S.K. Berry

PREFACE

This volume is a collection of papers presented at a two-day seminar organised by Samvad, the Centre for Creative Dialogue, in November 1991 at Bharatiya Vidya Bhavan, Hyderabad.

Samvad is a fledgling centre which believes in the intrinsic interconnections found potentially in various dimensions of manifest creativity. If creativity is basically effective surprise it is evident in all activities — secular and sacred. The formalising of this creativity is as significant as its relishing. To use the appropriate words from our own tradition, both *pratibha* and *pragnya* are necessary for creativity. Therefore, a dialogue involving the perception of the creative structuring and the critical restructuring is indispensable to a balanced view of things. The work of art, said the extraordinarily creative genius of our century, Ananda Coomaraswamy, is a product at once of wisdom and method, of reason and art. Putting this in terms of contemporary thinking, it can be said that every utterance, every sentence and perhaps every monologue is oriented towards an anticipated, implied response and it is in dialogue with utterances that have already been made. All this also interacts with the social situation around.

Samvad, therefore, is concerned with this complex of dialogue in which implicit responses interact reflectively with social structures. It believes in identifying the spectrum of these responses whether they manifest themselves in art, sciences, or other areas. The corresponding strategies demand discovery of a usable past. And nowhere is this past more pervasively present than on two cultural streams: literature and religion.

The Indian poet-saints were, from this perspective, great integrators responding to experience from the most earthy angle and yet catching a glimpse of divinity in its very mud and mire, its garlic and saphire. They wrestled with words only to discover the resultant distortion and in their awareness of the profanity masking the ultimate reality they sound a poignantly modern note which assaults us with a shock of recognition.

For instance, Tukaram in one of his *abhangas*, so very beautiful even in translation where the message comes through spontaneously and effortlessly, seems to speak to us with an immediacy that is peculiarly modern. He says:

> In this age of evil
> Poetry is an infidel's art.
> The world teemed with theatrical performers
> Their craving for money, lusting for women and sheer reproduction
> Define their values and priorities
> And what they mouth has no connection
> With their own being.
> Hypocrites, they pretend such concern
> For where the world is going
> Talk of self-sacrifice
> Which is far from their minds.
> They cite Vedic injunctions
> But can't do themselves any good
> They are unable to view
> Their own bodies in perspective
> Says Tukaram
> A tortuousome death awaits all those
> Whose language is divorced from being.
> (tr. Dilip Chitre, *Tuka Speaks*)

To explore the implications of this loss of being, the result of dissociation from redemptive language was the implicit intention of the seminar on the Poet-Saints of India. To discover strategies of redemption, to identify the paradoxes involved in such an attempt, and, above all, to appropriate the residue of the live, spiritual consciousness of these poet-saints constituted the overall cluster of intentions animating the seminar. The aim was to cover as many linguistic groups as possible so that a concerted, comprehensive picture would emerge.

The organisers are happy that scholars who have done considerable work in this area responded to their invitation. It was indeed heartening to see many young people enthusiastically welcoming this opportunity for an exposure to what is certainly a dimension of Indian creativity of enduring significance.

Preface

The editors would like to acknowledge their deep sense of gratitude for the privilege of having the Inaugural Address delivered by Rev. Paramarthanandaji of Ramakrishna Math, Hyderabad. In him can be found a rare blend of the Word both as language and as music. Therefore, his words provided the right tone and proper direction to the deliberations of the seminar.

Sincere thanks are also due to Shri B. Arogya Reddy, Principal, St. Mary's Junior College, Hyderabad. He is a dynamic figure whose college is itself a manifestation in the field of education of an irrepressible creativity. His eagerness to sponsor the seminar and his involvement with all the stages of its organisation speak about the breadth of his vision and commitment to values.

A word of appreciation for the authorities of the premier cultural organisation, Bharatiya Vidya Bhavan, for coming forward to co-sponsor the seminar. The organisers are especially thankful to Shri T.H. Chaudhury, the Chairman, and Shri Achutan, the Registrar, of the Bhavan for this spontaneous gesture of goodwill.

It is difficult to enumerate all the friends and well-wishers whose active help and cooperation have gone into the successful organisation of the seminar.

To Shri S.K. Ghai of Sterling Publishers we express our thanks for his unfailing cooperation on all occasions.

Since Smavad is dialogue, it seeks to free itself from the heat and dust of ordinary, academic, cerebral exercises. The participants in the seminar and the readers of this volume, too, it is hoped, are *sahridayas*, if not *sadhakas*, seeking, with a sense of togetherness, clarity, both secular and sacred, in these troubled, tortuous times. The aim of the discussion, therefore, is to illumine and enrich our beings.

M. Sivaramkrishna
&
Sumita Roy

CONTENTS

	Preface	v
	Contributors	xi

SECTION I

1.	Inaugural Address *Swami Paramarthananda*	2
2.	Bhakti Movement: Some Perspectives *M. Sivaramkrishna*	7
3.	Hindu Bhakti and Christianity: Some Comparisons *B. Arogya Reddy*	14
4.	Sufi Tradition in Indian Poetry and Music *Siddiq Ali*	17
5.	Bhakti and Music *M. Radhakrishna Sarma*	25
6.	Poetry and Religion *Rama Nair*	28
7.	Religious Note in Indian English Poetry *Sunaina Singh*	38

SECTION II

8.	Kabir *Indu Vashisht*	48
9.	Rahim *K.L. Vyas*	54
10.	Surdas *Rajkumari Singh*	61
11.	Sant Tulsidas *Kamala Ganorkar*	66
12.	The Divine Ferryman: Guru Nanak *Lalitha Jayaraman*	70
13.	Valmiki's Humanised Imagination *Y.L. Srinivas*	79
14.	Ravidas *Sheela Devi*	85

SECTION III

15.	Dadu Dayal *Sujatha Nayak*	90
16.	Tukaram *P.S. Deshpande*	101
17.	Mirabai *Shanta Subba Rao*	111

SECTION IV

18.	Tyagaraja *M. Suryanarayana*	124
19.	Krishnamacharya *M. Kulasekhara Rao*	139
20.	Annamacharya's Sringara Sankirtanalu: Some Poetic Strategies *R.M.V. Raghavendra Rao*	145
21.	Vemana *G. Lakshminarayana*	151
22.	Pothana *C. Murali Krishna*	155
23.	Bhakta Ramadas *A. Ramakrishna Rao*	159

SECTION V

24.	Haridasa Literature in Kannada *K.G. Narayana Prasad*	166
25.	Purandaradasa *B. Ramachandra Rao*	173
26.	Kanakadasa *N.R. Shastri*	181
27.	Bilwamangal *A.V. Suresh Kumar*	191
28.	Andal's *Tirupavai* *Mohan Ramanan*	193

SECTION VI

29.	The Bhakti Tradition and Ramprasad *Tutun Mukherjee*	206
30.	Bauls: The Singing *Sadhakas* of Bengal *Sumita Roy*	219

SECTION VII

31.	Ashtachap and Tallapaka Poets *R. Suman Lata*	232
32.	Mirabai and Mahadevi Verma *Moutushi Chakravartee*	241

CONTRIBUTORS

Swami Paramarthananda, Ramakrishna Math, Hyderabad.
Dr. M. Sivaramkrishna, Professor and Head (retd.) Dept. of English, Osmania University, Hyderabad.

The following teach English at Osmania University:
Prof. Siddiq Ali
Dr. Rama Nair
Dr. Sunaina Singh
Mr. Y.L. Srinivas
Mr. G. Lakshminarayana
Dr. C. Murali Krishna
Prof. N.R. Shastry
Dr. A.V. Suresh Kumar
Dr. Tutun Mukherjee
Dr. Sumita Roy

The following teach in Osmania University in other departments:
Dr. M. Radhakrishna Sarma, Professor and Head (retd.) Dept. of Ancient Indian History, Culture and Archeology.
Dr. Indu Vashisht, Dept. of Hindi.
Dr. K.L. Vyas, Dept. of Hindi.
Dr. M. Kulasekhara Rao, Dept. of Telugu.
Dr. K.G. Narayana Prasad, Dept. of Kannada.
Dr. B. Ramachandra Rao, Dept. of Kannada.
Mr. B. Arogya Reddy, Principal, St. Mary's Junior College, Hyderabad.
Dr. Rajkumari Singh, Dept. of Hindi, SRAS College, Hyderabad.
Dr. Kamala Ganorkar, Dept. of Hindi, Vanitha Mahavidyalaya, Hyderabad.
Ms. Lalitha Jayaraman, Assistant Editor, *Guardian*, Hyderabad.

Ms. Sheela Devi, Dept. of English, St. Mary's Junior College, Hyderabad.

Ms. Sujatha Nayak, Dept. of English, St. Ann's College, Hyderabad.

Dr. P.S. Deshpande, Dept. of English, Marathwada University, Aurangabad.

Ms. Shanta Subba Rao, Dept. of English, Vanitha Mahavidyalaya, Hyderabad.

Mr. M. Suryanarayana(retired), Dept. of Chemistry, DNR College, Bhimavaram.

Dr. R.M.V. Raghavendra Rao, Dept. of English, Bhavan's New Science College, Hyderabad.

Dr. A. Ramakrishna Rao, Dept. of English, JNTU, Hyderabad.

Dr. Mohan Ramanan, Dept. of English, University of Hyderabad.

Dr. Suman Lata, Dept. of Hindi, Hindi Arts College, Hyderabad.

Dr. Moutushi Chakravartee, Dept. of English, Pre-examination Training Centre, Ranchi.

SECTION I

1

INAGURAL ADDRESS

Swami Paramarthananda

Friends, I have come here neither as a very great authority on music nor a competent person to inaugurate this seminar. I have always loved music; therefore, I feel a oneness with the musical saints. When I was requested to come here I thought it was a great opportunity to renew my acquaintance with them. From that time onwards my mind and heart are constantly ringing with music.

I remember a story which I would like to share with you. Once a politician was invited to inaugurate a seminar on the qualities of mud. While introducing the guest the organisers said, "We have a distinguished person to inaugurate this seminar on the qualities of mud and his head is full of that now", meaning, indirectly, that his head was full of mud! Similarly, my head is full of music now.

I love music because music is the language of the heart. It is not the language of the tongue. You can captivate anyone by music — not only human beings but animals, too. Therefore, it is an honour to participate in such a function.

The seminar is about the Poet-Saints of India. There are two words involved in this: poet and saint. When we study the lives of saints we find that almost all of them were poets, though all poets may not be saints. But the saints were all poets. And this is not confined to any particular region, language or sect. We find saints from all parts of India, starting from Kerala to Kashmir, and Assam to Gujarat, wherever we go we come across poet-saints. They are a great force, a great integrating force amongst us. When other forces have been trying to disintegrate the country in the name of religion, caste and many other factors, these saints travelled from one end of the country to the other spreading the gospel of harmony, universal brotherhood and love. This has been their greatest contribution.

Narada Bhakti Sutras, one of the very important texts on bhakti, says in one of its *sutras*:

> Tirthi kurvanti tirthani
> Sachastri kurvanti shastrani
> Sukarmi kurvanti karmani.

What it means is this: we all go on pilgrimage to purify ourselves, to wash off our sins most of the time. But we come back from the holy places without any change. We remain as we were before.

Sri Ramakrishna used to say that Ganga has a purifying effect. In spite of bathing in Ganga people continue to be sinners. How is this? Has the river lost its capacity to purify? In his usual humorous manner Sri Ramakrishna analysed this by saying that when people enter the water of Ganga for a bath all their sins leave them and sit on the trees nearby. So long as they are bathing the people are pure. Once they come out of the water, the sins mount on their backs and return with them to their native places.

So Ganga has not lost its purifying power, yet we continue to be sinners and do our evil deeds. But when these saints travel from one place to another by their association the holy places become holier. The same thing happens to Ganga, too.

When Bhagiratha was bringing the river down from heaven, Ganga questioned him, "I am so pure; here I enjoy the holy feet of the Lord. You are taking me down to earth where lakhs of sinners will take their bath in me. What will happen to me? Who will purify me?"

Bhagiratha then assured her that many saints would come to bathe in her water and they would purify her.

So, when we take a bath in Ganga it is to purify ourselves. When great saints take a bath there they purify the water of Ganga. That is the effect of these saints. They move from place to place spreading the message of harmony, the message of peace, the message of interpersonal relationships. But we must be able to absorb this message and understand the spirit behind it in order to derive some benefit from the message of these saints.

Sri Ramakrishna often said that a monk goes to many places carrying his *kamandalu*, the water vessel made of bittergourd. In every holy river he bathes, he dips the *kamandalu* in the water. In spite of this, its bitterness does not go. It remains as bitter as ever.

Purandaradasa says something similar in one of his songs:

Manasudhi illedavage mantra da phala deno
Tanasudhi illedavage tirtha da phala deno

What he means is this: What is the use of sacred mantras to a man who has no purity of mind, and what is the use of going on a pilgrimage when he is impure in body?

The same song goes on to describe how the fish, crocodiles and other water animals living in a holy river get no purity out of the water they inhabit. Another illustration is of a crow in Srisailam. It seems there is a crow made of stone in Srisailam which always looks at the image of Siva. But no benefit comes to it. The crow remains a stone forever.

It is therefore said that to take a bath externally in hundred holy rivers is useless as long as a person does not take an inner bath, meaning, that he does not purify himself. To derive any benefit from external sources we should first have purity within us. For this the easiest and the best path is that of devotion, bhakti.

Moksha sadhana samagriyam
Bhakti reva gariyasi
(Of all the spiritual *sadhanas* the easiest and the best is bhakti.)

Bhakti can be attained either through singing or through the repetition of the divine name. It is no wonder, then, that all these great saints were inevitably poets, too. Take the representatives from the south: Swati Tirunal, Tyagaraja, Purandaradasa, Kanakadasa, Andal, Ramadasa; then in Maharashtra we have saints like Jnanadev, Namdev and Tukaram; in the north there are saints like Surdas and Mirabai; in the east Kamalakanta and Ramprasad, and in recent times, of course, we have Ramakrishna and Vivekananda.

All of them were poets and melodious singers too. They were poets not in the ordinary sense, stealing words from here and there. Their poetry sprang from the bottom of their hearts. It was the outpouring of their inner feelings. That is why their authenticity and power remain undiminished after centuries. Their songs continue to have a great impact and shower spiritual benefit on us.

Vivekananda believed that the greatest aid to the practice of keeping God constantly in mind is music. The Lord Himself told Narada, the great teacher of bhakti, "I do not live in Heaven. Nor do I live in the heart of the yogi. But where my devotees sing my praise there am I."

Thus, music has such tremendous power over the human mind that it brings concentration in a moment. Even the dull, ignorant, low brute-like human beings who never steady their minds even for a moment at other times cannot remain unmoved by music. When they hear music they immediately become charmed and concentration comes naturally. Even the minds of animals become quiet by music. Therefore, Vivekananda rightly said that music is a noble art and for those who understand it, it is the highest worship.

I would recommend a recital of devotional music after the two days of discussion on the poet-saints. There is, of course, an important purpose served by discussions — they create an awareness in us and a sense of appreciation for our tradition in religion and music. We are all musical in one way or another but we are not aware of this. Most of the time our music is confined to private enjoyment of it. But in devotion there is no distinction between private and public. It is open to all. It is a mode of expressing ourselves freely.

That is why Tyagaraja says in one of his songs that when music is combined with devotion it becomes sweeter. The same idea is expressed by Purandaradasa in another song. He creates a fine recipe for *payasam*: to Rama *nama payasam* you add Krishna *nama* sugar and then mix it with Vithala *nama* ghee. When you taste this you will find what an unforgettable taste it has.

So this is the music that has been given to us by these saints, these great musicians. They have given us this sweet music without any selfish motive behind it. Their only aim is to express their inner feelings.

If you read *The Gospel of Sri Ramakrishna* you will find it full of songs. The ideas that could not be conveyed through long hours of discussion and argument were effortlessly clarified by simple songs sung in a beautiful, soul-stirring way. People used to get elevated and transformed by it.

Music has this great capacity. And all the saints whom we are going to talk about in the next two days are musical saints. What a great contribution they have made towards Indian culture, religion and philosophy!

Unfortunately, modern day music is becoming a series of meaningless sounds. Music without devotion is useless and insipid. The combination of music and devotion gives great joy and spiritual benefit. One feels automatically elevated to a higher plane. This has been the contribution of all these poet-saints of India. We are very fortunate that Indian culture and heritage has innumerable such poet-saints whose contribution is immense.

Music knows no language barrier, it is immaterial whether you understand the text or not. When you hear a good song composed by a great saint, your mind naturally gets elevated. Therefore it is befitting that we should rethink and discuss the beautiful, lofty spiritual ideals and principles given to us by such great personages as the poet-saints.

I feel it a great honour conferred on me to be asked to inaugurate this seminar. As I have said, music is my life. I do not claim to be a great musician but I admit that I have derived immense spiritual benefit from music. Every day I sing for an hour in our Ramakrishna Temple. The whole day's stress and strain disappear in that one hour. That is my personal experience. Therefore, I feel extremely happy to come here and share my ideas with you and pay my homage, my humble homage, to all the great poet-saints of India.

2
BHAKTI MOVEMENT: SOME PERSPECTIVES

M. Sivaramkrishna

This note is structured after a traditional Indian rhetorical mode called *anubandha chatushtaya*. There are four components to this expository structure: *vishaya, prayojana, adhikara* and *sambandha*. *Vishaya* is, obviously, the subject matter, the thematics of the proposed area; *prayojana*, also identifiable with *phalasruti*, is the gain thereof, the concrete result of this exercise; *adhikara* is the target audience for whom this is meant, determined by the Hindu belief in competence crystallised in the complex called *samaskaras*, the antecedent predispositions which impel intellectual levels and existential practices. Finally, *sambandha* is the relational space the concerned subject occupies *vis-a-vis* the other disciplines.

I

Let me begin with *adhikara*. This expository exercise is primarily for those who share the basic belief in the possibility of apprehending truth through cultivation of the interior being. A cognate qualification is openness and receptivity to the experience of this truth as transcendental, as unavailable to ordinary sensate modes. Above all, it involves the assumption that language is both a trap and a mode of release, that the relation between the Word and its referent is *not* always arbitrary or conventional. In effect, the Saussurean linguistic system needs to be willingly, qualifyingly neutralised. There are areas where the Word is the truth. All these assumptions, one should add, are not necessarily inherent; they can be acquired as any other talent. But acquisition depends on intrinsically potential hinterland making the operative acquisitional process possible.

II

So far as *sambandha*, the relational space, is concerned, the poet-saint is neither an exclusive, purely creative artist nor a wholly saintly figure impervious to contingent reality. Thus, he/she is rooted in "the mud and mire, the garlic and sapphire" of "real" life but with antennae tuned to catch the truths denied to merely referential language dimension. This is, as it were, to cite Eliot, belief that poetry is more than "a mug's", merely verbal, "game." In effect, the area of awareness evoked through the word by the poet-saint has built-in resistance to secularising the literary text.

III

This resistance brings us to the *vishaya*: the thematics. In one of his poems — a typical cluster of intricately structured images — Kabir says:

> Speech is priceless
> if you speak with knowledge.
> Weigh it in the scales of the heart
> before it comes from the mouth.

This artlessly simple poem reflects the structure, function and ideology of the poet-saints. The weighing of words in the scales of the heart defines the *source*, speech subjected to a precedent process of knowledge and, experience before its emergence marks the *structure* of ideas and images. The logic of being is the being of language — language as an expressive as also a constricting mode, indispensable but inadequate, a glass through which we see, as it were, darkly. Whether it is the *doha* of Kabir, the *abhanga* of Tukaram, the *kirtana* of Tyagaraja or the *vachanas* of Kannada poets, the invariable process is dislocating language to deconstruct what traps us thereby: the word itself. Eventually the glass grins and, as Tukaram says:

> I pine
> For the truth
> It's therefore I worry
> About words.
>
> (Chitre, 1991:16)

This worry is central to the poet saint, for his/her sorrow is the sorrow that words are the awareness that words block. Says

Tuka:

> My knowledge of you
> Is reproduced
> From
> Learnt words:
> It's like
> A treasure
> Extracted
> From a mirror.
>
> (ibid.)

This "treasure" is a strange treasure, expressive only through paradox, obscurity, wit and conceit. It is, says Kabir,

> A flame without a lamp,
> a lamp without a flame,
> an unsounded sound that sounds without end.
>
> (Hawley and Juergensmeyer, 1988:57)

or, as Ravidas says:

> Your handiwork: the world;
> what could I offer more?
> I can only wave your name like the
> whisk before the gods.
>
> (ibid., 27)

The exasperation-fascination with words is not exclusive for the poet-saint. This "rough rhetoric", as Linda Hess calls it, is a shared one. In the words of Kabir:

> Everyone says words, words
> That word is bodiless.
> It won't come
> on the tongue.
> See it, test it, take it.
>
> (Schomer and McLeod, 1987:131)

Therefore, the job is to identify the difference between word and word but differentiate, simultaneously "the essence word" (Schomer, 1987:131). This parallel quest marks the transition through the *sant* from the medieval to the modern.

From this perspective, the language of the poet-saints is marked by a significant dimension. Surfacially, this is emergence of the vernacular, of anti-structure. Nevertheless, it also exemplifies the two basic dimensions of language described by Antonio T. de Nicolas, as that of integrating and that of transcending. This would mean not rejection of the Other but subsuming it as an invariable of an implicate order. Thus several worldviews are integrated without centralising any one. Says Nicolas:

> Disparate linguistic contexts embodying different ways of viewing the world...may be integrated within a transcendent context not by rejecting the reality of any of the previous frameworks, but only by changing to a transcendent 'viewing' of the world implicit in the internal dynamism of the languages themselves.
>
> (1976:10)

This would mean a fascinating creative tension between the cultural specifics and the residue of transcending significance. To use the philosophical typology suggested by Derrida the language of the poet-saints of India is both "specific" and "exemplary" — specific to the idiom of a culture and exemplary in possessing elements of universal significance. This is, in de Nicolas' insight, "a complemen-tarity of languages." He says:

> This integrating and transcendent context is a language, as well, and the totality of its manifestation is the result of viewing the world from the heights of a cultural embodied vision. In this manner, a complementarity of languages is suggested under a transcendent and unifying language; and each language is torn from its opposing demands of exclusivity in language in exchange for a way of viewing and acting in the world which is eternally (*nitya*) efficient.
>
> (ibid.)

Apart from these facets, the language of the *sants* also exemplifies what is called *sandhyabhasa*. This is "intentional language" — but intention camouflaged, usually by paradox.

From I *OR* Thou to I *AND* Thou

One invariable of modernity is paradox: the perception of incongruities yet retaining the nucleus of creativity which attempts resolution. Thus an uneasy *scepticism* is poised alongside a desperate search for faith. Committed to *image* and *symbol*, modernists are yet iconoclasts. *Sensuous*, they are also ascetic. Indeed, the *profane* and the *sacred* are in strange transposition. Above all, the modernist is fiercely *individualistic* with an irrepressible longing for a meaningful relation to the community. Songs, it is rightly felt, are composed in isolation but are communed with in public. Quintessentially, a *confessional*, the deeply idiosyncratic note with belief in redemption through language.

These elements of modernity are deeply imbedded in the poet-saints. For one thing, they represent temporally, the quest for authentic experience validated individually and not mediated by *smriti*, even the Vedic texts are not exempt from scepticism. In the post-modernist idiom, the foundational narrative texts are, to a large extent, decentred. As Vemana, the sixteenth/seventeenth century Telugu poet-saint puts it:

> Unless words are shed
> the Word is unattainable;
> Until the Word itself withers
> the mind remains wayward;
> Unless the mind focuses
> there is no freedom!

More forthright is Appar, the Tamil poet who says:

> Why chant the Vedas? Hear the Shastra's lore?
> Why learn daily the books of right conduct?
> Why know the six Vedangas again and again?
> No release except to those who constantly meditate on the Lord.

These are some of the paths mapping the typical cluster of complex responses which characterise the quest undertaken by the poet-saints.

IV

Finally, the *proyojana*, the necessity and the result that accrues from the exercise: this has a twofold impact. The poet-saint's involvement with questions, doubts, despair and disbelief, leading finally to some kind of acceptance, surrender, total faith brings him/her a gain which is one dimension while the listener/reader of these songs gets a gain of possibly a different yet comparable nature.

Both the levels speak of a preoccupation with the inward being but with no dearth of openness to existential frames of reference. The poet-saint sings to articulate the uniqueness of his/her experience which puts this implicit dimension in explicit terms, exploring the apparently incomprehensible in language which goes beyond mere literal meaning. This expression of the reality of their experience involves the exploration of a vast range of attitudes that are felt by the composers and intuited by the reader/listener tuned to that dimension of being.

The cluster of responses that the world of sense experience evokes may, in the case of certain temperaments, gradually or suddenly bring about a desire for something different; thus begins the inward quest. The initial effect of this transformation is one of defiance or revolt. The singer believes, but he/she is forced to this belief almost against better judgement. The result is the recurrence of doubt and despair alternating with deep faith. In the absence of what the mind considers as concrete proof of reciprocation from the Other there is a dominance of the attitude of defiance. The dimension of belief receives many jolts of revolt. The believer alternates with the rebel and demands proof of the authenticity and viability of this novel vision.

This involves the making of demands which leads to the next step — a different attitude — and that is one of supplication. The transition from total dependence on oneself to the acknowledgement and acceptance of the Other is an essential prerequisite for this frame of mind. It also circumscribes surrender which is a logical offshoot of supplication. Surrender dissolves the dimension of doubt/despair because the division between good/bad, welcome/unwelcome, fortunate/unfortunate, defined from the point of view of the experiences of the external world no longer have the earlier relevance. At every instance there is a total reversal of interpretation and comprehension from the earlier state. The entire world is seen in different hues and from this altered vision awakens total, all-encompassing love, that which has been identified in all modes of inward quest as the core of the redemptive principle.

Thus it is that the poet-saints enriched the tradition of inwardness by making available the individual and the particular to the community in generalised terms, involving as it does, one of the most ancient and inherent tendencies of human endeavour in terms which are startlingly modern; reading them affords a dimension of experience to the aspirant which may be unavailable through any other occupation. And that is the fruit of this whole exercise.

References

Antonio T. de Nicolas, *Meditations Through the Rig Veda: Four Dimensional Man*, 1976

Chitre, Dilip. *Tukaram*, Penguin Books, 1990.

3

HINDU BHAKTI AND CHRISTIANITY: SOME COMPARISONS

B. Arogya Reddy

This short note is an attempt to identify some points of comparison between the Indian views on bhakti and the Christian concept of devotion.

To begin with, both the perspectives are committed to a personalised approach to religion. As such, mystical experience — direct, immediate awareness, without any mediation — is given primacy. To apprehend the Ultimate Reality not scholastically, not cerebrally, but directly as one's felt being, is central to both the *bhakta* and the Christian mystic.

With primacy thus accorded to felt experience, we have in both the systems, an assertion of the individual. In the bhakti tradition, the sants were — unlike impersonal Vedic seers — given to affix their own signature to whatever they articulated. Thus we have the tag line associated with Kabir, Mirabai, Surdas, etc. Though this is not similar or exact to the Western traditions, we do have distinct mystical approaches associated with St. Augustine, St. John of the Cross, etc. These are, interestingly enough, both monastic and mystical schools. Thus a comparison between the "sant" and the saint is an area which sustains scrutiny.

Another interesting feature is that — contrary to the general trend in Hinduism — the bhakti school gave rise to "text"/guru centred mystical path. As in the Franciscan, the Augustinian and other groups, we have the *Kabirpanthis*, the Dasa followers, etc., among the poet-saints. Analogous to this is the concept of the prime *Acharya*, we have the Popes in the Christian Church. Both represent spiritual figureheads, though the role of the *Acharyas* —

such as Ramanuja, Madhava and Vallabha — is much more spiritually complex that the comparable figures in the Christian order.

One more significant point of comparison is the attitude towards the outer and the inner. As Rabindranath Tagore says, "true spirituality...is calmly balanced in strength, in the correlation of the within and the without" (1913, 1971:127). The neglect of one has led to imbalanced growth of the other. Thus the secular and the sacred are often allowed to become targets of dissociation of sensibility. The result, so far as India is concerned, is rigidities of caste, dominance of priestcraft and hegemony of the establishment.

In these terms the mode of protest implicit in the bhakti movement is easily comparable to the Protestant one in Christianity. Both attempted to free religion from ritualism, formalism and priestcraft. Implicit here is the attempt to democratise the accessibility to spiritual truth with salvation potentially available to all. In other words, theologically *both emphasise* "grace" and not "*karya*", so that action in this regard is possible for all. Indeed, once the caste rigidities are dissolved and bhakti identified as the residue of emotional recycling available to all, it is not birth, as in caste, but one's own individual volition that determines being.

It is significant in this regard that Chaitanya and Kabir are often compared to Martin Luther in terms of their sharing the element of protest. Another extension of this comparison is to consider, in depth, the parallelism between "Nirguna" and "Saguna" schools of bhakti on one side and the Protestant and Catholic groups on the other. Such a comparison would surely yield several points of contact. Indeed, recent studies noted the comparison that is obviously valid between Kabir and Amos or Jeremiah.

Finally, the emergence of vernacular languages as vehicles of sophisticated literary modes is a point worthy of comparison. Wherever bhakti poets appeared it led to the emergence of a strong, infinitely flexible language. Whether it is Marathi in Tukaram, Kannada in the Dasa *sahitya* or Hindi in Kabir, Gurumukhi in Nanak, Telugu in Vemana, we have the irrefutable evidence of a literature crystallising as the nucleus of an alternate tradition to the one available in the Vedic Great Tradition. This "little" tradition in its commitment to *"sabad"*, the "Word" is easily comparable to the authoritative nature of the King James Version of *The Bible*.

These are areas which need further scrutiny.

References

Tagore, Rabindranath, *Sadhana*, Madras: Macmillan and Company, 1913. 1971.

4

SUFI TRADITION IN INDIAN POETRY AND MUSIC

Siddiq Ali

Sufism or *Tasawwuf* is the mysticism developed by the Muslims from the seventh century onwards. *Tasawwuf* has been broadly defined as an emotional approach to the reality of life. The Sufis believe that the spiritual world can be reached only through feelings since intellect has no access to it. According to the Sufi belief a Divine essence permeates the whole universe and everything in it. The Sufi in a higher stage of mystical insight becomes oblivious of the material world through which divine truth is perceived and feels nothing except the existence of the Divine (Sadiq, 1984:8).

Tasawwuf can be interpreted from the spiritual, theological and philosophical standpoints. *Tasawwuf* is mainly concerned with the "relation between soul and God, various degrees of spiritual perfection on the Divine path, the merging of the individual will with the Divine will, the gnosis or the esoteric knowledge, the annihilation of all human qualities and realisation of the Divine Attributes, the soul's effacement (*fana*) and permanency (*baga*), the truth (*al-Haqq*) and the perfect man (*Insan-ul-Kamil*) which are personally experienced by the Sufis in their mystical states" (Bhatnagar, 1984:3).

Tasawwuf has very often been attacked for its advocacy of inaction. A study of the lives and teachings of the great Sufis, however, dispels this charge. *Tasawwuf*, in fact, advocates active benevolence and service to mankind. In a world increasingly becoming intolerant *Tasawwuf* has taught tolerance. The early Sufis held the view that all systems contained an element of truth and were divine in origin. They endeavoured to bring man close to man at a time when theologians were doing everything to breed violence and hatred. They condemned the clergy whose piety and devotion, they felt, were motivated by the desire for reward in the hereafter.

A Sufi strives to attain a mystical state in which a direct vision of reality is possible. He exercises great spiritual discipline in order to seek God. The eminent Sufi, Khwaja Banda Nawaz of Gulbarga, has said that the most important thing for a seeker of God is "*Ishq* or ardent love of God" (Waliuddin:11). He has given a detailed account of various disciplines a Sufi has to undergo to achieve the ultimate mystical state. These are:

1. *Zikr* or remembrance or recollection of God, performed silently or aloud;
2. *Muraqiba* or contemplation or meditation of God;
3. *Rabita* or close association with the *Pir* or spiritual preceptor of God.

Likewise, different stages and stations of Sufi path have also been described by scholars of Sufism. They are *tawba* (repentance), *wara* (abstinence), *zuhud* (austerity), *faqr* (poverty), *shukr* (gratitude), *tawwakul* (trust in God), *sabr* (patience), *rida* (satisfaction). The last stations on the mystical path are love and gnosis, *mahabba* and *marifa*.

Obscurity surrounds the early history of Sufism in India. However, the first Sufi known to have travelled to India was the celebrated Sufi martyr Mansur-al-Hallaj who went to the gallows for saying *anal-Haqq* (I am the Absolute Truth or I am God). It was during the eleventh century that India attracted the attention of many *dervishes* of Bhukara, Samarkhand, Iran and other countries. The most renowned among them was Ali Abu Hassan Hujwiri, the author of the well-known Persian manual *Kashf-al-Mahjub* who came to India in the later part of his life and settled in Lahore. The history of Sufism in India, however, begins with the establishment of the *chishtia* and *suharwardi* monasteries or *khankhas*, the two earliest orders, the former founded by saint Khwaja Moinuddin *Chishti* of Ajmer and the latter by Shaikh Bahauddin Zaki in Multan in the thirteenth century. Two other orders which gained acceptance were the *Qadrai* and *Naqshbandi* orders in the thirteenth and sixteenth centuries.

For a proper understanding of the Sufi tradition in Indian poetry it is appropriate first to examine the relationship between *Tasawwuf* and literature. According to authoritative commentators, *Tasawwuf* has played a significant role in Arabic and Islamic literature. Indeed, it is said that it has its beginning in Umayyas Dynasty (661-680). The origin of Sufi poetry can be traced to the woman saint Rabia of Basra who introduced the element of selfless love in the development of *Tasawwuf*. She was of the opinion that neither the desire for paradise nor the fear of hell should be the incentive for the prayer or love of God. She says: "In two ways have I loved thee — selfishly / And with a love that worthy is of Thee" (Rizvi, 1978:30). She prayed: "Oh God, if I worship Thee for fear of Hell, burn me in Hell, and if I worship Thee in hope of paradise, exclude me from paradise, but if I worship Thee for Thy own sake, grudge me not Thy everlasting beauty" (ibid., 31).

It was Ibn-al-Arabi, the twelfth century mystic poet who introduced the concept of *Wahdat-al-Wujud* (Unity of Being) which marked a watershed in the history of Sufism. Yet another aspect of Arabi's Sufi doctrine, *Wahdat-al-Shuhud* (Unity of Vision) is revealed in the following verse: "When my Beloved appears / With what eye do I see Him? / For none sees Him except Himself" (Schimmel, 1975:266).

Another dimension of Arabi's thought is reflected in the following verse: "He praises me, as I praise Him, / He worships me and I worship Him. / How can He be independent / When I help Him and assist Him? / In my knowing Him, I create Him" (ibid.).

The Sufis also made a significant contribution to the development of the Arabic language. In fact, a new language, that of experience and feeling, was born in the Sufi poetry of Arabia. A similar development can be traced in the literature of non-Arabic countries. The literary language of Iran is deeply indebted to the Sufi poets who gave voice to their yearnings. Persian poetry became the vehicle for the expression of transcendental love leading to annihilation of the self. During the twelfth and thirteenth centuries Sufi poetry reached its highest peak in the form of *masnavis* or narrative poems. The three great exponents of this style were the Sufi poets Sanai, Attar and Rumi.

In the poetry of Jalaluddin Rumi, Sufi poetry reached its greatest height. Rumi was the first Sufi poet to develop the theory of spiritual evolution. He believed that it is through *khashf* or Divine revelation in the heart that the mystic attains complete knowledge of God. Love, he felt was the driving force behind all revolutionary changes. In one of his *masnavis* he says:

> If this heaven were not in love, then its breast would have no purity,
> and if the sun were not in love, in his beauty would be no light,
> and if earth and mountain were not lovers,
> grass would not grow out of their breasts.
>
> (ibid. 293)

Rumi's attitude to love can be seen in yet another of his *masnavis*:

> From love bitterness became sweet, from love copper became gold,
> From love the dregs became pure, from love the pains became medicine,
> From love the dead became alive, from love the king is made a slave.
>
> (ibid.)

Literature of the Indian subcontinent, particularly poetry, has largely come under the influence of Rumi's work. Poetry written in Persian in India contains verses inspired by Rumi's thought and expressions. Most Indian poets considered Rumi a representative of the pantheistic school. He was also seen as a mouthpiece of Ibn-Arabi's ideas.

Urdu poetry not only imbibed the Persian tradition but also broadened it by adding Indian values to it. As a matter of fact, the development of Urdu language parallels the development of the Hindu-Muslim culture. The need for a language to give expression to the feelings and attitudes of a composite culture gave rise to the new language.

Sufi saint Khwaja Moinuddin Chishti was the first to learn an Indian language and use it for daily intercourse. In fact, the development of Urdu poetry owes a great deal to efforts made by the Sufi saints. Baba Farid of Pakpatan and Bu Ali Qalandar of Panipat also used Hindustani for their poetry. Amir Khusro, the famous disciple of saint Nizamuddin Aulia was the first major poet to use the Khadi Boli, sometimes referred to as Lahori or Dehlawi. His *dohas* continue to be popular and sung by the *Qawwals*. During the rule of the Delhi Sultans a number of *khankhas* were established by Sufi saints in Gujarat. The saints used another variety of Urdu called Gujur to communicate with the masses. Among the saint poets of Gujur who composed mystical poetry were Shaikh Bahauddin Hajan, Shah Ali Jiogani and Gazi Mohammad Rival. These poets also dealt with the Sufi doctrine of *Wahdat-al-Wujud*. Their poetry was influenced by the bhakti movement.

Khwaja Banda Nawaz, the Chishti saint of Gulbarga, was the first to use Decanni Urdu as the literary medium in early fifteenth century. Better known for his prose works, he did not neglect poetry. Though not a dominant feature of his poetry, *Tasawwuf* was a very important element of his poetry. Wali Decanni migrated to Delhi in 1707 and allied himself with the Naqshabandi Sufi order.

Interestingly two of the "greatest pillars" of Urdu literature belong to the Naqshabandi order. Mazhar Janjanan and Khwaja Mir Dard (ibid., 372). Mazhar Janjanan was held in high esteem as a mystic and according to one critic the reverence paid to him as a saint influenced the critical estimate of his poetry (ibid., 107). Nevertheless he is regarded as the first poet who made a departure from the *I'ham* school and gave currency to *Urdu-e-Muallah*.

Khwaja Mir Dard was the son of Mohammad Nasir Andalib (1697-1758), a Sufi poet in his own right. His father was the spiritual guide for him. A great mystic of the eighteenth century, Mir Dard is considered by many to be the first poet in Urdu poetry to strike an authentic mystic note (Sadiq, 1984:140). His greatest work is *Ilmul-Kitab*, his spiritual autobiography, in which he deals with his religious ideas and mystical experience. His poetry, he always felt, came to him by inspiration and he did not have to make any effort to write it. From his mystical verse it is possible to construct a whole system of Sufi doctrines ranging from the "unreality of life and its joys and sorrows, unity of existence, the greatness of man in the hierarchy of life, of self and suspicion of worldly life, pietism, contentment and resignation" (ibid., 141). The following verses of Dard illustrate some of the Sufi doctrines preached by Dard:

> Although Adam had not wings
> yet he has reached a place that
> was not destined even for angels.
> In the state of collectedness the single beings
> of the world are one
> all the petals of the rose together are one.
>
> (Schimmel, 377,82)

Sufi tradition is an integral part of love poetry written in Urdu and hence the Sufi strain is visible in modern Urdu poetry.

"Sufi poetry written in Hindi added a new dimension to Indian mysticism and a new lyrical and colourful way by which to achieve an ecstatic state," says a critic (Rizvi, 1978:379). Hindi indeed established a bridge between the Sufis and the bhaktas who also sought the higher reaches of Reality. Both the Hindi Sufi poets and bhaktas were radicals in the sense that they rebelled against all forms of religious formalism and orthodoxy. Their goal was to create a world of spiritual bliss. Kabir, through all his poetry, endeavoured to bring closer to each other the followers of Hindu and Muslim religions. In Hindi, Abdul Rahim Khankhana and Malik Mohammad Jayasi gave a new dimension to *Tasawwuf* by synthesising the Sufi and bhakti doctrines.

Several Sufi saints of India were obliged to use the vernacular in order to express the mysteries of divine love and devotion to their disciples. They abandoned high-flown theological Arabic or Persian and opted for the native tongue and its folktales to reach out to their disciples.

A common feature of Punjabi and Sindhi mysticism is the use of folktales for the expression of mystical experience. To the Sufis the popular tales of love were no ordinary love romances. The beloved to them was God Himself, the lover was the devotee or bhakta and the ordeals nothing but obstacles in the culmination of their goal which is union between the individual and the divine. The tragic tale of Heer Ranjaha was used by many poets to give expression to the mystical ideas about love. This story was given a classical form by Waris Shah. The greatest of the Punjabi mystical poets Bulleh Shah also deals with this theme in his poetry. In Punjabi and Sindhi Sufi poetry the longing soul represented by Heer is always a woman, a characteristic inherited from Indian influence.

The greatest of Sufi poets in Sindhi is Shah Abdul Latif. His collection of poems *Shaha-Jo Risalo* contains thirty chapters (*Surs*) named according to their musical modes, in addition to traditional Indian *ragas* like *Kalyan* and *Kebodh*. However, for the Sindhis the most popular poems are those in which Shah Abdul Latif relies on folktales dealing with the love stories of Sasui Punhu, Lila Chanesar, Mumal Rano, Sohani Mohar, etc.

The Sufis of India have made a significant contribution to the Indo-Muslim tradition of the country. *Sama* or the audition of music has always been a controversial issue in Islam. The Sufis of Chishti order considered *Sama* as a spiritual exercise and a means of revelation attained through ecstasy or *Waid*. *Sama* in Sufi terminology means listening to music, singing, chanting and measured recitation in order to produce religious emotion and ecstasy. This Sufi practice is reported to have been introduced in India by Hujwiri. Nevertheless, it is saint Khwaja Moinuddin Chishti who regularly organised *Sama* by holding music festivals very often and with increasing abandon and ecstasy. The great Sufi saint of the fourteenth century Shaikh Nizamuddin Aulia of Delhi continued the tradition and earned the wrath of the orthodoxy. While the theologians tried unsuccessfully to uproot the institution of *Sama* in their zeal to preserve the *Sharia*, the Sufis successfully endeavoured to establish this institution which was one of the best means of attracting the masses. For the Sufis of the Chishti order *Sama* was not just an ordinary mode of worship but was a specific path leading to God.

Amir Khan, a close friend and disciple of Nizamuddin Aulia and the best poet of the early sixteenth century, is considered to be the founder of the Indo-Muslim musical tradition. He is credited with the invention of the *sitar* and several melodies for it which he created by blending Persian and Indian tunes. They were designed to be sung in Sufi *Sama* gatherings in which he himself participated. The Sufi poets of India followed the example of Rumi in applying the symbolism of music and dance to poetry, and by practising *Sama* with their disciples. Notwithstanding the orthodox aversion to this aspect of Sufism, the activity continues. Even a sober mystic and poet of Naqshabandhi order, Khwaja Mir Dard felt compelled to write a book in defence of music. Dard was well-versed in music and is said to have composed *khayal*, *thumris* and *dhrupads*.

The interaction between medieval Hindu mystic traditions and Sufism is a fascinating subject of study. Conflicting hypotheses have been presented by scholars regarding it. However, it is not difficult to find correspondence between several aspects of Sufism and Hindu mystic traditions. One notices a striking similarity between Sufi conception of *Wahadat-al-Wuhaud* and *Advaita* conception of God. Similarly the Sufi conception of *fana* corresponds with the doctrine of *Nirvana* and *Moksha*. The position occupied by the *Pir* or *Murshad* is similar to the one given to a *guru* in the *Upanishads*.

References

Bhatnagar, R.S. *Dimensions of Sufi Thought*, Delhi: Motilal Banarsidass, 1984.

Rizvi, S. Akhlas Abbas. *A History of Sufism in India*, New Delhi: Munshiram Manoharlal Publishers Pvt. Ltd, 1978.

Sadiq, Muhammad. *A History of Urdu Literature*, New Delhi: Oxford University Press, 1984.

Schimmel, Annemarie. *Mystical Dimensions of Islam*, Chapel Hill: The University of North Carolina Press, 1975.

Waliuddin, Mir, (quoted). *Khwaja Band-i-Nawaz*, Hyderabad: Dairatul-Maarif Press.

5
BHAKTI AND MUSIC

M. Radhakrishna Sarma

"Even as human personality depends on the persistence of memory, social life depends on the persistence of tradition. Tradition is society's memory of its own past. If we tear up the individual from his traditional roots he becomes abstract and aberrant," points out Sarvepalli Radhakrishnan. If Indian nationalism is to survive meaningfully commanding respect it cannot afford to be divorced from its tradition.

Music is one of the most vital components of this tradition. If lifting up of the whole of lower life and the impressing upon it of the values of the spirit was, as pointed out by Sri Aurobindo, the characteristic of the post-classical period, the chief instrument chosen for this was music. Expressions of bhakti made the most effective use of music. Saiva Nayanars, Vaishnava Alwars, the Siddhas, Virashaiva saints, Haridasas, Maharashtra saints, Gujarat's Narasimha Mehta, Mirabai, Akho, Sindhi Shah Abdul Latif, Kashmiri Jalladevi, Sikh gurus, Sufi poets, Mithila's Vidyapati, Assamese Sankaradeva, Bengal's Ramprasad, Ramdas, Tyagaraja and many others evolved bhakti through music. Therefore, it would be quite profitable to take a look at the nature of Indian music which makes itself such a powerful instrument for the expression of and immersion into bhakti.

Indian music takes as its starting point the general laws common to all the aspects of the world's creation. Starting from metaphysical principles, it recreates the theory of sound. It analyses and classifies all the possible ratios and relations between sounds. Indian music makes two approaches to the theory of sound. The first approach is *Marga* (directional) and being based on absolute laws, is universal and unchangeable, while the other is *Desi* (regional) which varies endlessly according to place and time. Svaramarakatanidhi says, "The music which is called *Gandharva* (*marga*) is that which has been from time immemorial practised by the Gandharvas (celestial singers) and which leads surely to *moksha* (liberation), while the *gana* (*desi*) music is that which has been invented by composers (*vaggeyakaras*) in conformity with the recognised rules, and which pleases people. Gandharva music always follows the rules of theory." There is no sound without a meaning, say the Vedantists. In the guise of sound, it is only manifested idea that we perceive and it is logical to conceive a theory of sound based on the ideas represented by the sounds.

The essence of Indian music is lost when one studies it through a non-Sanskrit Western language like English. The reason is that the theory of Indian music is reflected in every one of its terms. Explaining the relationship between music and yoga Sutasamhita says: "*gitiganena yogassyat yogadeva sivaikyata,/ gitijnoya-diyogena sayati Paramesvaram.*"

Sivasarasvam gives supremacy to music over other paths leading to *moksha* in the following words: "*Trivargaphaladassarve danayanjnya japadayah/Ekam samgitavynanam caturvarga phalapradam.*"

The base of music is *nada* and it is defined as created due to the fusion of life and fire: "*Nakaram prananamanam dakaramanalamviduh/Jatah pranagni samyogattena nadobhidyate*" (without nada there is no *gitam*, no *svaram*, no *raga*).

Sruti means that which is fit to be listened to. "*Svatoranjayati sroto svara yabhidhiyate.*" The English word "note" does not suggest this. The musical term *murcchana* means that which captivates the listener. *Gamaka* delights the listener: "*Svarasya rampo gamakah srotru citta sukhapah*" (Sangitaratnakaram).

Raga which is the key to the uniqueness of Indian music is described as: "*Yasau dhvani visesastu svaravarna vibhusitah/ ranjokojana cittanam, saragakahkathito budhaih*" (Sangitaratnakaram).

Another characteristic *Tala* of Indian music is: "*Katomargah kriyamgani grahojatih katalayah/yatih prastara kaschati tala prana dasasmrutah.*"

These aspects of Indian music are to be deeply delved into. *Sankarabharan, Hamsadhvani, Mohana, Kalyani, Pantuvarali,*

Bhairavi, Bhoopati and the innumerable *ragas*, their characteristics, meaning and compositions in these *raganas* need extensive study. Then alone will the relation between bhakti and music become clear. When one of the great musicians of our times, Yehudi Menuhin says that "Indian classical music compared with our Western music is like pure crystal, it forms a complete perfected world on its own, which any admixture could debase. It can be seen that Western music is at this moment particularly ripe for Indian influence," probably he is providing an approach for us to study the problem we are investigating into, that is, the relationship between bhakti and Indian music.

6
POETRY AND RELIGION

Rama Nair

Poetry and religion are two indispensable components of the materialistic world we live in. To the sceptic these terms might appear redundant. For,

> under the influence of scientific assumptions, not only the psychic but the individual man and, indeed, all individual events whatsoever suffer a leveling down and a process of blurring that distorts the picture of reality into a conceptual average (Jung, 1958:13).

Poetry and religion belong to those realms of the human consciousness which are beyond the critical and logical assumptions of mere scientific enquiry. In today's highly industrialised economies, the relevance of poetry and religion towards the spiritual development of the human psyche is as important as it was in the past. Countless civilisations bear testimony to the fact that human beings do not live by bread alone, but "by every word that proceedeth out of the mouth of God." The "words of God" refer to those ideas expressed verbally, or visually by art, which bring about a communion between God and the human being. Poetry and religion enable the individual to free himself/herself from the tyranny of continuous anxiety caused by *avidya*, *kama* and *karma*, that is, desire and strife arising out of an ignorance of the ultimate truth. A person has to transcend this "egocentric" predicament if he is to achieve happiness. Poetry and religion, in different ways, pave the path towards spiritual liberation. As Marcus Aurelius Antonius had written:

> He who lives in harmony with his own self, his demon,
> lives in harmony with the universe, for both the universal
> order and the personal order are nothing but different
> expressions and manifestations of a common principle
> (Cassirer, 1956:23).

The theme of both poetry and religion is the representation of this "common principle". Before dealing with the interrelationship between poetry and religion, it is necessary to have a brief idea about the nature of the "reality" they deal with.

Religion is a social phenomenon that has existed since time immemorial. Neither can it be denied that the poetic utterance was the first mode of human communication. To the rational, religion might appear a "useful illusion" and poetry a "delightful fiction" — both seducing a person from what he/she would call "the harsh facts of reality." It is apparent that the nature of existence or "reality" has mystified people for centuries. In their attempt to understand the complex nature of "reality" which is beyond the power of words to define, humans brought into being various modes of interpretation. The materialist believes that each individual is a part and function of the material world in which he/she lives. The individual's actions are determined by the behaviour of the material world and are therefore limited in nature and scope. The idealist in the metaphysical sense believes that the world can be understood only through the ideas which the mind has of it. The world as we know it consists of finite facts. Cosmological and ontological arguments presuppose that the conditioned and incomplete realities we encounter should have some source which is not limited. It would assume that the harmony one perceives in nature could be the reflection/extension of a greater unity present elsewhere.

The presence of the Divine in nature was perceived in poetry and in religion. According to the Western and Eastern concepts of traditional metaphysical thought and art, the Pure Self is the principle by which all things "exist" as beings. This *atman* or self permeates all things. So it follows that the human individuality is only a reflection of the "Self". When the individual is isolated from the "Self" a person leads a meaningless existence, because reality is achieved only when the two are perfectly united. The individual exists only because it participates in the essence of the Self, and this essence transcends all existence, being the sole principle of all things.

The single unitary principle which pervades the universe is so vast and subtle that it cannot be easily comprehended. However, according to Tagore the poet has his own way of getting over this difficulty. Tagore believes this Supreme Principle capable of two functions: on one level it works as an impersonal force where truth is evident in its pure form. This level is comprehended by the philosopher and the scientist as it appeals more to the intellect. The Supreme Principle, on the other level, manifests itself on a different plane as pure joy. This is evident in the delightful display of beauty in nature. The poet reads in every movement of nature God's desire to shower love on him. Tagore asserts that in its emotional aspect the Supreme Principle manifests itself as a personality that reciprocates love.

Religious experience begins at the moment of apprehending that there is a "beyond". Since the nature of this "reality" is mysterious, the mode of acknowledging and articulating it in determinate terms is bound to be difficult. Human beings, through the instrument of language, aspire to reach the source of this mystery. The attempt, however, falls short; but they reach the nearest to it in language that is termed by Philip Wheelwright as "depth language" or "expressive language", the language that is to be found in poetry, in myth, and in religion. Their inferior attempts at imitation result in the "literal" or the "steno-language", which is the language of science consisting of precise logical denotation. Such language, then, could either be the result of logical reasoning which in today's world would be perfectly acceptable, or, it could be the result of an inner experience, an intuitive perception leading to a knowledge that ranged beyond ordinary perception and   day-to-day activities. This kind of illumination would take place in an intuitive mind, and not in the mind of an accurate reasoner. Such a mode of metaphysical enquiry could be termed as "transcendent" considering only that which lies beyond the reach of ordinary experience as what really exists.

The reality encountered in religion would be a transcendent reality. Religion attempts to discover the "beyond" within the human self. Religion at first begins on an incipient personal note. It is concerned, paradoxically enough, with the link between what is beyond and what is within. The ultimate reality is referred to as "God" because it is the embodiment of perfection.

But it is also designated as "God" when such a reality is apprehended in a personal way.

The religious experience of mystics begins in wonder at the ecstasy of the divine revelation. Poetic or artistic wonder comes closest to religion. The main reason for this is:

> that art has to do with reality in its more elusive individual form and exhibits to us those features of existence which touch off most readily the sense of the irreducible mystery in which all things, even by the mere fact of their existence, are set.... It makes the world, in its distinctiveness, yet more peculiarly and positively articulate, presenting us with significant mysteries which border on being religious and may merge almost into properly religious experiences. (Lewis, 1962:105-6)

Poetry and religion are based on wonder because both the poet and the religious person are fascinated by the realisation that the world in which we live is dependent on some absolute or unconditioned being of whom we can know nothing beyond the intuition of its unconditioned nature as the source of all other reality. The ambiguous nature of such an experience is the common factor in poetry and religion.

Of all the arts, poetry is considered to be the most condensed, intense and compelling form of communication. Some examples taken from the early history of religion confirm this. Primitive tribes, whilst performing their religious rituals, considered the incantatory power of words recited rhythmically to be most effective in stimulating their minds to a divine frenzy. It is the realisation of the word or "logos" that is most important in the highest form of poetry, that is, divine poetry. In Indian aesthetics, at the moment of transcendence, the word becomes a *mantra*. *Mantra* is generally described as "prayer" or as "mystic syllables" that are chanted during the performance of religious rituals. *Mantra* is a *sakti* or power in the form of sound which can evoke the primordial reality behind the uttered word.

The Romans called the Poet "Vates", that is, a Diviner, a Fore-seer, or Prophet. To Sidney the greatness of poetry lay in the fact that it imitated in antiquity and excellency the "inconceivable excellencies of God!" Sidney further states that.

Such were David in his Psalms, Solomon in his Songs, in his Ecclesiastes, and Proverbs, Moses and Deborah in their Hymnes, and the writer of Job, which, beside other, the learned Emanuell Tremellius and Franciscus Junius doe entitle the poetical part of the Scripture. Against these none will speake that hath the holie Ghost in due holy reverence (Sidney, 1977:49).

Poetry imposes order, harmony and a justness in our perception of reality. According to Shelley:

> Poetry in a general sense may be defined to be "the expression of imagination"; and poetry is connate with the origin of man.... Man is an instrument over which a series of external and internal impressions are driven... But there is a principle within the human being which produces ... harmony, by an internal adjustment of the sounds or motions thus excited to the impressions which excite them (Shelley, 1977:337).

Symbolism in poetry bring the divine and spiritual within the range of man's perception, as it embodies in concrete form the "intangible" aspect of God's power. Symbolism is an integral part of religious worship. The poet, through the use of image and symbol, apprehends the hitherto incomprehensible relationship between things, and makes this apprehension possible for others. Shelley defines poetry as "something divine," as it "makes immortal all that is best and most beautiful in the world" and "redeems from decay the visitations of the divinity in man" (365).

Wisdom which may be "external" to the ordinary person is conveyed by both poetry and religion. Their task is to direct one's thought to the existence of these "unfelt" values through a directly comprehensive mode of realisation. Though one cannot know God directly, yet one can know him expressly through symbols which make the transcendent significant in terms of the finite realities in which one is placed. In fact:

> The profane is the world of routines in which the whole is forgotten, the sacred is the individual seen in awe-inspiring relationship to the immensity of the universe (Thompson, 1981:65).

The great mystic poets attained a level of understanding that lay beyond the dogmas of science or orthodox religion. Those who did experience a vision of the logos used the language of myth and symbol to record the profundity of their spiritual illumination. Since language is an imperfect medium of communication, the intensity of such an experience is communicated through the poetic use of language where form and content, harmony and rhythm blend to recreate a symbolic vision of the poet's realisation.

According to William Irwin Thompson, there are four levels of myth. The most important is the fourth and highest level:

> The fourth level of myth is the vision at the summit, the vision where the mountain ends and the sky begins; gone is the arrogance of the positivist, and saint and scientist, philosopher and artist all sit down to listen to the music of the spheres. (82)

Poetry deals with the universal, and is indeed the transformation of Nature into an idealised state. While religion stresses the rationality behind the principle, poetry is concerned with the emotional absorption of its essential principle. Poetry and religion deal with the contemplation of the divine archetypal forms. The traditional concept of art believed that there is an eternal source of life. This source was variously called "the God of religion, the Absolute of philosophers, and the Truth, Beauty and Good of the artists, poets and mystics" (Raphael, 1977:7).

However, poetry and religion have a limited dimension. Though both help to heighten the perception of the individual consciousness to the various levels of reality, the state of the highest transcendence is available only to the mystics. Poetry can never be divorced from morality. The poet, like the prophet, in a state of divine inspiration, reaches the height of poetic excellence. Poetry *can* make one aware of metaphysical reality, but it affords only a temporary release from the natural world of misery and suffering. A mystical experience on the other hand, leads to total freedom from the material bondage of this world. Through poetry an individual experiences a temporary state of *ananda* or bliss. This state is not one of *moksha* or true enlightenment as it is not one based on perfect knowledge. This bliss can be experienced permanently by the saint, or the *jivan mukta*, who has attained perfect knowledge.

Poetry helps to dispel emotional ambiguity while religion helps to articulate the belief in an unknown force. While religion adds stimulus and depth to artistic activities of various kinds, the artist orders the universe in a way that appeals to our imagination. Poetry acts as an instrument which reveals these religious insights. The creative power which religion releases is viewed as a source of inspiration by the poet. Religious imagination needs to be controlled and made objectively viable. Poetry and religion are integrated as the former disciplines the latter. If religion is concerned with worship, then the material factors which affect worship are undoubtedly of the utmost significance. Carlyle referred to poetry as "musical thought" embodying the essence of the divine in its lyrical notes. In worship, as H.D. Lewis observes:

> we are not merely aware of God, and of His dealings with us, we react to this awareness and adopt certain attitudes towards God, reverence, love, submission, penitence, and so forth (1962:175).

These worshipful attitudes have to be elicited and expressed through the material elements of worship. One of the ways in which such reactions can be elicited is through the poet's song. The poet expresses a certain attitude, mood or a nuance of feeling in his verse. These, by an affinity with, or a resemblance to the religious mood it evokes, create an appropriate personal relationship between the devotee and the object of his worship. Such moods can be expressed spontaneously by the mystic poets. In finding ways to express their love for God, they make their surrender complete. Words cease to become mere conventional symbols for things. They are not merely heard and understood but are experienced by the inner consciousness as living entities. Religion and poetry attempt to realise the "truth" of existence. But this truth becomes more profound and accessible when religion and poetry blend as in the verses of the mystic poets.

In poetry, as in religion, the individual consciousness is alerted to a new awareness of one's physical and mental environment. The poet may not be a teacher of moral precepts in the traditional sense. But by presenting a finer and objective view of the relationships that exist, he presents a particular illumination that enhances the worth of the world we live in. We are in a position, then, to view things with greater detachment and with a truer perspective. The devices the poet uses generate new images out of themselves, and further his attempts at unravelling the mystery of reality. In religion the same process occurs. Traditional symbols generate new images and new ideas, which in turn sharpen our perspective of the world. But while the poet is concerned with the finite environment, in religion the apprehension we gain about our environment is conditioned by its relationship to an unconditioned source. H.D. Lewis points out that:

> The inherent character of this experience points also in its own way to the appropriate focusing of it and predisposes it to a certain representation. This is where art is taken up into religion and serves to give firmer form and continuity to the religious insights, just as it may also predispose us to have them by the character it gives to the antecedent situation (ibid., 203).

In his own vision of the world the poet comes closest to the religious visionary or prophet, since he too deals with the ultimate mystery of things emanating from a transcendent source. Poetry shapes the creative religious images, and thus gets merged into the religious process. But while the prophet's revelation is determinate and particular, evoking a particular practical response to God, poetic revelation is concerned with a contemplative realisation of human existence. In poetry, the prophet might divine the message of God. Then, the poet becomes a visionary and a seer, too.

The Divine poet is one who has experienced the reality of the word or Logos, and who enables others to see the Divine. He is one who reveals his own self-realisation so that others can transcend the limitations of their self. God is viewed as the Beloved showering His Grace of Divine love on his disciples. The Divine poet of the East is an *avatara*, or God in human form. True poetry emancipates one from the illusions and ignorance of this world. Religion is the art that is born out of the inner freedom that results from the attainment of such divine bliss. Freedom lies in the realisation of the Divine within one's soul. Anyone below this level of inspiration may be poetic, but cannot be truly called a poet.

Every religion believes in devotion, discipline and self-realisation. The mode of realising it is through worship and prayer. There is a basic unity that binds all religions. Most religious thinkers have adopted a view that synthesises all these essential components into an integrated whole. Poetry assimilates, refines and absorbs the essence of these beliefs through myths and symbols. For instance, the love of Radha for Krishna cannot be interpreted as a standard of conventional morality. Rather, it expresses the fulfilment which the individual soul realises when it merges with the Divine Soul. Brindavan is symbolic of the field of human consciousness. Religious poetry is full of such symbolism. Great poetry has always been motivated by God and religion. The verses of the *Vedas*, the *Gita*, the *Bible* and the *Koran* are signifcant instances.

But, here again, there may be differing opinions. As Nizzim Ezekiel observes:

> poets who have mystical experiences and project them in verse have occasionally been successful but mystics who write poetry do it badly. Religious hymns, however notable the religious sentiment they express, are not notably poetic. Great religious poetry undoubtedly exists but the greatness is unequally divided between the poetry and religion, while perfect integration between the two is rare. To be good, poetry has to be an independent art (1987:230).

Religious knowledge arrives at the deepest truth. But the poet is qualified to do so only when he fuses thought and emotion in images which have moral and philosophical implications. When he does attain this level of transcendence, then poetry merges into the religious. Otherwise, we may be left with lower levels of poetry.

References

Cassirer, Ernst. *An Essay on Man*, New York: Doubleday and Co., 1956.
Ezekiel, Nizzim. *Critical Thought: An Anthology of Twentieth Century Indian English Essays* (ed. S.K. Desai and G.N. Devy). New Delhi: Sterling Publishers, 1987.
Jung, C.G. *The Undiscovered Self*, London: Routledge and Kegan Paul, 1958.

Lewis, H.D. *Our Experience of God*, London: George Allen and Unwin Ltd., 1962.
Raphael, R. *Ananda Coomaraswamy. Spiritual Frontiers of Art, Literature and Culture*, Madras: Rayappa Publishers, 1977.
Shelley, Percy Bysshe. "A Defence of Poetry" in *The English Critical Tradition. An Anthology of English Literary Criticism*, Vol.I (ed. S. Ramaswamy and V.S. Sethuram), Delhi: Macmillan Company of India Ltd., 1977
Sidney, Sir Philip. "An Apologie for Poetry" in *The English Critical Tradition. An Anthology of English Literary Criticism*, op. cit., 1977.
Thompson, William Irwin. *The Time Falling Bodies Take to Light*, London: Rider/Hutchinson, 1981.

7

RELIGIOUS NOTE IN INDIAN ENGLISH POETRY

Sunaina Singh

The scope of this paper is initially to trace the growth of spiritual or religious mode in the modern Indian Poetry in English; secondly, the form that their individual quest for God takes. It will be essential to understand the terms, religious, moral, spiritual, theistic, mystical *vis-a-vis* the material, non-theistic, rational and secular, before we analyse the nature and quality of religious poetry. We should then be in a position to recognise the similarity and the difference in the religious poetry written by adherents of different faiths.

To be religious in the commonly accepted form is to believe in God and all the supernatural adjuncts of such a belief. God is conceived with qualities as *saguna* and without qualities or attributes as *nirguna*. When He is invested with qualities like all-merciful, omnipotent, omniscient, the devotee seeks to enter into a personal relationship of adoration, awe, worship and love with the Almighty Father figure praying for redemption from evil and for spiritual enlightenment. The ways of providence appear strange and inscrutable, therefore, hardships and suffering inflicted upon the devout and virtuous have to be borne with unswerving faith in God. For the believer, God's ultimate judgement will be in favour of the virtuous — if not here, then in the hereafter. The concept of hell and heaven and the cycle of births and rebirths strengthen this belief.

The class of believers who do not cherish a personal God but have faith in a supreme, cosmic force, the oversoul of Emerson, envisage the immanence of such a force within the human soul, they need not necessarily have to believe in any form of *deu-ex-*

machina or God's direct intervention in human affairs or personal matters, or even in the supernatural props of heaven and hell. Sufis and mystic poets, who have such an unflinching faith in the spiritual resources of their own being, in *Atma-sakti* or liberated ones who are free from fear, cherish the oneness of God and the human being preach the principle of love, fraternity and peace against the forces of greed, hate and violence. One can categorise poets like Kabir, Tulsi and Mirabai who in their ostensible adoration essentially recognise the soul force energy of God in themselves in the form of Rama and Krishna. One can also include the mystic poetry of Tagore in this class.

A person's threefold relationship with God, other people and the universe (nature, ecology) has been the subject-matter of great poetry. The interconnection between these three form the bedrock of the philosophic thought in these poets.

The religious poets like Dante and Milton have their moorings in orthodox belief but are able to transcend the formalistic and ritualistic faith to perceive the deeper conflicts between good and evil, virtue and sin — in them religion gets pristinely spiritual.

There are other writers who cannot be labelled as religious or even theists as commonly understood, but are spiritual and sublime in essence like Shakespeare, Kalidasa and Dostoevsky.

One need not have to be religious in order to be spiritual. Even an atheist, a non-believer, a pagan can scale spiritual heights without binding himself to any organised dogma.

The spiritual is connected with the soul-force latent in every human being. This force includes and transcends the physical, rational and intellectual. The spiritual is also basically linked with the moral whose realm is the code of conduct in human relationships that lead to stability and strength of goodness and peace amongst people. Without such an ethical foundation, one cannot conceive of spirituality in the vacuum.

Against this perspective one has to analyse and interpret the religious or spiritual strain in some of the modern Indian poets in English. The post-independence poetry evinces a discernible rebellion against the earlier modes; it started in the early 50s and acquired shape and character in the 70s and later.

The salient features of the movement as suggested by P. Lal are a revolt against the pre-independent British romanticism and sentimentalism, and a rejection of mystical and spiritual poetry. If one agrees with the first assumption, one would certainly have reservations about the latter. The modern poet reveals a changed sensibility and a new awareness of his environment — and one does discern a religious strand of a totally different kind. As T.S. Eliot said, doubt and disbelief are a "variety of belief". Or, more aptly, to quote Tennyson, "There lives more faith in honest doubt, than believe me, in half the creeds." One gets acquainted with this trend in Modern Indian English Poetry like that of Kolatkar and Ramanujan. Hence, the religious poetry of our times takes into its ambit scepticism and scientific rationalism.

Religious poetry is expressed in different moods — often opposed and conflicting, for example, praise which rests on an intense eruption of faith, self-abnegation, self-remorse, a questioning of God's ways, a highly mellowed reconciliation and a petition to God. All these trends could be seen as the dynamics of religious change — part of an ongoing culture.

Helen Gardner evinces the reasons for the vital changes in religious poetry through the ages, thus: "Religious thought and practice, forms of worship and methods of prayer, personal religious experiences and religious feelings and religious conceptions of the good life are no more static through the centuries, *than are the arts*. Both change and develop by reason of their own inner principles of growth, and in accordance with, and in interaction with, social changes and intellectual movements" (1971:143). Some of the modern poets have literally eschewed the traditional reverential note. The poets write under the stress and strain of socio-economic pressures, and secular concerns, the end result being a demythicised strain bordering on protest underscored by parody and irony.

When one reads Kolatkar or Mahapatra the first impression is that one should know the tradition and culture before criticising it. Another reaction could be that their poetry functions as a search for the self — or one's cultural roots — this in some sense could be true of Ramanujan and Ezekiel, too. Although Kolatkar, Mahapatra and Ramanujan have a firm grip on the tradition of the past, they refrain from entertaining a celebratory attitude towards them. They do not subscribe to the blind acceptance of the orthodox version of our cultural heritage. Hence the probing of self, quest for roots and demythicised attitude.

Kolatkar's *Jejuri*, a poem with 30 sections, came into limelight with the award of the 1977 Commonwealth Poetry Prize. It is a poem where the traditional concept of pilgrimage to a holy place is mixed up with the idea of a weekend tour to a picnic spot, and the result is not a happy one. Manohar and Makarand make a one-day visit to the pilgrim centre of Khandoba. The details of the visit are presented to us through the consciousness of Manohar. A typical modern sceptic youth, his attitude to the place, its gods, myths and legends are unconventional, irreverent and mocking. The pilgrimage to Jejuri turns out to be more of a secular journey. It is this secular stance that makes the poet aware of some of the social evils which reflects in turn the poet's essential humanism. Whereas the devout do not attach importance to the incongruities, highlighted by the poet, to Kolatkar divinity co-existing with the exploitation, poverty and misery in Jejuri, or for that matter any pilgrim centre, is atrocious. Hence, there is a clash between belief and non-belief which has its roots in the bicultural conflict. This bicultural tension is explained by Sudhir Kakar (in a letter to Naipaul) thus:

> In India it is closer to a certain stage in childhood when the outer objects did not have a separate independent existence but were intimately related to the self and its affective states. They were not something in their own right, but were good or bad, threatening or rewarding, helpful or cruel, all depending on the person's feelings of the moment.

For an Indian external reality cannot be objective, very often it is interiorised/internalised. Hence the conflict in Jejuri.

In *Jejuri* the spatial distribution of thoughts could be seen as highly disproportionate. If the first section is about the bus-ride, from the second to the 29th it is devoted to various major and minor details of Jejuri, and the 30th section is "Between Jejuri and the Railway Station". This kind of distribution exposes the poet's stance of ridicule and mockery of the various aspects of the pilgrim centre. The very first poem evinces Kolatkar's secular attitude:

> You seem to move constantly forward
> to-wards a destination
> Just beyond the caste mark between his eyebrows.

The intention is to probe deeper and perhaps beyond the caste mark — into every aspect of the place with objectivity. In the next poem he exposes the hypocrisy of the priest — who is neither pious nor dedicated, as he is expected to be. Rather, he is a priest known for his avarice, waiting for the gullible pilgrims:

> Is the bus little late?
> The priest wonders.
> Will there be a puranpoli in his plate?

He is described further as a "lazy lizard" waiting to fleece the pilgrims of their money. The description strips the priest of his holiness. In "A Song for Murali" he is described as an "old lecher" for whom the carnal pleasures are more attractive than devotion and worship.

The poet's description of the Maruti Shrine reveals the uncaring attitude of the priest and devotees who seen to be oblivious of the dilapidated condition of the temple — occupied by a mongrel and its pups. In another "temple" one is greeted by a "wide-eyed calf" which has now turned into a cowshed, the dividing line seems to have become very thin:

> What is God
> and what is stone
> the dividing line
> if it exists
> is very thin
> at Jejuri.

Apart from the razor-edge irony one notices the close observations of the poet which permeate through the poem. However, despite the sarcasm, it is difficult to overlook the human traits in the poem. The protagonist ostensibly finds it difficult to reconcile myth and fact, miracles and failures; one finds him uneasy at the dilapidated condition of temples, the ignored gods, bad water supply, poverty, odious sanitation. All this reveals his quest for serenity and divinity — probably a new myth too. In his irony and observation he strikes a more religious note than the poets celebrating the god. Jejuri also reveals the influence of saint-poets such as Tukaram and Janabai to name two.

By way of illustration I would like to quote Kolatkar's own translation of Janabai and Tukaram:

> I eat God/I drink God /
> I sleep/on God
> I buy God/I count God /
> I deal/with God /
> God is here/God is there /
> Void is not/devoid of God /

Jani says:

> God is within/God is without /
> and moreover/there is God to spare.

Tuka 6 (Tukaram)

> Lacking the guile/of a mass hypnotiser /
> I merely extol your name/and sing your praise.
> Not being a miracle worker/or a faith healer /
> Without a train/of disciples to boast of /
> Being the patriarch/of a monastery /
> But a mere/shopkeeper /
> No high priest/no seer /
> No necromancer/No exorcist /
> No witch doctor/...
> There's no voodoo about Tuka /
> Tuka is like/None of these /
> Hell begotten lunatics. (1982:114)

The influence of these two poets on Kolatkar is obvious in his use of irony and satire to deflate the trappings of religiosity and priestcraft, without genuine spirituality. It is, perhaps, his quest for the religious or spiritual that has made him translate the works of these saint-poets.

Ramanujan, on the other hand, is preoccupied with the live-wire of tradition and culture. It is a quest for roots — hidden and half-forgotten — hence the need to probe and reacquaint oneself with it. The deep influence of the culture is manifest in his imagery, setting, milieu and the *spiritual vis-a-vis* familial preoccupations. His *Prayer* to *Lord Murugan* lays bare his close association with the classical Tamil form — it is a poem influenced by Nakkirar's *Tirumaru Karrupattai*. Ramanujan's poem is a happy blend of irony and prayer — the poet is trying deliberately to be irreverent:

> Lord of answers,
> cure us at once
> of prayers.

Ramanujan's criticism and sarcasm deflate the myths, folklore, rites and faith clustering around Lord Murugan. The speaker sounds rather cynical apart from being a sceptic. The poem proceeds from a joyous traditional fervour to turning away sharply into doubts and despair.

Ezekiel, experiencing rootlessness, both cultural and religious, faces an identity crisis. He seeks to turn from alienation to a sense of belonging. His *Hymns in Darkness* evinces his changing predicament.

> The Indian landscape sears my eyes.
> I have become a part of it.
> ... I have made my commitment now.
> My backward place is where I am.

The desire to belong is recurrent. Although an outsider to Indian culture, tradition and religion, he has made use of the Indian traditional ethos in a highly intellectual fashion. Ezekiel treats life as a journey where poetry is the chief source of "discovering and organising one's self" (Karnani, 1974:14). His religious poems wear the tone of irony:

> Do not chose me, O Lord,
> to carry out thy purposes
> O well, if you insist,
> I'll do your will
> please try to make it coincide with mine.

His poems reveal the "spiritual degradation" of modern man — and for him poetry has "therapeutic" value — there ostensibly is a need to speak aloud. In his *Egotists Prayer* he starts with a feigned submission to God, the cynic in him challenges God to teach him, reform him. There seems to be an odd mixture of defiance and submission bordering on arrogance.

> Who can rescue Man
> If not his maker?
> Do thy duty, Lord.

But gradually the arrogance is tamed, the egoism is displaced by piety. Throughout *Hymns in Darkness* the stress is on the individual quest for the durable value system.

The modern religious poetry derives its subjects from the stress and strain of socio-economic pressures. Hence, the need to agree with Frank Kermode's observation (although written in a different context): "It is sometimes said to be a characteristic of our times that we undo the spiritual structures of our ancestors; whatever they sacralised, we desacralise" — this is characteristic of modern religious poetry — which also reveals the poet's tendency to recycle the spiritual/cultural values of our ancient tradition. The emotion is kept under tight control and a severe objectivity seems to be a part of the poetry, be it of Kolatkar, Ramanujan or Ezekiel.

References

Gardner, Helen. *Religion and Literature,* London: Faber and Faber, 1971.
Kolatkar, Arun. "Tukaram and Other Saint-Poets" in *Journal of South Asian Literature,* Vol.x, VII, Winter-Spring, 1982.
Karnani, Chetan. *Nissim Ezekiel,* New Delhi: Arnold Heinemann, 1974.

SECTION II

8
KABIR

Indu Vashisht

There are no accounts or reliable sources giving information about the exact date or year of birth of Kabir. In the 1,200-year-long history of Hindi literature there has been no other philosopher-poet to stand comparison with Kabir except Tulsi, the devotee of Rama. Kabir exerted a lasting influence on Hindu thought and Hindi poetry through his extraordinary intellect, social commitment and magnetic personality. For the Hindus Kabir is a Vaisnavite bhakta, while the Muslims revere him as a peer, the Sikhs call him a *bhagat* and the Kabir *panthis* worship him as an *avatara*. Modern nationalists respect Kabir as the bridge between Hindus and Muslims; modern philosophers view him as an advocate of the religion of humanity. In the opinion of radicals he was a reformer, an opponent of the caste system, a strong supporter of the downtrodden. He is hailed as a revolutionary who spread the message of universal brotherhood, social justice and equality.

There is a story in vogue that at the time of his death at Maghar his Hindu and Muslim followers had a dispute among themselves about his last rites. This clearly indicates that Kabir was respected by both the communities, mainly due to his broadmindedness. Even the Sikhs feel that Kabir and his teachings are close to their religion. In the words of Dr. George Grierson, "Kabir's doctrine of the word *(sabad)* is a remarkable copy of the opening verses of St. John's Gospel."

The powerful character of Kabir is greatly appreciated by Western scholars. This has been most eloquently summed up by Grierson as follows:

> What a wonderful man Kabir must have been! A lowly Muslim weaver who by a stratagem gained accession to a Vaishnava community — universally despised and hated by both Mussalman and Hindu, maltreated by the Muslim emperor and persecuted by the Brahminhood of Benaras — with unparalleled audacity he dared to set himself face to face against both Islam and Hinduism, the two religions of the 15th century India, and won through. Each he attacked in its tenderest point — its shibboleths and its rituals — and over both he rode triumphant, teaching and converting thousands who became his devoted followers. Not only did he find an eclectic monotheism that survives in India to this day, but he became the spiritual father of Nanak who founded Sikhism... (1918:151).

Due to this great influence Kabir has been called the "Indian Luther". By the 18th century the voice of Kabir echoed even in Europe. Around the year A.D. 1758 Father Romba, an Italian cleric, translated Kabir's works into Italian. Western scholars like Mechalif, H.H. Wilson, Garsa-da-Thusy, Smith and others have made deep study of Kabir.

Indian society at the time of Kabir was full of evils, like blind faith, hypocrisy, caste distinctions and many more. Nineteenth century was the era of Renaissance. It was during this time that institutions like the Brahmo Samaj, Arya Samaj, Ramakrishna Mission and others launched powerful social reforms. Kabir was a great source of inspiration to them. Tagore and Gandhi too were greatly influenced by Kabir. The latter adopted the doctrines of Truth and Non-violence from Kabir's philosophy. Tagore considered Kabir's poetical utterances as the highest achievement among all Indian vernacular literatures. He declared that what Kabir had expressed in Hindi about mysticism has no parallel in Bengali. Gandhi is said to have claimed that his mother was a Kabir *panthi*.

Dr. Peethambardatt Barthwal in his book entitled *Gandhi and Kabir* has discussed the great influence Kabir had on Gandhi by saying that "The source of the Ganges of Gandhism is Kabir's teachings, which he imbibed along with his mother's milk"(51).

Comparisons such as these between Kabir and Gandhi abound in the Indian nationalistic literature of the 1930s and 40s.

As I. Madan writes: "If Gandhi had lived in the times of Kabir, he would have done what Kabir did. And, in turn, Kabir would do in our times exactly what Gandhi is doing" (1973:5). Like Kabir, Gandhi was also an ardent supporter of Truth.

In order to understand the true nature of Hindi bhakti literature we need to study the social, religious and political conditions prevalent then. The literature of the eighth to the fifteenth centuries is important. Those were the days of religious fanaticism. Slowly this started influencing the common man. The educated few veered to the popular opinion of the majority. Language and thought, too, moved towards the folk forms. There were social and political upheavals arising from repeated invasions. Unlike the earlier invaders the Moghuls did not attempt to establish an understanding with the people of this land for whom it was like a challenge. This can be viewed from two angles: first, the upper class were steeped in the hollowness of rituals, hypocrisy and narrow-mindedness; when they were harassed by the Muslims they would automatically abuse the lower castes and make them the target of their anger; second, the lower castes were ill-treated both by their social superiors and by the Muslims.

Due to the conservative attitude of the Brahmanic religion, these castes were attracted towards Islam. To them this new religion seemed more liberal. Therefore, the Muslims found it very easy to convert the lower castes and untouchables to Islam as soon as they conquered India. Of course, there were many people who accepted conversion on their own while some were also forcibly converted. In these circumstances the emergence of Kabir gave a great boost to the downtrodden people.

Kabir belonged to the community of weavers which was considered as a low caste. There are not many authentic sources narrating Kabir's life. The writings of his contemporary and successive generations of bhakti poets speak of Kabir more with reverence and devotion than with historic authenticity. There are a few references by Kabir himself, that he was born in Maghar and then came to Benaras. After extensive research it is widely accepted now that the birhtplace of Kabir is a place called Laharatara in Benaras. Kabir called himself neither a Hindu nor a Muslim. He preferred to be called a weaver. He may look a Muslim by appearance but he was a Hindu by *samskara*. He has

Kabir

constantly used the names of Hindu gods and goddesses, sages and other references from Hindu mythology in his writings.

Inducted into the sant *dharma* Kabir spent most of his time in *sadhana* and *satsang*. Even his married life was more oriented towards spirituality than worldly preoccupations. In spite of his being a *grihastha* he spent long hours in activities of inner transformation.

Kabir was greatly influenced by Hindu traditions. He was a strong supporter of *satya* (truth) and *ahimsa* (non-violence). He gave the utmost importance to the *guru* (teacher). He said that the path of *sadhana* cannot be pursued without the teacher. Teachers, according to him, are of three kinds: *manava guru, siddha guru* and *divya guru*.

The *manava guru* of Kabir was Ramanand from whom he received the initiation of *Ramanama*. His *divya guru* was none other than God himself. It is possible that he was blessed with His *darshan*, the vision of the Divine.

The works of Kabir can be classified into three categories: *Ramaini, Sakshi* or *Sakhi* and *Sabad*. The Ramaini describes the wanderings of the *soul (jeeva)* in this world; the *Sakshi* or the observer is a *doha* or couplet; and the *Sabad* or *shabda* is the word of the Master.

In *Ramaini* Kabir has mainly dealt with the creation, the soul and the world or *jagat*. *Doha* and *pada* forms of verse are used to express these. There is much space devoted in these verses to Kabir's ideas about *maya*.

The word *Sakhi* originates from the Sanskrit form *sakshi* meaning the witness of truth. Kabir has chosen this name because in these verses he has mentioned only those incidents which he witnessed through his senses and grasped/analysed through his intellect. There is no reference here to knowledge acquired through books.

Sabad can be used in two different senses: it can refer to the word of the Master or to a form of *pada*.

Kabir's *sadhana* was of the Advaita variety; he elaborated this in the *Ramaini, Sakhi* and *Sabad*. In Advaita the dominant feeling is that of the union of the *atman* with the *paramatman*. Kabir described the soul as a part of the *paramatman*. The *atman* is created by and finally unites with the supreme *paramatman* at the time of the body's destruction. To explain this idea Kabir has used a beautiful simile: a pot filled with water is floating in a river; once the pot is broken the water inside and the water outside mingle to become an inseparable whole.

Kabir acquired all this knowledge through "love" and not through books. He was illiterate. He believed that *yoga* was one of the means of attaining to the Supreme. Of course, he was not in favour of the difficult or tortuous ways of *yoga sadhana* practised by cults such as the Nathas and Siddhas. He vehemently condemned all hypocrisy.

By way of experience Kabir imbibed some *yoga sadhanas* of Natha *panthis* and *tantriks*. But the most powerful aspect of his devotion can be termed as "love". He gave utmost importance to love, though he did not deny the path of *jnana*.

In Kabir's usage the word *unman* popularised by the *tantriks* signifies the state which is above the ordinary mental state. It is akin to the state of *sahaja samadhi* which the followers of Natha doctrine subscribe to. Kabir's usage becomes evident in his famous verse:

bahari khoj janam gavaya
unmani dhyan dhan bhitar paya.

In Kabir's philosophy "love" is all-encompassing. *Yoga* and *jnana* are also founded on the base of love. Kabir professed his love for *Nirguna Rama*. He was of the opinion that there is no need for the Supreme to have any form because It is pervasive everywhere. In order to attain to the *Nirguna brahman* he described three stages of love: *anurag*, *virah* and *milan*, in other words, affection, estrangement and final union.

In the first stage Kabir drowned himself fully in *Rama rasa* with his heart full of *prema rasa*. This is a different order of emotion from passion which has its foundation on worldly desire; whereas love of this kind has its ultimate goal in finding the essence of life. There is a complete surrender in this love, followed by a purity of thought and mind, loss of self or ego and constant preoccupation with the object of love — God.

The second stage symbolises the great sorrow felt in estrangement. This is in proportion to the intensity of the love for the Divine. The sorrow of Kabir is for the love of Rama which has reached its climax. In addition, there is anxiety about the delay in union with the beloved. The *bhakta* or devotee has only one desire: that his body be made into a lamp, the *jeeva* be a wick, his blood the oil to keep the lamp burning. After lighting the lamp with the light of love he waits patiently wondering when he will be able to get a vision of his beloved. In Kabir's view it is not easy for everyone to find the Lord. Those who have found Him had to cry first. Unless the soul burns itself in *viraha* there can be no *milan*. In this state even the agony of separation is welcome because it keeps the mind engrossed in the beloved. The bonds of love become stronger during separation. This constant contemplation of the absent Lord is *sumiran*. The depth of love is so great that its impact is indelibly etched on the physical body. The urgency of complete dedication comes into love only due to separation. Kabir has repeatedly stressed the fact that he is like a pet dog of Lord Rama. He follows the Lord as per the dictates of His pulling the chain. He would like to stay with his Lord constantly. Separation for even a fraction of a second is unbearable to him.

Like all *bhaktas* Kabir attributes many qualities of greatness to his beloved, God, and laments his own pitiful state. There is great pleasure to be derived from this expression. Kabir feels that to get the beloved one has to completely sacrifice himself. We have to make much preparation before we become suitable to enter His house.

Kabir has loved that God who is imperishable. He could visualise that his beloved is *ananta*, He cannot be destroyed. Although Kabir lived in this materialistic world of squalour and evil he created within himself a beautiful world filled with the glory of the Divine.

(Translated from the original Hindi by Dr. Suman Latha and Dr. K.L. Vyas)

9

RAHIM

K.L. Vyas

I

Chah gai chinta gai, manua be parwah
Jinko kachi na chahiey, we sahan ke sah.

(Desire is gone and anxiety is over; the mind is free from care. Those who have no wants are the king of kings.)

Rahim, in this deceptively simple couplet, *Doha*, rightly describes the qualities of a saint who has no worldly desires, who neither longs for material wealth nor craves for political power. A saint is a detached soul who strives for higher values of life and spiritual bliss.

There are many examples of this: Kumbhandas, the great singer-poet of the *Ashtachap* school, the disciple of Vallabhacharya, was once invited by the great Mughal Emperor, Akbar, to adorn his court. The poet turned down the emperor's invitation and said:

ka sant sikri so kam
awat jat panhaiya tuti, chuti gayo hari nam.

(What work have the saints at Sikri, the Mughal capital? Our footwear is worn out and broken by travelling up and down there which has finally made us forget the name of our Lord.)

In other words, Kumbhandas was telling the great ruler: what if you are a king? We are saints, that is, we are the king of kings. Even Kabir, the great mystic poet of Hindi, though poor and illiterate, had the courage to say almost the same thing to Sikandar Lodi, the ruler of Delhi.

These saints were the torch-bearers for the entire humanity. They rose above the narrow dogmatic religion and dwelt on the plane of universal consciousness.

For attaining this spiritual unification with the Lord one has to gradually get rid of the ego that divorces the soul from the Supreme Being. As Rahim says:

> Rahiman gali hai sankari, dujo nahin thaharahi
> apu aye to hari nahin, hari to apu nahin.

(The lane of love is very narrow. It cannot accommodate more than one at a time. If "I" is present, God is not, and when He is present "I" is not.)

In this couplet Rahim underlines the fact that a devotee can attain oneness with the Lord only when he/she gets rid of the ego.

Through such immortal words Rahim, or Abdul Rahim Khan Khana, continues to live in the hearts of all Indians. He occupies a unique place in Indian history, culture and literature. He was one among the nine jewels in the court of the great Mughal emperor, Akbar. He was adept at both war and diplomacy; he was a patron of poets and artists and a great help to the poor and needy. He was a true representative of the secular and composite Indian culture. Rahim has an unassailable position in the history of Hindi literature and his memory remains evergreen among the millions of common folk for the simplicity of his language and expression.

II

Rahim was born on 17 December, 1556, at Lahore. At this time his father was away fighting a war on the Western front. Bairam Khan, Rahim's father, was a brave and faithful Amir who served many Mughal emperors like Babur, Humayun and Akbar. Unfortunately, the Amir died in the battle. After the death of this loyal warrior Akbar interested himself in the welfare of the young child. Young Rahim was placed under royal protection and the title of Mirza Khan was later conferred on him.

Rahim was a very intelligent boy, ready to learn all that he came across. From his father he inherited valour, sagacity, charity, statesmanship and artistic interests. Rahim's mother was a Mewati Rajput lady of royal descent. Hence he had in his veins a combination of many traits: the fiery toughness of Turks, the culture of Iran, Rajput chivalry and other distinctive traits bred on the Indian soil. Rahim succeeded in assimilating the spirit of these two countries and cultures completely. He grew up to be a fitting disciple of Akbar's genius — intellectually, politically and spiritually. The Emperor's court served as a school for him where he learnt courtly manners and the courteous ways of aristocrats.

From his childhood Rahim had great enthusiasm for learning. He was equally fluent in Persian and Turkish languages. He was commissioned by Akbar to translate *Tuzuk-e-Babari* from Turkish to Persian. In addition, he learnt many other languages and dialects. He became well-versed in Sanskrit, Braj, Avadhi, Khadi Boli by his constant and prolonged association with poets of these languages. It also gave him an extensive knowledge of Hindu literature, religion and philosophy. His Hindi verses bear testimony to the fact that he had a fairly good knowledge of Hindu mythology. For example, in one of his *dohas* we are told:

> *ocho kam bado karae, to na badai hoe*
> *jyo Rahim Hanuman ko, Giridhar kahe na koe.*

(Even if small people do big deeds they do not get any credit. No one calls Hanuman Giridhar though he carries a bigger mountain than Sri Krishna did.)

In another *doha* Rahim says:

> *mange ghatat Rahim pad, kito karo badi kam*
> *teen pair vasudha kari, tau bapane nam.*

(Whatever great work a person does, his stature is lowered when he goes out to beg. Though Vaman measured the three worlds in three steps, he is referred to as a dwarf.)

Apart from such direct uses of Indian mythology Rahim's verses often convey his interpretation of some common observation in mythological terms. An illustration of this is found in a *doha* which says:

> *dhur dharat nij sees pai, kahu Rahim kehi kaj*
> *jehi raj muni-patni tari, so dhudat gajraj.*

(Seeing an elephant sprinkle dust on its own head Rahim is puzzled. Then he concludes that just as Ahalya was changed back to the human form by a touch of the dust of Sri Rama's feet, the elephant too is probably trying to find the sacred dust which will give it salvation.)

III

Rahim survives even after centuries as he tried to win the hearts of common people through his love and sympathy for them. He served them by creating a literature in a language closest to the people. He was a master of the sword as well as the pen. He was a gifted poet who wrote with equal felicity in Persian, Turkish, Hindi and Sanskrit. His Persian letters bear an evidence of his mastery over the Persian language. But his poetic genius is best expressed in Hindi. He was also a translator par excellence.

Rahim's long life was eventful, his experiences were both sweet and bitter. He acquired first-hand experience of a variety of human behaviour. He was acquainted with both affluence and poverty, power and neglect. Hence, his poetry is a reflection of common human experiences, morals and emotions. His genius was not suited to the composition of epic poetry. He was incomparable in shorter poems like *dohas* and *barvai*. His lines on the ethics of life and human nature are oft-quoted in ordinary conversation. They display his deep knowledge and understanding of the vagaries of human behaviour. As he writes in a couplet:

ekai saade sab sadhe, sab saadhe sab jaye
Rahiman mulahi sinchibo, phulahi phalahi adhaye.

(To achieve a goal one must concentrate on one thing at a time. Other achievements automatically follow. But if we scatter our concentration on many things we lose all. It is like watering the plant: there is no need to water all parts of the plant; if we water the roots plenty of flowers and fruits result.)

Again he says:

pawas dekh Rahim man, koyal sade maun
ab dadur wakta bhae, hame puchahen kaun.

(Rahim observes that the cuckoo has become silent on the approach of the rainy season. Now the frogs have become vociferous and the poet fears that none will care for the words of others.)

Referring to adverse circumstances as the "rainy season" Rahim puts forward his view that in times of trouble wise people — cuckoos — keep silent while fools — frogs — loudly express their opinion.

Similar words of wisdom are contained in almost all his *dohas*. For example, he says:

> tute sujan manaieh, jo tute sau bar,
> Rahiman puni-puni pohieh, tute mukta har.

(In case of a dispute with a good person one should make up and affect a compromise just as when a garland of pearls is broken, we collect the pearls and string them together again.)

According to Rahim, good people are as precious as pearls and under no circumstances should we lose them.

IV

Rahim's poetry is not overtly mystical like that of Jayasi, nor full of devotion like that of Raskhan. Yet it bears testimony to the purity of the heart which served as an impetus for his composition. Rahim wrote on ordinary subjects, illustration laudable moral tenets. He tried his hand at various metres. He cultivated mastery over Sanskrit and Hindi poetics. His *dohas* sparkle with wit and humour; his *barwais* express deep emotions and celebrate various aspects of beauty. There is admirable freshness and everlasting appeal in his verses which touch the heart. Rahim's name has been a house-hold word for generations of poetry lovers. His simple and subjective renderings catch the imagination of all.

Rahim's writings can be divided into the following categories: *Dohas* or couplets, about four hundred in number written in Braj bhasha; *Barwais*, written in Avadhi dealing mainly with various aspects of love; *Baraw Naika Bhed*, a famous work dealing with poetics.

Another important work of Rahim is *Madanastak* in which he presents a harmonious blend of Sanskrit, Persian, Braj and Khadi boli. The subject of this collection of poems is love and devotion. A typical verse from this work reads as follows:

> sharad nishith, chand ki roshabai.
> saghan wan nikunje, kanha bansi bajai.
> rati, pati, sut, nidra, saiyan chod bhagi
> madan shirshi bhuyon kya bala aan lagi.

(The time is midnight on a moonlit autumn night. In the woods Krishna plays his flute in a charming melody. The music is so tempting that the womenfolk run towards it, leaving behind their home, husband and sons. Rahim's comment is that Madan, the god of love, has brought about this trouble.)

V

In addition to being a man of great learning and impeccable morals, Rahim was also a very kind-hearted person. he never turned down anybody who sought his assistance. he even went out of his way to help the poor and needy. While offering help he never used to look into the eyes of the receiver. On being asked the reason for this he said:

> *denhar koi aur hai, bhejat so din rain.*
> *log dharam hum pain dharain, yate niche nain.*

(The giver is not me. It is someone else who sends money day and night. Since people mistake me for the giver, I keep my eyes lowered.)

Another reason for this may have been that Rahim wanted to cause no humiliation to those who accepted the alms. He may also have tried to save himself from becoming proud of his generosity to others, thus falling into the trap set by his ego. This was the nobility of his character.

Rahim was undoubtedly a devout Muslim but he was not a fanatic. He had great respect for the scriptures and teachings of other religions. He had an attitude of veneration towards Tulsidas.

VI

Due to some political misunderstandings Rahim was deprived of his wealth and power during the reign of Jahangir. He remained in disgrace for two long years. It was at this time that Rahim composed some of his best couplets.

Adversity brought him to such a state that he had nothing to offer to the others. Under these circumstances he warned his friends and those who depended in him by saying:

> *ye Rahim dar dar phirahi, mangi madhukar khahi,*
> *yaro yari chodiye, wo Rahim ab nahi.*

(Friends, do not seek my company. This Rahim is not the former Rahim. Now he himself lives by begging.)

Unfortunately the people did not leave him alone. There was a constant stream of men and women who continued to expect his assistance. His helplessness depressed Rahim. Often he sent these needy people to his friends in high places like the King of Oudh.

Thus Rahim encountered many ups and downs during the course of his existence. In his last days, his rival Mahabat Khan gave him the worst shock of his life by sending him as "gift" the severed head of his son. This tragic end of his son and grandson broke the heart of the old man. In the year 1627, at the age of 71, Rahim left his mortal frame. He also left behind him his invaluable compositions and the story of the rise and fall of a great general and an equally great artist.

VII

Rahim was a great lover of books and learning. He established a library at Ahmedabad in the year 1583 which possesses a rare and rich collection of manuscripts.

Rahim was a poet of the Indian soil. He loved Hindi, he loved Hindus, he loved Hindustan. His poetry throbs with Indianness, Indian mythology, Indian scenery — rivers, mountains, birds and animals, the Indian way of life, its customs and traditions adorn his poetry. His reverence and love for his motherland was an inheritance from his Rajput mother. His association with the poet-saints of North India added to this and attracted him to the rich cultural heritage of this country.

Rahim was not only a brave warrior but was a refined and cultured person, too. His intellect and aesthetic sensibility were very well-developed. Art and poetry were the springs which nourished his character.

Bharatendu Harishchandra has paid a fitting tribute to the secular spirit of Rahim by saying that he could sacrifice crores of Hindus for one such Muslim.

Rahim respected all the creeds of this country. He never knew any hatred. His love sprang from the cordial attachment he had for even the most insignificant objects of this nation. He sang praises for the Hindu gods, advocated the efficacy of Ram-naam and expressed his heartfelt love and devotion for Lord Krishna. His attachment to music and painting and other fine arts found reflection in his poetry.

Rahim is therefore a true representative poet-saint of the composite Indian mind and culture.

10

SURDAS

Rajkumari Singh

Surdas, the great poet and devotee of Sri Krishna, shines on the horizon of Hindi literature like a sun, not only due to his works but also due to his personality. His life history continues to be a source of controversy among scholars. In spite of this his greatness is undoubted and none can deny that even a common reader is moved by his verse. One gets immersed in his beautiful poetry only to enjoy thoroughly the *sringara, vatsalya* and *shanta* rasas found in them. Being so engrossed, the reader forgets to enquire about the biographical details of the poet, remembering to identify Surdas only in and through his verse.

Like most other poets of his time Surdas too did not leave behind much mention of his personal life. He hoped to be immortalised by his works; he wanted them to be the reflection of his personality. The very fact that his writings continue to be popular after centuries bears testimony to their exceptional calibre.

In the beginning of his life Surdas sang *bhajans* at Gaughat. A chance meeting with the great sage Vallabhacharya changed the style of his devotion and compositions. It can thus be said that the contribution of Vallabhacharya to the moulding of Krishna *bhakti* literature of which Surdas is a major exponent is very decisive. The school of philosophy expounded by Vallabhacharya is known as *suddhadwaita* or *pushti marga*. In it Krishna the child is worshipped. This inspired all the Ashtachap poets including Surdas who holds the highest position among those exponents of Hindi literature whose works are devoted to the veneration of Sri Krishna just as Tulsidas is the leader of the poetry devoted to Rama.

To understand Sur and his verse it is necessary to study the society and culture of his times. Prior to the devotional poetry of the *bhakti* movement venerating Rama and Krishna, the tradition of religious verse was dominated by Nirguna poets.

Dr. Namvar Singh has described this age as the age of internal conflicts or *antharvirodh* (242). The reason for this was that society was divided between the haves and the havenots and there was a wide gulf between the two. The feeling of high and low among the castes was glaringly felt. The result was the downfall of religious tenets and this in turn gave rise to serious social discord. The situation worsened with the passing of time. The deterioration was also aided by the complicated teachings of yoga put forth by the Natha and Siddha poets. All these factors were responsible for the increasing restlessness felt by individuals in society. To counter this situation came the great Saguna bhakti poets like Surdas and Tulsidas. Theirs was the true and natural message of love as the highest manifestation of religion. In their worship they necessarily believed in the existence of God with form. Sur himself admitted that he had tried various paths before he came to bhakti. Hence it can be concluded that bhakti poets wrote with the authenticity of felt experience to guide them. The poets of the bhakti movement truly understood the deepest feelings of the common people. Though there may be minute differences in the various forms of bhakti literature, the basic concepts remain unaltered in their numerous renderings.

In any attempt to study the works of Surdas it is essential to take into consideration the social, economic and political situation of his contemporary India. One major upheaval of the period was the Muslim invasion which resulted in a political revolution on the surface together with deep-seated cultural changes not so easy to discern. This new cultural movement left a lasting impression on the fields of art, literature and religion, and altered the thinking of the people widely.

Talking about the prevalent trends in those times, K. Damodaran writes that the bhakti movement began at a time when the selfishness of the priests of both Hinduism and Islam was at its height (328). It became imperative to fight against their dogmatic orthodoxy. The masses were steeped in superstition, exploited by those in positions of authority and needed to be awakened to the real meaning of existence. It was in this context that the poetry of Sur acquired immediacy.

Dr. Devraj admits that the art which does not point to reality cannot be considered significant (221). Literature should be a mirror of society. It is to the credit of Sur that in the age of feudal oppression he took up his pen to portray the simplicity of the life of the common people like farmers and shepherds. Sur took up the task of depicting the natural and supernatural *leela* of Sri Krishna who was a cowherd boy. The aim of his verse was to set a moral code for the Hindus in an era of Muslim tyranny. He succeeded in strengthening the self-esteem of the common folk.

Lord Krishna whose *leela* was enacted in Braj was a true representative of the culture of shepherds. There is also an element of the supernatural present in the activities of this popular hero. The poet stresses this from time to time. For example, Sur describes how a heavenly shower of flowers heralded the birth of Krishna, followed by the killing of Pootana, Kaliya and the lifting of the Govardhan mountain; the defeat of Indra by young Krishna is one more instance of his divinity which the poet mentions.

In the literature of Krishna bhakti the folk life of Braj is vividly portrayed and Sur is possibly the best exponent of this form. Indian rural life is enshrined in all descriptions, with importance given to agriculture and animal rearing. Cows formed an important source of income and many verses are connected with them: *madhu van* — the pasture, cowherd boys; milkmaids, the making of curd and butter, all form the subject matter of poetry. Krishna's adventure in childhood with butter entitled *makhan leela* are episodes rich in philosophic cadence as well as the lifestyle of the community into which he was born. Surdas attempted to improve the prevailing social conditions of his times by such verse.

There are two dominant strains in these verses: the urban life represented by Mathura and the rural one of Braj, symbolic of simplicity. With these backdrops Sur wrote numerous verses on traditional festivals such as Fag, Jholan, Vasant, introducing the romance of these celebrations. Many of the verses in *Sur Sagar* are borrowed from popular folklore which make the poetry of Sur colourful. In the descriptions of Holi, for instance, we find music, dance and ecstasy.

The main attempt of poets devoted to Rama and Krishna was to find viable alternatives to the oppressive feudalistic tyranny of the times and they succeeded remarkably in this. Their goal was attained by making their chosen deity the representative of the best virtues and highest values of life. The verses also humanise these divine personalities so that they would serve as models for the common people to emulate.

In the *Bhramar Geet Prasanga Krishna* is as desperate and depressed at his separation from the Gopis as the latter are for him. Sur composed some poignant verse to describe his grief. Such lines abound in philosophic overtones in addition to establishing an ideal of religion. Sur shows how the ideals perpetrated by Krishna have more sociological import rather than individualistic value. This was crucial because he was trying to achieve integration in a society that was disintegrating rapidly.

In all the works of Surdas, namely, *Sur Sagar, Sahitya Lahari, Sur Saravali, Bhramar Geet* the central theme is his undying devotion to Krishna. He could not bear to leave the geographic location associated with his beloved Lord Krishna even for once in his life. Consequently, he could describe with great vividness all aspects of the life of the Lord. Sur was a skilful poet in addition to being a veteran musician and an incomparable devotee. He invented many new ragas. He devoted his entire life to the service of his Lord.

Music has its own importance in the works of Surdas. Music and poetry are inseparably linked and interdependent. The right blend of music and poetry is the most sublime form of literature as is found in the compositions of Surdas. Being a great devotee, Sur clothed his devotion in music. To please his Lord, to plead with Him, Sur used music. The treasury of verses left behind by this great poet-saint is in two forms: those that have an inward dimension and those having an outward dimension.

Sur Sagar is, as it were, a dictionary of hundreds of ragas. The credit of inventing *Rag Malhar* and *Sur Sarang* goes to Surdas. His music represents the classical trend popular in his times: with the tunes of *Rag Bhairavi* the day begins and during the midday we hear *Rag Sarang*, etc.

Surdas used many interesting innovations in his verse. For instance, the personification of Krishna's flute, the anger and jealousy of Radha and the other Gopis towards it are unique in the history of the world poetry. Other examples are descriptions of the various dances of Krishna: that of child Krishna, or the classical dance on Kaliya, the demon serpent, his *Ras Leela* with the Gopis on the banks of river Yamuna. Thus dance and music form an integral part of Sur's writings and also the most important contribution of the poet-saint to Indian art and culture.

Surdas had great insight into the psychology of a child. His depiction of child Krishna is very sensitive. Sur's numerous verses have immortalised the beauty of the childhood pranks of Sri Krishna. In *Sur Sagar* there are verses describing the birth of Lord Krishna, his childhood, youth, adolescence. In these compositions the dominant strain is of *Sringara rasa* with special stress on *sanyoga* and *viyoga*. Descriptions of the beauty of child Krishna alternate with endearing tales of rivalry between Krishna and his elder brother Balaram.

Surdas has drawn beautiful pen-pictures of child psychology. Krishna is seen after he has been caught red-handed for having stolen and eaten butter from other houses. The Gopis complain to mother Yashoda and she scolds the child. Krishna pretends innocence. He proves his alibi by saying that he has been with the cows since early morning and out of mischief, the others have plastered his face with butter.

In his verses Surdas has described in minute detail each phase of the child's growth: his crawling, smiling, crying, playing and his naughtiness. These portraits are incomparable. Here the dominant *rasa* is *vatsalya*.

After the child grows up, Surdas depicts Krishna as the hero of the Gopis. This stage of the Lord's life is equally attractive. When Krishna migrates to Mathura, the Gopis, Yashoda and his cows, and the whole of Brindavan is immersed in tears.

In conclusion it can be said that Surdas, the blind poet, has great insight into the many-faceted human mind. This became the main theme of his poetry. Sur's verse is a rare blend of poetry, music and philosophy. Yet it is extremely simple and has universal appeal. Through his writings Sur performed a twin task — he took poetry to new a height and developed the inexhaustible treasure of *Braj Bhasha*. The greatness of Surdas lies in the fact that his verses are the true embodiment of Indian culture and way of life of the people.

(Translated from original Hindi by Dr. Suman Latha and Dr. K.L. Vyas).

11

SANT TULSIDAS

Kamala Ganorkar

Sant Tulsidas is probably the most popular of the Hindi poets. He belongs to the tradition of the devotee saint-poets of North India. The basis of his immense popularity is his immortal epic, *Ramcharitmanas*.

Tulsi's bhakti was of the *dasya* type, that is to say, he considered himself as the servant of the Lord. He had implicit faith in and unshakable devotion towards Lord Rama. In his unprecedently popular composition, the *Ramcharitmanas*, Tulsidas not only retells the story of Rama but he also tries to harmonise and synthesise different sects. At the time he wrote this epic there were many paths of devotion and worship prevalent in Hinduism. Tulsi attempted to illustrate the inherent unity amid all this apparent diversity. At the end of Rama's life history he explained elaborately and in convincing detail the differences between *jnana* and *bhakti*. Such is the powerful attraction of this epic to all that even after four centuries of its composition it is found in every house in North India. This is more so because it is widely believed that the regular and repeated study of this holy work rescues people from sins, relieves doubts and protects them from evil.

Tulsi was an incomparable devotee and a remarkable genius who could translate his personal spiritual experience of Rama bhakti into poetic expression, making it accessible to common people. Though he wrote his *Manas* for his own edification it has assumed the status of an epic of the people because it contains the eternal message of the welfare of all humans.

Tulsidas defined *bhakti* as the path of devotion, moral living and surrender to the divine by way of conquest of the eternal senses:

> *priti Ram so niti path chaliye ragris jiti*
> *Tulsi santan ke mate yehai bhagati ki riti*

According to Tulsidas the devotion which spells overwhelming love for God is called *ragatmika bhakti*. He practised and propagated this in order to attain perfection. In the *Bhagavad Gita* it is described that people of different temperaments and different situations choose the path of bhakti. They are: a person who is troubled, one who is desirous of knowledge, one who craves material wealth and finally a person who desires only the love of God. Tulsidas attempts to synthesise all the varieties of desires leading to devotion under one head, that is, his *ragatmika bhakti*. The best illustration of this is found in four incidents of the *Ramcharitmanas* which refer to the four paths of bhakti.

The first of these is a dialogue between Siva and Uma where the latter pleads with the former to be told the story of Rama so as to get rid of troubles. The second is a dialogue between Garuda and the crow. Being an eager learner, Garuda wants to know the improbability of the imprisonment of his God who is omnipotent and omnipresent. In spite of this the Rakshasa had been able to bind Him in Nagapasha. Garuda put this question first to Lord Siva. Instead of answering Garuda himself, Siva sent him to Kaaka Bhushandi, the Crow, who was to tell the story to Garuda. Hearing the narration of this episode of Rama's life from the crow Garuda's thirst for knowledge is quenched.

The third instance is depicted in a dialogue between the poet and a commoner. Their discussion reveals that some people listen to a story because they are eager to learn something from it; others listen out of curiosity; some for enjoyment and still others because they hope that the process of listening will bestow them with worldly attainments:

> *man kamana sihi nar pawa*
> *jo yah katha kapat taji gawa*

The fourth category of devotees are the *jnani* or those who have attained knowledge. This is illustrated by the dialogue between Yagnavalya and Bharadwaja *rishi*.

In addition to this Tulsidas describes *navadha bhakti* or devotion of nine types. The special feature of the devotion which Tulsidas describes is its singleness of purpose (*anaya*). He recounts how he held Rama in his mind constantly even while worshipping other gods and goddesses.

Tulsi's *bhakti marga* included both the variations of devotion: *saguna* and *nirguna*. He admitted that of the two the former is easier and the latter more difficult. In *Kavitavali* he acclaimed *saguna* path of bhakti:

> *antat jamihu te bade bahir jabhi*
> *sagun roop ki bhakti*

Tulsidas accepted image worship as the first and most concrete manifestation of devotion. This makes the bhakti of Tulsi free from narrowness. It is neither singular nor self-centred. It contains elements pertaining to the well-being of one and all as is ordained in the *Upanishads*. Therefore, it can be said that using the story of Rama as his vehicle Tulsidas gave the divine message of devotion to the common people. In the words of the great critic Ramchandra Shukla:

> The voice of Tulsi as heard through his work, the *Manas*. was equally pleasing to king and beggar, the fool and scholar, the great and small. Tulsi succeeded in bringing Rama to all; Rama dwelt in all hearts through his efforts. Every Hindu, irrespective of class or sect finds solace in Rama.

Tulsi held that whether it is the state of joy or sorrow, whether the place is a palace or a jungle, in times of both war and peace, people should hold on to the security of devotion to Rama. Tulsi made the life of common people full of Rama. His ideal was the *chataka* bird which is unshakable and unalterable in its constant cry:

> *kabahu kaho yah rahani rahogo*

Like the other saints Tulsidas strove to be rid of pride, anger and other bad habits. He preached the value of being contented with whatever one has; to be helpful, pleasant in speech and good in all matters were the greatest of virtues in his view.

The entire creative genius of Tulsidas found appropriate expression in his endeavour at synthesising the discordant elements of religion into harmony. He spent his lifetime in attempting to synthesise various diversities, for instance, *saguna* and *nirguna bhakti marga*, the Vaishnava and Saiva sects, the ideal and the actual, as well as many other dimensions of religion prevalent in his age.

Thus, we can conclude by saying that the entire body of work composed by Tulsidas was a great effort to revitalise the cultural heritage of India.

(Translated from original Hindi by Dr. K.L. Vyas).

12

THE DIVINE FERRYMAN: GURU NANAK

Lalitha Jayaraman

One of the unique socio-cultural movements of fifteenth century India was the bhakti cult, which brought together poetry, music and religion in an evocative, powerful synthesis that happens but rarely in the history of a nation. The galaxy of eminent poet-saints who gave a whole new scripture to the Indian people—a scripture simpler, more accessible and more in touch with the rhythms of their own life—were instrumental in transfiguring the very face of traditional religion, with their revolutionary concept of bhakti as the essence of faith and the true way to God. But in transforming religion and society they also succeeded in transforming Indian literature with songs, hymns, poems and musical compositions that were, paradoxically, both intensely popular and intensely classical: simple and direct in their message, yet with levels of complexity reaching far beyond the translucent beauty of their surface.

Nanak — later Guru Nanak, the founder of a new faith — occupies a revered place in this genre of poet-saints who, for the first time, brought God to the people in a form, a language and an idiom that they could understand. Born into a poor family in 1496, legend has it that Nanak underwent a miraculous, mystic experience in 1507, which revealed to him his true mission in life. In the years following this, Nanak wandered over the country, composing beautiful hymns which would be set to music by his Muslim companion, the rebeck player Mardana. The *Adi-Granth* contains nearly a thousand such hymns, divided not according to their thematic content but by their ragas into eighteen subdivisions. Like the other great poet-saints—Kabir, Tulsidas,

Mirabai, Namdev—Nanak's was an eclectic, intensely liberal faith which denied the distinctions of traditional religion, questioned the validity of caste and revealed rituals for what they often were — meaningless rigidities meant to divide the believer from God.

Central to Nanak's creed — as to the bhakti movement throughout the country — was the affirmation of the oneness of God, although His manifestation and the names He is called by are myriad. Nanak states this with moving simplicity and utter clarity in a song from *Japji*, the morning hymns which scholars consider to be the epitome of all that Nanak taught:

> There is one God.
> His name is Truth.
> He is the Creator.
> He is without fear and without hate
> He is beyond Time, immortal
> His spirit pervades the universe
> He is self-existent. (14)

This is the *mool-mantra*, the root teaching which forms the basis of all Nanak's hymns and recurs, stated in different ways throughout the *Adi-Granth*. Contained here is the essence of the Guru's teachings: his emphatic rejection of polytheism and of the elaborate Hindu pantheon of gods, and his deeper identification with the Hindu concept of the Brahman, the non-iconoclastic, omnipresent, omniscient pervading spirit that manifests itself in the entire created universe, and is both *nirguna* (beyond all qualities) and *nirakar* (without form). Here is Nanak's invocation to this over-arching presence:

> Thou art primal.
> Thou art pure,
> Without beginning, without termination,
> In single form endure forever. (20)

This assertion of the oneness of God questions completely all traditional distinctions between the Hindu and the Mussalman, the Saivite and the Vaisnavite, the brahmin and the shudra: it declares the merging of all faiths, sects and religions in the timeless quest of God and for the truth. For, as Nanak states in a beautiful metaphor:

> Just as there are many seasons,
> But the sun that makes them one;
> so, O Nanak, the creator has
> many garbs, but is one. (114)

Given this eternal and unchanging quest, the quest to tear the veil of illusion (*maya*) that covers our eyes and to know the true God who is both within and outside us, the *Adi-Granth* places central emphasis on the role of the guru, as the teacher, the enlightened, the guide who leads us to God. In a sense the *guru*, because he shows the true way to the devotee, is almost as worthy of reverence as God himself. As Nanak states in a hymn for *Sri Raga*:

> I am forever beholden to my guru,
> Through the guru's teaching we attain honour,
> To the guru be all praise for uniting me to him.
> *O brother I know that without the Guru,*
> *there is no knowledge,*
> The guru is like the tree in full leaf
> casting a vast shade . . . (39)

This central concept of the *Sat Guru* ("sat" encompassing in its connotative sweep, both the truth and the essential reality, as opposed to the delusions and shifting mirages of the sensual world) as the bridge between the devotee and God, is in keeping with the *guru shishya parampara* and the Sufis *Peer Mursheed*. Khushwant Singh in his commentary on Nanak sums up the exalted position of the *guru* in Nanak's *Adi-Granth* in the following words:

> The guru applies the salve of knowledge, *"gyan anjan"*, to our eyes, so that we can see the truth that is God; *he is the divine ferryman who ferries us across the fearful ocean of life— the bhava sagar;* he interprets the ordinances of God and shows the difference between the genuine and the counterfeit. The guru instils the fear of God in his disciple so that out of that fear may spring the love of God.

As important as implicit faith in the guru—" He who would know, must have faith" states Nanak—is his emphasis on that "inner purity" which transcends all outward rituals and the hypocrisies of mere formalistic worship without the piety and

The Divine Ferryman: Guru Nanak

love that alone gives meaning to them. This is the message in song after song of the *Adi-Granth*: the truth—and therefore God—are not accessible through dry knowledge, or academic learning, or the egotistic self-exaltation of the self-appointed guardians of religion:

> The Pandit knows it not, nor is it writ in his Puran,
> The Qazi knows it not, though he read and copied the Koran.
> The yogi knows not the date and day of the week...
> Research-weary scholars have delved, but do not know. (18)

Equally distant from God are those who resort to outward pieties—"prayer, austerity, control over the senses, pilgrimage to holy places, giving alms, charity..."—to find what is really within the precincts of their own soul.

> The fire of pride is not extinguished,
> By wandering over distant lands,
> The dirt of the mind is not cleaned,
> By wearing clean garments.
> Fie! the life of falsehood! Fie, the mask of divinity! (31)

The only way to God, therefore, is through an active, dynamic life of goodness — a humanism that permeates every aspect of our behaviour, and manifests itself in our practical, everyday conduct towards our fellow-beings. For, as Nanak sums up in a line that crystallises the entire philosophy of the *Adi-Granth*: "Worthless is prayer without good acts done" and "Unless truth enters the soul, all service and study is false."

This is because to Nanak God is Truth, "both a spiritual concept, and a code of life." And so, every personal violation of purity and every little act of transgression — lying, cheating, cruelty, stealing, even an unkind or angry word — is also a violation of God, and the sullying of His name. The greatest virtues that the *Granth* adjoins, therefore, are the simple traditional virtues which have timelessly been associated with goodness in its most essential sense: patience, austerity, love, grace, humility, simplicity, love for one's fellow-beings, renunciation and faith. One hymn states these qualities and the attitude of mind which should go with them — in words of transcendent wisdom:

> As a beggar goes a-begging
> Bowl in one hand, staff in the other,
> Rings in his ears, in ashes smothered
> So go thou forth in life,
> With ear-rings made of contentment,
> With modesty for thy begging-bowl,
> Meditation the fabric of thy garment,
> Knowledge of life thy cowl...(20)

From early childhood Nanak, it is said, loved Nature with an adoration bordering on the mystical. It is hardly surprising then that Nature forms the inspiration behind many of the most passionately devotional songs of the *Adi-Granth*: and metaphors, similes, images, symbols from the natural world strew nearly every page of the *Granth*, infusing the hymns with the colour and vitality that brings them joyously, vividly to life. From the soft, muted shades of autumn to the bare and silent stillness of winter evenings; from the drowsy heat of summer noons to the burst of colours in spring; from dark monsoon clouds and the crash of thunder in rumbling skies to the poetry of magical nights bathed in moonlight glow — every facet of the ever-changing natural landscape finds a reflection in Nanak's songs of celebration of nature.

And yet, paradoxical though it may seem, this very love of the natural world is, for Nanak, eventually only a path, a by-lane that leads as everything ultimately does, to the transcendent love of God. For Nanak, while gazing in wonder and gratitude at the "forms, colour, attire of Nature", at the "breezes, the water, the fire", the "lands, the earth and the spheres", "the thunders and lightning, the moons and suns, the world and its regions", sees not Nature itself but a divine manifestation of the God who fashions these "myriad forms" and infuses them with life, vitality and spirit. And so, even the sensuous beauty of the natural world is for Nanak tinged with a simultaneous joy and anguish: because he was searching for the reality of that truth which does not change with the changing seasons, of that beauty which does not fade, and wither, and die, as the flowers of spring do; of that lasting repose of the mind which does not rely on a capricious natural world for fulfilment. In nature, then, even at the very instant that he celebrates her, Nanak only found deeper and deeper lessons of the transcendence of human life, and the eternity of the world hereafter, of the impermanence and pettiness of the ephemeral mortal world when set beside God's changeless realm of Truth and His unchanging love for His devotees:

> In the realm of action,
> Nothing...prevails.
> In the realm of Truth is the formless One
> Who, having created, watches his creation,
> There, by a myriad forms are a myriad purposes fulfilled,
> What he ordains is in them instilled.

One beautiful passage from the *Rag Basant* epitomises Nanak's response to Nature and God most completely. "Months and seasons ever come and go, and come again," he wrote. "Trees and bushes attain foliage at one season and lose it at another. The grape only receives its juice at one season. But the good man receives his reward at all times of the day and night. Those who do evil, wither and die; those who take the name of the Lord ever have spring in their hearts." One message, then, emerges again and again, with increasing fervour and passion, as we read the hymns of the *Holy Granth*: that everything is finally but a "whirlwind of ego" — beauty and power, joy and sensual fulfilment, name, fame, riches, wealth, and all that we behold and strive for in the transient world of illusion that we call "life". Only one thing abides, enduring alike the vicissitudes of Time, the mortality of the flesh and the changing of the seasons — the name of the Lord and His holy Word.

Stylistically the songs and poems of the *Adi-Granth* display a fascinating range that often defies the traditional categories, and baffles simple classification. Indeed reading the hymns with their inexhaustible variations of dialect, diction, form and style, of metre, and syllable and line-length, one is almost tempted to believe the beautiful legend about Nanak: that he would compose the songs even as they came to his lips and then put them into a bag which he carried slung on his shoulders as he travelled over the country. Only such joyful enforced spontaneity can account for the springs of creativity that well up almost unbidden in the songs infusing them with the freshness and immediacy so characteristic of the semi-oral tradition of religious poetry. Nanak used rhyming couplets and quatrains, rhythms and refrains, reiterated images and snatches of lines that recur through song-sequences — all to great poetic effect. Yet the final impression conveyed by the hymns is not one of deliberate studied craftsmanship, but rather of an ecstatic outpouring of devotion for the divine Master — with the words, symbols, images tumbling out, as it were, and patterning themselves almost of their own volition. Perhaps it is this quality of immediacy which renders the hymns of the *Granth* so potent in the oral, as well as the written tradition: for they are, in the most essential sense of the word lyrical born out of the song in the heart, born of our need to communicate a message in the simplest most transparent words with nothing no unnecessary complexities of style, no intricacies designed to impress or merely decorate — standing between the poet and his message.

Indeed, simpicity is at once the most outstanding quality of the hymns and their greatest strength. Like Kabir, like Tulsidas, like Mirabai, Nanak wrote for the people and his songs are almost single-mindedly moved by a fundamental aim — to make the most transcendent religious experiences the most metaphysical of concepts, the highest flights of philosophy accessible in simple homely terms, terms that every householder can relate to.

And so, Nanak finds material for his hymns in the greatest, most ordinary, most quintessentially mundane of everyday experience — a housewife washing her grimy bundle of clothes in the stream, a merchant counting his coins at the end of a working-day, a gardener tending his flower-beds, a bride waiting for her beloved in the bridal chamber, a farmer looking to the skies for rain. Yet each homely metaphor gleaned out of the prosaic round of undistinguished daily life, becomes a vehicle for conveying a profound, timeless truth: each simile, reflecting the experience of ordinary men and women in the commonality of their day-to-day lives, rises to evoke a divine transcendent experience. Here is a hymn from far distance in which Nanak describes the meeting of the soul with God in an extended metaphor which relates it to the simple act of lighting an oil-lamp:

> Let your body be the lamp,
> From the holy books take wisdom,
> And use it as oil.
> Let knowledge of his presence be the wick,

> And with the tinder of truth,
> Strike the spark,
> Thus light you the oil-lamp
> And in its light meet the Lord. (34)

In another song, the difference between the life of truth and falsehood is stated in an image which connects it to the familiar, worldly business of buying and selling, of profit and loss:

> Without goods to sell, a trader sits idly,
> He knows not how to start, his merchandise earns no profit.
> Without anything to trade in, he suffers heavy losses,
> Thus one who trades in falsehood suffers,
> And is afflicted with sorrow. (38)

This movement from the physical to the metaphysical, from the sensual to the spiritual, the worldly to the divine and the tangibly real to the ineffable and the eternal is a pattern which underlines nearly all the hymns of the *Adi-Granth*. It is a stylistic device which reflects the root of the entire bhakti movement, and its underlying philosophy to bring God and religion, metaphysics and mysticism, theology and philosophy to the people in terms that they could instantaneously identify with, and immediately recognise. Even a theological concept as complex as evil and good, sin and virtue, faith and corroding doubt becomes almost childlike in simplicity when Nanak expresses it through an image which every Indian farmer would know — of a stone dam holding back the flooding waters of a river:

> A stone dam can hold the flood,
> but if the dam bursts,
> you cannot repair the breach by plastering mud.
> Evil is like the flood,
> the stone-dam like faith.
> If faith weakens,
> the dam will give way,
> and the flood will sweep all before it. (8)

And contained here is the secret of the timeless appeal of Guru Nanak's songs, their unchanging relevance in a changing world. For Nanak shared with the other great saints and mystics of the bhakti movement — as indeed with great religious teachers all over the world—the most difficult of all qualities — the ability to express a lasting, changeless truth in the simplest, yet the most beautiful of all words. In a rare moment in one of the hymns, Nanak reflects upon his own art as a poet bard and with moving humility admits the awesome impossibility of the task he has set himself:

> O Nanak, had I a hundred thousand tons of paper,
> Pen plying with the speed of wind,
> Dipping in an inexhaustible ink well,
> Even so,
> I know not how great thou art,
> How then can I praise thee? (24-5)

Yet with no "inexhaustible ink-well" at his service and in the brief space of only a thousand-odd hymns, Guru Nanak came as close as a poet-mystic could hope to, to expressing the inexpressible. For within the pages of the *Adi-Granth* lie the deepest essence of those religious experiences which do not lend themselves to words, of that knowledge which by its very definition is beyond form and beyond verbal communication. And to Nanak, as to some of the greatest modern writers this dilemma —" the necessity to tell and the impossibility of telling"—becomes the knowledge out of which is born true humility, true wisdom and the most profound literature.

References

Singh, Khushwant(tr).1991. *Hymns of Guru Nanak*. Bombay: Orient Longman Ltd. (All page numbers given in the essay are from this book.)

13

VALMIKI'S HUMANISED IMAGINATION

Y. L. Srinivas

The true history of the world always must be the history of the few. We measure the height of the Himalayas by the height of the Mount Everest. We must take true measure of India from the poets of the Vedas, the pages of the Upanishads, the founders of the Vedanta and Sankhya philosophies and the authors of the oldest law books and not from the millions who are born and die in their villages and who have never for one moment been roused out of their drowsy dream of life.

Prof. Max Muller

There is a relation between the present and the past. We cannot escape the influence of the past even if incomplete unless we study the history of India. If we turn the pages of Indian history we do not find the prototype personalities of the present day but we find personalities hiding behind the great works. Thus we do not know the names of the composers of the *Vedas* and the *Upanishads*. There are many great epics which depict in their immortal pages the accounts of the lives of great personalities who revealed immense potential and add a fresh chapter to India's glory. A meticulous study of the creators of epics reveals another remarkable dimension. For instance, the biography of Valmiki, the creator of the *Ramayana*, depicts the major upheaval brought about by the emotional conflict of a moment which resulted in the creation of the national epic.

Since every human being is potentially divine, wickedness is only a product of circumstances. Divinity requires a minor inspiration to manifest itself and endow the person with wisdom. Such a person understands the sufferings of others. Valmiki, a picaro turned pilgrim, started as a dreadful dacoit whom the death of a bird stirred to heights of noble emotion. It can be said that the hunter who had killed the bird had actually killed the wickedness in Valmiki.

Valmiki's *Ramayana* is a text composed in a heightened mystic state. This sublime recital conveys a myriad of messages to the world. Many legends are told about the life of Valmiki. It is said that his name is derived from the fact that during his penance he was buried under an ant-hill. Among the other stories two are worth recording.

One of them describes the child Ratnakar walking with his father through a forest with his face glowing with celestial radiance. While the father was praying fervently for their safe passage through the forest, the child was enjoying its tranquillity. When they were out of the forest the old man heaved a sigh of relief but Ratnakar was reluctant to leave the forest. He said he would like to go back there. After much persuasion he followed his father. But around midnight Ratnakar's father realised that the boy was not in bed. Finally Ratnakar was found in the forest, not afraid of the wild animals. He lost his way in the forest and reached the hamlet of some tribals. Their leader was amazed to see the heavenly radiance on the face of the strange boy. He was received by them as a gift of the gods; they taught him hunting and their profession of robbing the passers-by. When he grew up Ratnakar assumed the leadership of the tribe and continued the tradition of robbing and killing people.

During one of his attempts he met Narada, the *devarshi* who had nothing with him except his *veena*. Narada told the dacoits that neither his *veena* nor the wealth of knowledge which he had would be of any use to them. He pointed out the mistake of their ways and said that those who shared their ill-gotten gains would not be willing to share their sins.

Ratnakar felt the stirring of the first seed of doubt at these words of Narada. He rushed home to his wife and family to find out the truth of the holy man's words. When every one of them refused to accept a share in his misdeeds, reminding him that he was only fulfilling his responsibility towards them Ratnakar was shocked. He rushed back and fell at the feet of Narada repenting for the past and starting a severe penance in atonement. No amount of persuasion from his people could make him return to his family.

Valmiki's Humanised Imagination

Seeing the earnestness of Ratnakar's penance Indra, the king of Gods, was afraid that his position would be usurped by the former. He tried his best to distract Ratnakar's attention from this single-minded pursuit but failed. Long years passed by and an ant-hill grew on Ratnakar's body as he was transformed into a wise man. Thus he got the name of Valmiki.

Once Narada visited Valmiki's *ashrama* which had become beautiful where cruel animals turned soft due to the power of his penance. Valmiki invited Narada with all reverence and asked him, "Oh great *rishi*, who is the perfect man: possession, of strength, aware of obligations, absolutely truthful, firm in the execution of vows, compassionate, learned, attractive, self-possessed, powerful, free from anger and envy but terrifying when in fury?"

Narada said that a combination of characteristics in a single person is rare but one such is the very person whose name he had venerated, that is Rama. Valmiki heard Narada's pious words with total devotion and together with his disciples made obeisance to him. Narada blessed Valmiki and departed. Valmiki then went to the banks of the river Tamasa. The river's pure water fascinated Valmiki. He told his disciple Bharadwaj, "Look how beautiful this spot is! Free from all stains of dirt. Its stream is transparent like the hearts of pious men. I shall bathe in this sacred stream."

On his way back from the river Valmiki saw a pair of birds engaged in amorous ecstasy. At that very moment a hunter killed the male bird and the female raised cries of despair unable to bear the sight of her mate in a pool of blood. Valmiki's heart was overwhelmed with grief to hear the pangs of separation in the bird's cry. Waves of anger and agony surged from Valmiki's heart in the form of poetry. After uttering the words charged with emotion Valmiki was struck with awe and wonder at his own creative upsurge. He told his disciple about the rhyme and meter of what he had just spoken. Valmiki's emotional outburst expressed his *shoka* and transformed into a *sloka*.

As Valmiki was pondering over his spontaneous composition, Brahma blessed him. The pain of the evil act made a deep impression on his mind and he was engrossed in thoughts of separation. It was a silent protest against the cruelty of human beings. His mind had long been contemplating the perfect being whose presence and power would destroy wickedness in this world. Narada's words left a deep impression on his heart. He passed into a sublime mystical state where he visualised that perfect being born to perfect *dharma*, destroy *adharma* and to serve humanity. This resulted in the creation of the *Ramayana*.

Valmiki's main purpose in creating the epic was to spread the ideals of love to the world so that it would be a bond between human beings, and extend even to other creations. The *Ramayana* has lessons applicable to all times and conditions of life. We see prototypes of Ravana in all walks of life though it may not be possible to find an equal number of Ramas to counter the evil. In delineating the character of Rama Valmiki was portraying the character of an ideal king, an ideal son, an ideal brother, an ideal friend, a devoted husband, a valiant soldier, the protector of truth and, above all, a lover of humanity. The epic lays more stress on the humanity of Rama rather than his divinity.

It becomes clear that Valmiki's aim was to make the *Ramayana* a spiritual guide for the people of all times. Valmiki believed that the lack of higher values would have a devastating effect on the human psyche. His creation should tell the people about the demerits of *adharma* and the need for *dharma*. The character he created followed various paths and faced different consequences. His aim was to picture an utopian world free of sinners.

Another point to note is that the *Ramayana* is the result of the great Rishi's wounded heart, his *shoka rasa*.

The *Ramayana* as a treatise on education bears scrutiny. In the epic we find many Ashrama schools. The aim of these schools was to train students in such a way as to have a complete development: promote character, individuality, etc. Great sages like Gautama, Vishwamitra, Atreyi, Bharadwaja were in charge of these institutions. Valmiki's concern for such an ideal education stemmed from the fact that he himself had been deprived of the formative influence of a meaningful education. He had become a dacoit and followed the path of *adharma* because he had never learnt about *dharma*. He did not want the future generations to be so deprived.

Among the social concerns of the *Ramayana* is its discussion of the various aspects of monarchy. Valmiki spoke about democracy and the involvement of the people in administration. For instance, King Dasharatha had to seek the approval of the *royal* court before appointing Rama as the heir-apparent.

Valmiki also emphasises the responsibility of the individual in serving humanity and improving society. This is reiterated by Anjaneya, Rama and Bharata many times in the course of the narrative. The tradition of the 'Raghu Vamsa' is the service of humanity.

According to Valmiki, if a person commits a crime, he should be punished irrespective of his social status. Marichika and the other demons were punished because they destroyed the *yagna* of the rishis. Parasurama was punished for causing agony to the newly wedded couple. King Dasharatha inadvertently killed an ashrama boy and had to face the consequence of the curse of the child's parents.

When Ravana defended the abduction of Sita by saying it followed the dictates of *Rakshasa dharma* Sita is made to speak, defining *dharma*. She says that *dharma* is that which does good to people and harms none.

In the *Ramayana* we find many addicts who suffer because of their addictions. Vali is fond of women, Sugreeva is addicted to wine and Ravana to power. All the three suffer because of their obsessions. Lust and anger are the two things which steal the jewel of human wisdom. Hence we must be away from these passions. When anger dominates Ravana, he abducts Sita. Thus Valmiki warns people against these addictions.

Like human beings, birds and animals are the creation of God. They must be treated as we treat humans. Rama, for instance, performs funeral rites for Jatayu who sacrificed his life in an attempt to rescue Sita. Some animals like the squirrel tell human beings that they should not desist from duty on the plea of inability. One must do whatever one can. Thus, the squirrel itself helps Rama to construct a bridge to Lanka. One can achieve great tasks through unity. Rama could have killed Ravana directly without any effort given his divinity. But instead he organises a united attack to show the efficacy of a combined effort.

The epic teaches us that we must not forget our motherland even when we find a Disneyland. Lakshmana likes Lanka but Rama convinces him that the motherland is the best.

These and other such lessons indicate that Valmiki was attempting to drive away the ignorance of the people which compels them to commit crimes. It is an indication that Valmiki had deep insight into human psychology. *Ramayana* combines sublime poetry with a serious ethical message. Each character in the story has a message to convey which is pertinent eternally. The perennial philosophy that takes shape in the epic has sustained Indians for centuries. The intrinsic value of the epic has remained undiminished by time. Even today the *Ramayana* continues to pervade our cultural life in one way or another.

References

Avadhani, Venkata Divakarla. *Adikavi Valmiki.* Hyderabad: Samskritha Bhasha Prachara Samithi, 1980.
Lal, P. *The Ramayana of Valmiki.* New Delhi: Tarang Paperbacks, 1989.
Nagaiah, S. *Valmiki Ramayana - An Appreciation.* Madras: Super Power Press, 1981.

14

RAVIDAS

Sheela Devi

Saint Ravidas opened the floodgates of bhakti in the realm of Indian poetry. He wrote:

> I've never known how to tan or sew
>   though people come to me for shoes
> I have not the needle to make the holes
>   or even the tool to cut the thread.
> Others stitch and knot, and tie themselves in knots
>   while I, who do not knot, break free.
> I keep saying Ram and Ram, says Ravidas,
>   and death keeps his business to himself.

As death keeps his business to himself, Ravidas kept himself immersed in his devotion for his only lord, Lord Rama. An untouchable born into the family of cobblers, Ravidas surpassed the brahmins of Benaras in his devotion. The Brahmins saw a divine right in cornering the glory of the Lord by the sheer virtue of their birth. To them Ravidas said:

> Oh well-born of Benaras, I too am born well-known:
> My labour is with leather. But my heart can boast of the Lord.

Thus spoke Ravidas. He saw wisdom in the way God worked his way through mother nature. He chided the high caste thus, using familiar images from nature, "And this toddy tree you consider impure, since the sacred writings have branded it that way, but see that writings are written on its leaves."

The bhakti of Ravidas, then, is a gritty, personal faith so it is fitting that the response of the outcastes to it and to him has a number of facets — social, liturgical, conceptual and, of course, personal. The first of these responses is indeed the demand for social reform, and at various points over the past decades it has been couched in frankly political terms.

Casting aside all that is said and analysed about Ravidas as a social crusader, we can find in his poems a sweetness which attracted even brahmins. Whether they hated him or respected him, it did not matter to him; they could not just ignore him. Ravidas was a special poet and singer, and the hymns he sang evidently had such a ring that the upper castes especially came to hear them. His poetic charisma must have been equally powerful for he says that the brahmins actually bowed before him, in a total inversion of religious and social protocol. (1977:191-204)

One thing that lingers in the minds of those who read and admire Ravidas is whether the bhakti is a message of social protest. Is the equality it celebrates fundamentally a social reality — and therefore something revolutionary in its Indian context — or is it only spiritual in which case it can coexist with brahminical Hinduism even if it does not endorse it?

On the one hand it seems clear that a poet like Ravidas raises crucial questions about the social order. His approach towards brahmins and other upper castes who set store by standard Hindu texts and rituals is scarcely complimentary, and he has contempt for all who denigrate people belonging to other sectors of society than their own. He insists:

> A family that has a true follower of the Lord is
> neither high caste nor low caste, lordly or poor.

The number of times he refers to his own case position suggests that Ravidas was always mindful of it. On the other hand he does not propose any religious legislation that would change the current social order. Instead, it often seems that he values his own lowly position as a vantage point from which the truth about everyone comes clearly into view. His ideas of bhakti seem to be not so much that God desires to reform society as that He transcends it utterly, and that in the light of the experience of sharing in God, all social distinctions lose their importance. In one of his poems he speaks of how the person of faith may "flower above the world of his birth" as lotuses float upon the water. He often dwells on the miracle that God has come to him as an implicit sign of how remarkable it is that he should touch any human life.

Ravidas's bhakti, then, is an answer to caste ridden Hinduism, but not explicitly a call for its reform. Even though he speaks of a kingdom "where none are third or second" — all are one and where the residents "do this or that, they walk where they wish," still he admits that it is his "distant home" and he gives no direct call for realising it here on earth.

Indeed, when Ravidas speaks of the earth his emphasis is quite different. He characterises life in this world as an inevitably difficult journey and asks God for help along the way. Death stands waiting at the end of the road, he knows, and when it strikes, even one's closest relatives scurry to keep their distance. As for the body, it is a friction of air and water, nothing more than a hollow clay puppet. Above all, there is nothing to do in such circumstances — as bewildering to human beings as the wider world is to a frog in a well. It is useless to cry for help. Fortunately, there is a remarkable friend who answers that lonely call, someone who is at times confusingly, disconcertingly near, someone to whom people are tied by what Ravidas calls on several occasions "the bonds of love". That friend, of course, is God, as we see in the following lines:

> Your handiwork the world
> what could I offer more?
> I can only wave your name like
> the whisk before the Gods.

References

Sant Ravidas: Vicharak aur Kavi. Jalandhar: Nav Chintan Prakashan, 1977.

SECTION III

15

DADU DAYAL

Sujatha Nayak

That saints live for the sake of humanity is an indisputable fact; that most of them do not chronicle their own lives is also irrefutable. Much redundant and often unseemly controversies rage over many a saint's life. Dadu Dayal, a poet-saint of Rajasthan, is no exception. But as often happens with poet-saints, Dadu's convictions and his upbringing concern us here. As the inimitable Kabir rightly says:

> *Jaati na poocho sadhu ki pooch leejiye gnyan;*
> *Mol karo talwar ka, pada rahan do myan.*

This paper attempts to analyse some of Dadu's writings. For this purpose I have divided this paper into three parts. Part I tries to discuss Dadu's spiritual teachings; Part II his attempt at socio-religious reformation, and Part III the literary value of his *distichs*. I have based my readings on two books which contain a selection of his writing. They are : Monica Thiel Horstmann's *Crossing the Ocean of Existence—Braj Bhasa Religious Poetry: A Reader* and *Sant Dadu Dayal* edited by K.N. Upadhaya of which *Dadu: The Compassionate Mystic* is a translation. All the translations of verse rendered in English are theirs, none mine.

Part I

THE SPIRITUAL TEACHINGS: Dadu believes that the human form is the only vehicle that can provide escape from the cyclical play of life and death.

> *Baar Baar yahu tan nahin, nar nara yan deh;*
> *Dadu bahuri na paiya, janam amolika yeh.*

Dadu Dayal

> This body, a veritable manifestation of Divinity,
> In human form, is not available again and again.
> This priceless birth, thou canst not obtain again sayeth Dadu.
> (Dadu Dayal, 1980:28)

Only those who can estimate the value of this priceless treasure can hope to attain salvation. Otherwise it becomes the proverbial treasure on a donkey's back.

A very thin veil separates us from God and the veil is made up of a complex web of the ego and the mind:

> *Man hasti maya hastini, saghan ban sansar;*
> *To mein nirbhay havai, rahya Dadu mugdh ganvar.*
> The mind is the male elephant, Maya the female,
> and the world is the dense forest.
> Therein the stupid, demented creature has grown fearless.
> (ibid.,158)

The mind craves sensual pleasure taking it to be the only reality. Such is the spell cast by *Maya*. But there are antidotes to both the mind's restlessness and *Maya's* vice-like grip on it. And that is the constant and concentrated repetition of God's names—Allah, Ram and so on. The names Allah and Ram do not represent either the Islamic Godhead or the anthropomorphic form of the Hindu mythological king of Ayodhya. They represent *a bija mantra* which will help the devotee penetrate the layers of *Maya*:

> *Naav bhulave deha gun, jiv dasa sab jai;*
> *Dadu chadai nav ku, tou phiri lagai ai.*
> It is the Name which enables one
>   to forsake bodily qualities, and to rise
>   above the limitations of individuality.
> When detached from the Name, one is attached
>   to the world again,
> O Dadu. (ibid., 118)

Dadu regards the *mantra* as a fence which can achieve what millions of efforts cannot. It can destroy all the accumulated *karma* of the aspirant and unite him/her with its Divine Regulator. The distributor of this antidote — the *mantra* — is the guru. The greatness of the *guru* is conveyed in the following verse:

> *Satguru milai to paiye, bhagati mukti bhandar;*
> *Dadu sahajain dekhiye, sahib ka didar.*

> If the true Guru is found, the storehouse
> of all devotion and freedom is found.
> Then see thou with ease the vision
> of the Lord, sayeth Dadu. (ibid., 88)

God and the *guru* are verily one. But woebetide the disciple who breaks the *guru's* words.

> *Satguru sabad ulanghi kari, jini koi sish jai*
> *Dadu pag pag kai hai, jahan jai tahu khai.*
> Transgressing the Word of the Perfect Master,
> Let no disciple go his (/her) own way,
> *(Kal)* Time dogs his (/her) wherever s/he goes, O Dadu.
> (ibid., 21)

Dadu repeatedly cautions aspirants embarking on spiritual ventures on their own. It is a necessity and a blessing indeed to find a good *guru*. The *guru* is the veritable Satguru who can appraise and then guide us on the path of the razor's edge. Dadu recommends not only the *Nirakar* but also the *Akar* paths of God-realisation:

> *Niraka mansurati son, prem priti son sev;*
> *je pujai akar kow, tow sadhu partashi dev.*
> Full of love and affection, serve
>   the Formless with thy mind and soul.
> If thou worshipest the Form then
>   the saint is the manifest God. (ibid., 82)

The other attitude that Dadu endorses is that of the lover towards the beloved:

> *kyon bisari mera piv piyara, jiv ki kidan pran hamara;*
> *kyonkar jivai min jal bichure; tum bin pran sanehi*
> *chyzntamani jab kar thain chuthai; tab dukh pavai dehi.*
> Why hath my dearly Beloved forgotten me?
> Thou art my very life-breath.
> Like a fish separated from water,
> How can I survive without thee, O my Lord? (ibid., 150)

In order that this love may develop, purity of the body, mind and soul are prerequisites. In this connection, Dadu recommends a vegetarian diet. Eating non-vegetarian food is harmful because some day meat-eaters are bound to meet the fate of the beings they killed and consequently spiritual attainment might get postponed.

> (Dau) Ja kow maran jaiya soi phir marai;
> ja kai taran jaiye, sai, phir tarai.
> Whatever beings thou killest, the same
>   ones will kill thee in turn;
> Whatever beings thou savest, the same ones
>   will save thee in return, O Dadu. (ibid., 189)

Purifying the body, regarding it as the abode of God along with intense internal spiritual practices will help the aspirant. Any other external practices are exercises in futility. Once these basic tenets are set, then the devotee yearns for communion with God and finally learns the truth behind this creation which Kabir neatly puts across as:

> *Jal mein kumbh kumbh mein jal hai*
> *Bahar bhitar pani.*

And once the earthen pot breaks, once bodily distinctions break, the *atman* finally unites with the Paramatman to stop once and for all the cyclical play of life and death.

Part II

Dadu's Attempts at Social and Religious Reformation:
The poet-saints of India did not confine themselves to matters metaphysical and spiritual. They were intensely aware of their society and have much to say against three important manifestations of the establishment — formalism, ritualism and priestcraft. They condemned sham and religious priggery. Being object-lessons themselves, they illustrated that *nirvana* was by no means the prerogative of the upper classes nor eternal servility the fate of the lower.

The faith that Dadu propagated won him many followers and detractors. His detractors condemned him for preaching "heresy" — the Hindus because he denied the authority of the Vedas, rituals and casteism and the Muslims because he scorned the *namaz* and other dogmas.

> *Pathas pivai dhoi kari, pathat pujain pran*
> *Anti kal pathar bhaye, bahu bhude yahi gnyan.*
> They love stones and drink the water;
>   living souls worship stones,

> In the end they are converted into stones,
> Many have thus been ruined by this practice. (ibid., 200)

Again:

> *(Dadu) gal katain kalma bharai, aya bichara din;*
> *panchow bakhat nimaz gujarai, syabit nahin akin.*
> While cutting the throat of the poor,
>   innocent goat, they mutter holy syllables;
> They offer their holy prayer all five times
>   Yet they have no integrity whatsoever. (ibid., 188)

And, again:

> *Kaji kaja janhi, kegad hath kateb;*
> *Padhta padhta din gaye, bhitar nahin bhed.*
> The Qazi (who sentences others to death)
> While holding the Holy Book in hand,
> Knows not his own (impending) death.
> His days are spent in reading, but
> The Truth penetrates not within. (ibid., 10)

The addresses are unmistakable. Dadu firmly believed that God is for everyone because:

> *Isak Allah ki jat hai, Isak Allah ka ang;*
> *Isak Allah auvjud hai, isak Allah ka rang.*
> God belongs to the caste of love,
> Love is dear to Him;
> Love is His body,
> And love alone is His colour. (ibid., 14)

The social implications of the above are obvious. Since God belongs to the creed of love, God's creations too cannot belong to any other parentage. Dadu then sets out to define who a true Hindu or Muslim is:

> *jogi jangam sevde, boudh sanyasi sekh;*
> *Shat darsana dokhava lok ka, bhitari Ram dikhai.*
> Yogis, mendicants, Jains or Buddhist monks,
> Also the Muslim priests and the six
> Orthodox systems of Hindu philosophy
> All are forms of deceit, O Dadu,
> If they are bereft of devotion to God. (ibid., 195)

At a time when the country was rife with religious bigotry, such a definition was obviously unacceptable to many who professed various religions. As was to be expected Dadu and his followers were termed infidels. Dadu has something to say about that, too:

> *So kaphir jo bolai kaph; dil apna nahim rakhe saaph;*
> *Sain ko pehchana nahin; kud kapat sab us hi mahin.*
> Infidel is one who tells a lie;
> One whose conscience is not clear;
> Who has no recognition of the Lord;
> And is full of blemishes and deceit within. (ibid., 10)

Dadu's was an unconventional definition. Devotion to God, he felt, could be expressed in the aspirant's own way which might not necessarily be conventional. Though he often mocks idol worship and calling out to God from minarets, he says that they are justified when they stem not from superficial and dogmatic observance of rituals but out of love for God. He, however, continually recommends inner prayer because external worship tends to become showy:

> *kora kalas avah ka, upari chitra anek;*
> *Kya dijai Dadu ast bin, aise nana bhesh.*
> A new pot taken from the potter's furnace
>   may be decorated with many pictures outside;
> But of what use will it be to thee, O Dadu,
>   without any contents?
> Such are the ones who make outer display of religiosity.
> (ibid., 192)

One can infer from the above that Dadu tried to bring about changes, social and religious, via the medium of religion itself. This was perhaps because of the fact that religion dictated the system of society. It was not surprising, therefore, that especially of his stand on the caste system and religious bigotry Dadu stirred a hornet's nest. But the hornets could do nothing except rage impotently because in his lifetime itself, only a very small section of society was against him. The others realised that for a long time they has been so involved in concretising artificial barriers that the actual purpose of life was being overlooked.

Part III

Dadu's Work as Literature:

Like many other corpuses of the *"sant-kavi"* tradition, Dadu's works consists of two group's — *sakhis* and *padas*. The *sakhis* are religious didactic distichs while the *padas* are religious songs (*bhajans*) set to certain *ragas*.

The term *sakhi* is derived from *sakhya* or *sakshin*, meaning, the testimony of a realised soul whose knowledge is based not on perception but immediate, direct, revelation. In this tradition the *sakhis* were considered the mark of a saint, the proverbial *hayagriva*. Since the *sakhis* had to express a philosophical or spiritual maxim in the space of a couplet, it could not obviously develop any particular image or thought as could the *padas*. It had to be precise and concise. The *padas*, on the other hand, are often in couplets and sometimes in quatrains. A single image is sometimes developed in a song to convey Dadu's spiritual/mystical message.

In *"Par nahin payere, Ram bina nrivahan hay"* the image of river and ocean is used conveniently to talk of worldly existence and its innavigability without a Ferryman (God). This image enables Dadu to use other related images of shore, floods, vessels and in the final couplet he maintains:

> *That aughat viram hai re, dubat mahi sharira;*
> *Dadu kaya Ram bina, man nahin bandhai dhira.*
> The vessel of flesh is impassable and rough,
> The subtle transmigratory body is drowning in it;
> Dadu says: if the body is without Ram
> the mind cannot be controlled.

Dadu believes that the human form is the only vehicle that can provide escape from the wheels of life and death. He uses the images of a vessel, a ship, threshold, doorway, and unbaked earthen pot, etc., to speak of this potential medium of *mukti*.

But the human form also consists of a mind which generally believes in playing truant. The images of "mad elephant", "beggar", "jester", "frog", "serpent", "waves", "fish" and so on in Dadu's verses are symbolic of the vagrant mind.

The name or word of God can control the restlessness of the mind. Much importance is given to *Nam* or *Shabd* in Dadu and it seems to occupy the same position the "logos" occupies in

Christianity—" in the beginning was the Word. The Word was with God and the Word was God."

> *(Dadu) Sabdai bandhya sab rahai, sabdai sab hi jai;*
> *Sabdai hi sab up jai, sabdai sabai samai.*
> All are bound by the Word;
> The Word abides in all.
> All arise from the Word and
> Into the Word do all merge. (ibid., 109)

Dadu often uses the device of personification. *Kal/Time* when the personified is the hunter. It stands for temporal time, but by extension, also symbolises Death—the destructive aspect of time.

An oft-repeated device to speak of an aspirant's yearning for God is that of a lover aching for the beloved:

> *Birhani bapu na sanbharai;*
> *Nis din talaphai Ram ke karan, antari ek bicharai.*
> . . . .
> *Byakul bhai sarir na sajhai, bishn ban Hari marai;*
> *Dadu darsan bin krun jivai, Ram sanehi hamare.*
> The separated one controls not her body
> Writhing day and night for the sake of God,
> She thinks only of the One within.
> Restless for the sake of meeting the
> Beloved, she calls out for God again and again.
> God shoots her with the dreadful arrow of (poison)
> separation; she is restless with no awareness of her body.
> How can she survive, O Dadu? Without the
> vision of her beloved God? (ibid., 151)

The opening of this *pada* also testifies to the fact that whereas all the *sakhis* are in rhymed couplets of equal number of syllables, the *padas* follow a slightly different mode. Often the opening line might not have a rhyming line in which case it acts as refrain or even if it does not have one, the first two lines might not have an equal number of syllables. The lines that make up the rest of the song, however, are in couplets and sometimes in quatrains.

A noteworthy feature, though by no means an original one, is the signatory word "Dadu" in most of his writings. Since it occurs very frequently one tends to overlook it but it actually symbolises Dadu's iconoclastic stance. For signatory/words/names are in stark contrast to the anonymity of the Vedic texts. But Dadu is an individualist or "modernist" with a difference. Unlike many present-day Western-tradition-based poets that we read, his (Dadu's) name in his writings does not draw attention to itself.

Monica Thiel-Horstmann points out Dadu's extensive use of Nath-Yogic symbols. In the song *"Tab ham ek bhai re bhai"* Dadu uses the phrase "the secret of Malayagiri". Trees of two kinds, Thiel-Horstmann says, are contrasted in both Nath Yogic and Sant poetry. One, the creeper of delusion, rooted in *ahamkara* can be uprooted through intense spiritual practice. As a result of the sadhana the *sadhaka* derives the tree of Brahman or *tattva* which has no roots and is upside down.

Yet another poem *"Ulthi aputhaaya"* (consciousness has been discovered in a reverse manner) describes a central idea of the Nath-Yogic philosophy and practice, the latter called the *"ulta sadhana"* "the regressive practice".

> The human physical and psychic processes are conceived as moving in a downward direction. The movement during the evolution is free from the stable primeval matter to the diversified evolutes which are bound to decay, die and re-enter the process of the cycle of re-birth. Hence until all normal processes are reversed the human being cannot attain full liberation. (Thiel-Horstmann)

As far as his ideas are concerned, Dadu makes extensive use of Braj bhasa. Use of words like *karai, janai, chahya, saunpya, bhayau, nahin, kabahun, kahai,* etc., in place of *kare, jane, chahiye, saunpa, bhaya, nahin, kaba, kahate hain*, respectively testifies to this. Though he does make use of Nath Yogic symbols, his idiom is most often commonplace in the sense that he uses everyday words to symbolise spiritual insights:

> *Andhe kon dipak diya to bhi timir na jai;*
> *Sodhi nahin sarter hi, tasani ka sam jhai.*
> The blind was given the lamp,
> Yet his darkness was not removed;
> What is the use of teaching one
> Who has not purified the body. (Dadu Dayal, 1980:23)

Those lives which are not used for the purpose of seeking the Divine are as fruitless, Dadu says, as the *nagar* creeper. The comparison is apt because it is common knowledge that *nagar* (betel) creepers do not yield any fruit. Dadu also compares such people to parrots. Parrots often break open a cotton seed fruit expecting to find something edible. But they get only cotton seed inside which is insipid. Needless to say, cotton seed fruit symbolises materialism, parrots are those human beings who are involved in the meaningless pursuit of transitory things.

But once God's blessings are on human beings then their thirst for the Divine is not easily satiated. They are like "fish...writhing restlessly/ when separated from water" until they realise the Truth:

> *Dadu yahu ghat kacha, jal bhar ya binasat nahin bar;*
> *yahu ghat phuta, jal gaya, samajhat nahin ganwar.*
> This body, sayeth Dadu, is like an unbaked
> earthen pitcher filled with water.
> The foolish one does not understand
> that the moment the pitcher breaks
> the water flows out. (ibid., 82)

But once the *atman* unites with the *Paramatman*, the aspirant is:

> *Khir nir jyoun mili rahai, jal jalahi saman;*
> *Atman pani lun jyoun, duja nahin an.*
> Like water mixing with milk, like water merging into water,
> Like salt dissolving in water, he is unified with
> no duality whatsoever. (ibid., 80)

The only people who can redeem the aspirants are saints. They are qualified to act as our guides because:

> *Bhouja ap tirain te tarain, pran udharan har*
> Having themselves crosses the ocean of the world,
> they take others across. (ibid., 81)

The comparison to Ferrymen immediately drives the point home.

The more we read Dadu's teachings, the more scope does it give us for literary interpretations. While assessing his literary merit one should remember that two centuries of Sant tradition had preceded him. (Dadu is supposed to have been born in A.D. 1544 and died in A.D. 1603) The literary and religious tradition was in the main, a floating tradition, and, therefore, gave abundant scope for a complex network of influences and by extension, overlapping, to occur. Yet in one respect he is slightly different from his predecessors, say Kabir: Dadu accepted worship of God with form, while Kabir in the main did not. Kabir's derision of idol worship can hardly be forgotten: *"Pahan pujai Hari milai to, main pujun pahar / Tate ye chaki bhali, pis khaiye sansar."*

Though not very original in his utterances, Dadu's spiritual convictions more than his literary merit seem to have won him a large following. Indeed the profoundness of his thoughts garbed in everyday idiom makes him relevant today. For, did he not believe in and practice liberty, equality and freedom, in a word, democracy, which is today a much sought after, but little understood and much less practised utopian ideal? His ideal of selfless service among many other virtues makes him one of the brightest stars in the galaxy of the poet-saints of India.

Finally, Dadu approximates to the idea of poet as "Vates" in Greek and *Kavi* in the Indian literary tradition. He is not only a composer of verse but a *Darshanika*, a seer, who through his access to the realms of the Highest Truth, shares in his infinite compassion his experience with others.

References

Dayal, Dadu. *Sant Dadu Dayal* (ed.). Upadhaya K.N. Punjab: Radha Soami Satsang Beas, 1990.
Thiel-Horstmann, Monika. *Crossing the Ocean of Existence—Braj Bhasa Religious Poetry: A Reader.*
Upadhaya, K.N., *Dadu the Compassionate Mystic,* Punjab: Radha Soami Satsang Beas, 1980.

16

TUKARAM

P.S. Deshpande

Tukaram has been recognised all over India as one of the greatest poet-saints of Maharashtra. His poetry has great political, economic and religious significance. Tukaram has used it to express and illustrate his poetic and spiritual vision of life. It captivated the reader by the quality of life and the soul that it reveals and by its mellow grace. It has a wide popular appeal to the uninitiated on account of the beauty and simplicity of language and a special appeal to the learned and initiated because of its power of communicating with felicity, ease and directness the highest truth of spiritual realisation. R.D. Ranade (1933:19) considered Tukaram as the glorious pinnacle of the mystical edifice in Maharashtra founded by Gyaneshvara and erected by Namadeva and other saints. In every village of Maharashtra there are people who are well acquainted with the poetry of Tukaram along with the poetry of other poet-saints. Their familiarity with these works have sustained them through their lives and kept the Hindu society united. It is because of the works of these poet-saints that religious, moral and human values still survive in our villages. Throughout history our society has passed through many crises but has retained its inner strength and identity because of the sustenance it has derived from the works of these poet-saints. People still continue to look up to these poet-saints for inspiration and for assimilation of their succinct exhortations on each one of life's concerns and on the *summum bonum* of human existence.

According to a widely accepted account Tukaram was born at the village of Dehu in Poona district in A.D. 1608. He belonged to a family of tradesman who had worshipped Vithoba ever since Tukaram's ancestor Vishvambhara had made an eventful pilgrimage to Pandharpur.

The picture of Tukaram's early years is that of a happy and prosperous family. Besides the mother Kanakai and the father Bolhoba, there were three brothers, Savaji, Tukaram and Kanhoba. When his father became old, he asked Savaji to take charge of the family business. But he begged to be released from such an arduous task and the choice then fell upon Tukaram. Tukaram carried on the business for several years with success. But unfortunately a series of disasters overtook the family. Both parents died as also Savaji's wife and Savaji became a religious mendicant. Tukaram began to lose money in business; gradually he fell into debt and became an easy victim to many rogues.

Tukaram's first wife Rakhmabai was an asthmatic patient. He, therefore, married a second wife Avali or Jijabai who was the daughter of a Poona shopkeeper.

Tukaram faced a severe crisis in his life in 1629 when a terrible famine broke out in Maharashtra. His first wife died of starvation. His son Santu also died. His family began to starve. In less than eight years his dream of a successful family life was completely shattered. At 13 he entered business, at 17 his parents died. Soon his brother's wife died, which was followed by the death of his first wife and son. At 18 his brother became a *sannyasi* and at 21 he found himself totally bankrupt. Closing his eyes he cried, "Hari, O Lord, can I behold Thee? How can I bring Thee before my eyes? How shall I deal with the world?"

After this crisis Tukaram severed his ties with the world and his family business. He threw into the river Indrayani all his family account books, withdrew from the world and spent all his time in silent communication and in religious devotion.

Though his failures and moments of crises in life contributed towards Tukaram's *vairagya*, his initiation in the esoteric path of *sadhana* by his teacher Babaji in a dream was a great event in his spiritual life. Tukaram himself tells us that his spiritual line may be traced from Raghava Chaitanya to Keshava Chaitanya and Babaji Chaitanya (Abh. 3427). Bahinabai, one of Tukaram's greatest disciples, says in one of her *abhangas* that Raghava Chaitanya was a spiritual descendent of Sachchidananda Baba, who was himself a spiritual descendent of Gyaneshavara. From this account it becomes obvious that Tukaram comes directly in the spiritual line of Gyaneshavara. Next to Babaji, Tukaram refers to the influence on his life, exercised by Gyaneshavara,

Namadeva, Kabir and Eknath (Abh. 2787). Tukaram was persecuted by Rameshvara Bhatta, Mambaji Gosavi and many others who later became his admirers and disciples. Tukaram makes many references to his wife who he says had a biting tongue and who quarrelled frequently with her husband. But it must be said that her trials were many, and being loyal to him as she was, and in keeping the family intact in spite of dire poverty, her contribution to his life-work was not inconsiderable. As a husband he loved his wife in spite of her cantankerous nature. He thanked God for blessing him with a cursing consort as it helped him to get detached from family life and concentrate wholly on his spiritual seeking. He earnestly tried, by precept and example, to wean her from excessive worldliness (Abh. 3489). Tukaram was not an ascetic, he led a normal life. "Neither punish nor pamper the body", was his golden rule. His sainthood was rooted in his humanity and his humanity extended to all that throbbed with life (Abh. 119). Though Tukaram was familiar with the poetry of Gyaneshavara, Eknath, Kabir and Namadeva and dived deep into the *Bhagavat Gita* and *Bhagavad Purana*, he cannot certainly be called learned. But his poetry has greatly enriched the Marathi language and literature. His poetry is endowed with originality and religious inspiration. His poems are spontaneous and are given out in the enthusiasm of his *kirtans*.

Tukaram has left us over 4,600 *abhangas*. Since their chronological order of composition is not known, it is rather difficult to trace systematically the important phases of his spiritual development. The *abhangas* reveal a high degree of religious depth and a wide range of practical knowledge. But there are also apparent contradictions and inconsistencies. There are sublime visions and trifling matters, noble sentiments and crude emotions, sometimes high-seriousness is mixed with banality, idolatry is upheld in some and rejected in others, rituals are recognised in some and criticised in others. His tendency to brevity sometimes results in obscurity. Though the language is sometimes not refined, it goes straight to the very heart of the readers.

His teachings in his poetry can be summed up in the broad tenets of the *varkari* sect: to recognise and worship the Divine in every object of manifestation, not to discriminate on the ground of sex, caste, religion, creed and dogma, to worship God Vitthal, an incarnation of God Vishnu as the principal deity, to believe in the unity of all deities and in the unity among the basic tenets of all religions, to practise non-violence in thought, word and deed, to practise truthfulness, to transcend passions, to give up the feeling of doership in action, to achieve tranquillity of mind, to refrain from malicious gossip, to feel compassion for all creatures, to achieve a state of complete detachment, to have a feeling of humility and a sense of shame in doing things not sanctioned by the scriptures or usage, to practise forgiveness, fortitude, external and internal purity.

The poems of Tukaram cover a great many topics. There are autobiographical *abhangas* relating to incidents in his own life, *abhangas* referring to his religious experience, on God and his relation to the world, on God's relation to his worshippers, on sin, on the means of salvation, on the obstacles to salvation, on the moral ideal, on the saints, on renunciation and the state after death, etc.

The poems are written in a familiar *abhanga* metre with its variations in rhyming and arrangement. There is no hard and fast rule about the length, and although most of them are short some have more than fifty lines.

Tukaram strengthened the *varkari* cult and contributed to the social and religious history of Maharashtra. He was also instrumental in aiding the political rise of Shivaji and the Maratha power which was an answer and challenge to the Mughal imperialists. But the religious and spiritual significance of his work was even more profound. It signified an extension of the renaissance which had begun in the thirteenth century and a reassertion of the Hindu spirit which had been on the decline during the period of Muslim aggression. It created self-confidence in the masses and awakened them to their glorious tradition. Tukaram removed the apparent contradiction between the intellectualists' monism and the devotee's dualism and showed that self-realisation transcends both monism and dualism.

Aspiration, devotion, action, consciousness, steadiness of consciousness, transcendental devotion and self-realisation are the stages of individual evolution outlined in the *Tukaram Gatha*.

Tukaram is recognised in Maharashtra as one of the greatest devotees. By strengthening the *varkari* sect he revived the

Bhagavad Dharma in Maharashtra. Tukaram's poetry reveals mainly three phases. The first phase consists of his spiritual career, where he is resolved to withdraw himself from the life of the world with a determined effort to achieve spiritual realisation. This can be called as the stage of positive affirmation. Then comes the phase of warring with himself. Finally, there is a phase of new affirmation, a period of a final vision of the Godhead, which supersedes the earlier two phases.

In the first phase he becomes aware of the mystic treasure, passed on to him by his guru Babaji Chaitanya in his dream. He is determined not to part with it and bids farewell to all idleness, to all forgetfulness, to all shame and vices which stand in the way of the attainment of God (Abh. 2774). He impresses upon himself an extreme severity in social relations. He shuns the worldly objects and affections which are the causes of sorrow, becomes impervious to praise and blame, happiness and sorrow, compassion and anger (Abh. 594). He avoids people because they are involved in all sorts of futile activities. He at one stroke comes out of the manners of the world (Abh. 1514). He invites deliberate suffering, requests God to make him homeless, wealthless, childless so that he may remember God. He considers wealth and fortune as a calamity (Abh. 2084). "Let me get no food to eat, nor any child to continue my family line, but let God have mercy on me. Let my body suffer all sorts of suffering but let God live in my mind. All these things are really perishable says, Tuka, for God alone is eternal and a source of happiness" (Abh. 247).

As a spiritual aspirant, Tukaram advises us to cease to take care of the body. Old age brings the news of death, so the mind should get alert at such a message (Abh. 1914). He constantly remembers death and calls it a thief, a robber and advises us to protect our inmost treasure (Abh. 248, 1006, 1106). He tells us that nobody can rescue us from the clutches of death except God himself. We cannot rely on money, parents, wife, children, relatives and friends in this matter, on anyone, except God (Abh. 2178, 2035).

But Tukaram was conscious of the great merit that belonged to the body. He asks us to use the body well and make it pure.

The most important help Tukaram considers for the realisation of God is the company of saints and he expressed earnest desire for the company of those who love God. He wants to meet like-minded people. His mind plans to meet them and his eyes keep a watch for them (Abh. 1316). He wants to be saved from false prophets. He finds only arrogance in the learned. Those who are well-versed in the Vedas only delight in quarrelling with one another. The so-called gurus are full of anger (Abh. 980). He does not know how to express his obligations to the saints. They keep him always awake. He shall not be able to repay their kindness even if he sacrifices his life. They impart great spiritual knowledge even in their normal conversation (Abh. 2787).

But with all his efforts to know God, Tukaram finds it difficult to reach Him. He becomes extremely restless. He compares his self with the old saints and thinks that perhaps he is still a slave of his senses and is not able to curb a single sense (Abh. 319). He intensifies his internal and external warfare which he has been carrying on in his life. "I am always warring," he says, "with the world and with the mind. Accidents befall me and I try to ward them off by the power of Thy name" (Abh. 3140). He is afraid on account of the darkness of the journey. All the quarters become lone and dreadful to him. He loses all courage when he sees herds of dangerous beasts. The darkness prevents his journey and he stumbles at every step. He finds numerous paths opening out before him and he is afraid to take any one of them though his guru had shown him the way. He thinks that God is yet far away (Abh. 2504). He finds desolation in the external as well as in the internal world; he asks God to save him from the wanderings of his mind. His mind is very agile and does not rest even for a moment (Abh. 1136). He becomes keenly conscious of his defects. His introspective mind puts him to torments and self-calumny (Abh. 1902). He elaborates on his vices and sins, his egoism, censure, betrayal, adultery. He enumerates them at length and says that his mind trembles to think of them (Abh. 2062).

Tukaram asks the saints to intercede. He begs for God's grace to save him. In *abhangas* 1485, 1279, 1923, 2527 he loses his patience and calls God impotent, cruel, shameless, thief, an adulterer, one who forgets his Godhood, an ass, a dog, an ox and a liar. He is now provoked to quarrel with Him and says that nobody can gag his mouth (Abh. 1531). He prepares himself to curse his God now (Abh. 3548). He loses all patience with his

God. He threatens Him with dire consequences if he does not appear before him. "I shall spoil Thy fair name, I shall refuse to utter Thy name, Thy name shall be dishonoured." "In my opinion God does not exist — I have lost both the life of the world and the life of the spirit" (Abh. 3303). "In my opinion," says Tukaram, "God is dead - I shall no longer speak about God. I shall not meditate on his name. Both God and I have perished - vainly have I followed Him, and vainly have I spent my life on Him (Abh. 1597). Finally he is determined to commit self-slaughter. "Thou hast no anxiety for me — why should I now continue to live? — My hopes are shattered and I shall now commit self-slaughter" (Abh. 2266). His heart-rending cry was at last heard by God. Tukaram had God's vision and bowed at His feet. He narrates this blissful experience in *abhanga* 4065.

For Tukaram the path of light begins with moral discipline and devotion to Vitthal. It ends in spiritual freedom when the individual feels that he has himself become Vitthal. It is thus a gospel of spiritual life with particular emphasis on the ethical stages. Spiritual life is nothing but fellowship with God through service, through devotion and through contemplation. True spiritual life begins with moral discipline and faith in God. He condemns in severe terms all evil doers, atheists, religious hypocrites who without making a sincere attempt to reach God traverse the downward path. He criticises rituals, sacrifices, popular forms of worship, severe penances, ascetic ways of life and rigid rules of traditional ethics in a spirit of sympathy and love and replaces them by a purer and more inward and living religion. He tolerated neither the arrogant free-thinker who discards all scriptures and becomes a law unto himself, nor the blind literalist who makes a fetish of his scriptures and follows the letter of the law and kills the spirit. Tukaram asks the aspirant to shift the goal of his life from the external material world to the internal spiritual world, to abide in it constantly, to feel that he is no longer a separate self with interests of his own, but an agent of God carrying out his high purpose. There is no happiness beyond serenity. All else is sorrow. Therefore, if you hold on to serenity you will cross over to the other shore. If desire and wrath get stirred, the body becomes a nest of tribulations. "Tuka says: when serenity is attained all troubles end as a matter of course." "Keep your mind serene: it is the secret of all achievements — O ye seekers of happiness and contentment. By the mind the mind is worshipped. Wishes are fulfilled within the mind. Mind is the mother of all. Mind is master and disciple. It renders valuable service to itself. Seekers, pupils, pundits, listeners and speakers hear what I say: there is no deity whatsoever other than this declares Tuka."

Tukaram's God was everywhere, not confined to Pandharpur nor manifested in stone alone. Nevertheless, like other saints, he did not deny himself the liberty to worship Vitthala just as he liked. At the same time he had no illusions about the nature of true worship. He adored Vitthala without being "idolatrous". He clearly distinguishes between God and his material representation. "We make a stone image of Vishnu," he says, "but the same is not Vishnu: the worship is offered to Vishnu, the stone remains the stone."

Tukaram gave utmost importance to inner contemplation. "Inner contemplation," he says, "is the real worship. Know this to be the secret, if you wish to know." His Vitthala was standing no doubt with even steps on a brick, so full of charm, on the banks of Bhima but he is also "Bliss without parallel, eternally pure. That which is the objective of constant contemplation for the Yogis." "Tinier than the tiniest atom Tuka is vast as the sky." "My native land is the whole universe!" This is what Tukaram says about himself. He further tells us, "I have built my home in the stainless, my everlasting residence is the formless, I am completely one with the reality beyond illusion. I have attained individual unity. The day of divine light has dawned for me, and I am merged in the mindless state free from anxiety."

Tukaram rises above idolatry, above all conventions, above traditional ideas and above himself. He asks the aspirants to keep his mind radiant because it is the root of all achievements. The mind, according to him, is both the guru and the disciple; it renders service to itself, it bestows grace on itself.

The *mantra* he received from his guru in a dream was after his own heart: it was also very simple; it was "Ram Krishna Hari". For him Hari is all-pervading. This faith is the very essence of *Vedanta*. He makes no distinction between Hari and Hara. He says, "there is no difference between Hari and Hara — each is in the heart of the other." Tukaram practised what he preached. He found his happiness in the happiness of others and felt unhappy to see others suffer. "I cannot see these people sunk in misery," he said. "Whatever his family, clean or untouchable if he should call himself a slave of God, Tuka says, he is a blessed man."

Tukaram had realised the vision of the Unity of the universe in God and of God in himself. "While God is in yourself, says Tuka, in vain do you wander about places of pilgrimage. The musk deer has the perfume in its own navel, but it roams about the whole forest in search of it. Why don't you see the God in your own person, O you foolish people?" Like Eknath, Tukaram too goes to see God and finds himself metamorphosed into God. Those who are blessed by the illumination of a guru are indeed happy. Knowledge dwells in their hearts. Tuka says: knowledge verily is Vitthala in all fullness. He vitalises even the minutest atom." Then he gives his final state of realisation in the words, "My speech is silent; dying I live. Existing I do not exist. In enjoyment is my renunciation, in association my detachment. I have broken all bonds, I am not what I appear to be. I have witnessed my death by my own eyes — I am now far from limitations of I and mine." In another *abhanga* Tukaram says, "Tinier than the tiniest atom I am as vast as the sky I have abandoned triplicates. The light is within the lamp. I now remain only for the service of all."

The greatness of Tukaram lies in his transcendence of traditional ideas—in one of the *abhangas* he boldly declares: "In my view God is verily dead. Let Him exist for others; but in your own mind know that the truth is otherwise."

The secret of Tukaram's greatness and his ever-increasing appeal lies in his essential humanity, his simplicity, his frankness and above all his capacity which he displayed to transcend himself. Born as an ordinary man he transformed himself into an extraordinary poet-saint. With all his achievements he remained a humble until the end. He was a paradox to many when he was alive and he has not ceased to be an enigma ever since. He experienced the worst and the best of life: the hell of human misery and the heaven of superhuman delight. His songs are like the stars, they show us our path even in the darkest night of the soul. He acted his part well as a son, as a brother, as a friend, as a tradesman, as a devotee, as a husband and as a lover of man, bird and beast. He teaches his fellow beings not chiefly by what he says but by what we realise him to have felt and experienced as aspiration, struggle and realisation.

References

Deming, W.S. *Selections from Tukaram*, Madras: Christian Literature Society for India (the *abhanga* numbers given in the essay refer to this volume), 1932.

Ranade, R.D. *Indian Mysticism: Mysticism in Maharashtra*, Poona, 1933.

17

MIRABAI

Shanta Subba Rao

The name Mira evokes a very complex and paradoxical image, a multifaceted personality in whom polarities meet. To the egocentric, vainglorious Rajput community which prided itself on its deep-rooted royal tradition, social customs and hierarchical caste system, Mira is a self-assertive, non-conformist rebel whose name and memory should be wiped out of the annals of Rajput history as she has tarnished the image of the royal family of Sisodia. To the feminists she is the most liberated woman and to the whole world she is the greatest of the devotees of Lord Krishna for whom she sacrificed everything in her life. She is a gentle figure, clad in white, with *ektar* in hand, dancing in deep ecstasy, singing the glories of God, drinking deep the divine nectar, unmindful of her physical surroundings. Today, all these images of Mira are as alive and relevant as they were in the past.

At a time in the sixteenth century when the word feminine evoked only the image of someone physically beautiful, delicate and graceful and mentally meek, gentle and docile, Mira was the first feminist in the broadest sense of the term, who broke away from the narrow bonds of tradition, rigid social and religious customs, class and caste distinctions and discriminations, and sought absolute freedom. She surmounted all the physical, territorial as well as sexual, mental and spiritual barriers and limitations. Her protest is not a half-hearted, slogan-raising interspersed with a few symbolic gestures. Her very life is a translation of the protest into action and the fulfilment of her ambition, a reaching-out to the goal. Her triumph is not limited to the freedom gained from the superficial, limited, materialistic level of the physical world, with its legal, social and economic implications but extends to the region of the spirit where the individual soul is liberated totally and merges into the universal consciousness. Mira's life as the Queen of Mewar who travelled from Mewar to Dwaraka through Brindaban, her life as a devotee of Krishna who bears her soul in her *padas*, is a journey both in the literal and metaphorical sense, from the profane to the sacred.

Mira's rebellion begins with her refusal to accept as her husband anyone other than Giridhar whom she has chosen. She refuses to surrender to her human husband as an object of pleasure and yet paradoxically she throws all womanly modesty to winds and audaciously declares in the most suggestive and erotic manner her yearning for the physical presence and the love of Krishna whom she adores.

> Giridhar is my true lover
> On beholding His beauty I long for Him much.
> As night falls I set out to see Him
> And at break of day I return
> Day and night I sport in his company,
> I please Him in any way I can,
> Whatever He clothes me in, that I wear
> Whatever He offers, that I eat
> My love for Him
> Is ancient and long-standing
> Without Him I could not live. (20)

She surrenders herself to Gopal completely and unconditionally, physically, mentally and materialistically, *tan, man, dhan*. She is left with no will of her own to protest. She is totally besotted by the beauty of her beloved and has submerged her identity into His. The very thought that she can live without Him and apart from Him is inconceivable; she is one with Him. Yet she is a unique lover who reverses the roles of the lover and the beloved, who instead of being sought after and wooed seeks Him and courts Him not secretly but openly proclaiming her love.

Mira the non-conformist, instead of observing *purdoh* and remaining cloistered in the palace according to the dictates of Rajput tradition, comes out into the streets, associates herself with saints, sages and common people who are socially her inferiors. She sings and dances openly with the other devotees, with utter disregard for family honour, *kulmaryada* and reputation. The threats of the king of Sisodia, his attempts to put an end to her life, her mother-in-law's accusations that she is a *kulnashi* do not deter her from giving full vent to her devotion with total abandon. Though she drank the poison, slept on the bed of thorns/nails without a murmur or protest, she defies both the mother-in-law and the Rana, the former a symbol of suppression and oppression at the domestic, home level and the latter, the ultimate in worldly power and authority.

> *Sanp pitara raja bhejya, Mira hath diya jaye*
> *Jahar ka pyala raja bhejyo, amrit dinh banay*
> *Sul sej raja ne bheji, dwijyo Mira sukay.*

Much to the displeasure and annoyance of the members of the royal family who observed caste distinctions very rigidly, Mira accepted Ravidas as her guru. To Mira he was not a cobbler but an enlightened soul worthy of occupying the seat of a guru.

> I have found a guru in Ravidas
> He has given me the pill of knowledge
> I lost the honour of the family,
> I went astray with the sadhus.
> I don't follow the norms as the oldest daughter-in-law
> I have thrown away the veil,
> I have taken refuge in the great guru
> And snapped my fingers at the consequences.
> (Madhu Kishwara and Ruth Vanitha, 1989:80)

Discarding the riches and comforts of the palace Mira embraces a life of poverty. She proves the true spirit and courage of a Rajput woman by laying herself open to all types of dangers on the way to Brindaban. However, she does not put a high price on the family honour and *suhag*, the concept of *sati* and *jauhar*. She does not observe *sati* when her husband Bhojraj dies for she considered herself *chirasuhagini* as she is married to the *ajara amara* Giridhari. Nevertheless, she is a *sati* as she has experiences *sat* or truth in her union with her beloved Giridhari.

Rising above the binary opposition of male/female principle she has liberated herself from the constraints of sex. In fact, she turns her female body which is considered a hindrance and limitation into an asset to win love of the divine bridegroom.

Though the twentieth century may recognise Mira as the first feminist born four centuries ahead of time, before the concept of feminism had come into existence and interpret her work as feministic writing belonging to the third phase, "the Female phase" (Elaine Showalter, 1979) where female experience becomes "the source of autonomous art" yet her role as a feminist is limited to the world of academics. To the rest of the world Mira is a Rajput queen who experienced innumerable hardships, persecution, calumny, in her path of devotion. She is the greatest of mystic poets who trod the path of bhakti and took *madhurabhava* to its highest peaks. She is the ideal lover who surrendered herself to Lord Krishna in deep devotion and immeasurable love.

Mira stands as the symbols of a *mumukshu*, an aspirant who is eager to comprehend that invisible, yet all-pervading supreme Truth or Brahman who is addressed as "the bare Pure One" (Plotinus), "Perfect Beauty" (St. Augustine), "Wilderness of God" (Eckhart) whom Mira addresses as Giridhari, and to establish an unbroken connection with Him and ultimately become one with Him. Her life is a metaphor for an individual's awareness of the limited individual soul and the overwhelming, all-powerful consciousness of God and an endeavour to reach out to that consciousness.

Mira's mystic approach or *rahasya vada* is the devotional mysticism of the *Puranas*, especially of the *Bhagavata* where interpersonal, human relationship between God and man is highlighted. The bond between God and man is so close that God is considered as the nearest and dearest and the role He plays is that of a friend or a lover or a bridegroom. "God may well be loved not thought," declares the author of *The Cloud of Unknowing*. Plotinus describes this coming together of individual soul and the universal soul, the devotee and the Lord as "the veritable love, the sharp desire." "It is the burning within...the flame of love for what is there to know—the passion of the lover resting on the bosom of his love" (Underhill, 1960). Therefore, the very language and symbols used are entirely different from the "icy method of negation". The words are surcharged with emotional exuberance, exhilarating joy, burning passion, and deep and touching pathos.

This divine-human relationship which is not restricted by time and space but is eternal and non-physical, applicable to all ages, races, cultures, religions and regions is conceptualised in the metaphorical presentation of Krishna lila at Gokul and Brindaban, the *rasalila* of the gopis and Shyamsundar, the love of the *munipatnis* for *Kanahyya*, the yearning of Radha for Yoshodanandan and the pangs of separation of Mira from her beloved Giridhari.

Though Mira did not belong to any particular school of devotion either *Nirguna* or *Saguna* exclusively, we find in her traces of *Nirgunabhakti* of the Sant and the Nath *sampradaya*, of Sufism that expresses the devotion of a lover to his beloved and the *kirtan sampradaya* of Sri Chaitanya, where a devotee loses his bodily consciousness experiencing a bacchanalian frenzy or *unmadinibhakti*.

Some scholars hold that Mira has taken Andal of the Alvar tradition as her model while others feel that gopis are her model for in one of her songs she states that she was a gopi named Lalitha in her previous birth who pined away for Krishna and is still pining for Him as Mira in this birth.

Mira's *padavali* reveal that her *madhura bhav* is something unique. Her agony, her anguish is a purely subjective personal experience which can have no parallel. The pangs of separation, *viraha*, the torture of estrangement and the inconsolable grief find a framework in the most spontaneous and natural flow of the *padas*. The personal element which is one of the chief qualities of *gita kavya* reaches its peak in Mira's *siddha kavya* (songs by the realised soul).

Peerki Akriti or the anguish that wells up from the innermost being, the unity and brevity of thought, the cadence and melody of the verse, meticulous adherence to rules of prosody, that is, *atmabhivyakti, bhava pravranata, anviti, samkshipti* and *sangeetatmakata* which are consciously and assiduously cultivated by the composers of *gita kavya* come naturally and spontaneously to Mira establishing her as a peer to the great masters such as Vidyapati, Surdas, Paramandadas and Hitaharivamshi. Though Mira is not an exponent of classical music, her songs naturally lend themselves to the classical tunes of Todi, Bhairavi, Sorat, Lalit, Bihag, Maru and others according to the mood that is delineated in the *pada*. But their significance and importance lie in their being an effective mode of *sadhana* to attain the highest, viz., to be with the beloved and to become one with Him. Therefore, the songs are a metaphoric representation and realisation of the physical, mental and spiritual aspiration of a lover being united with his beloved. It is divine ecstasy achieved through agony.

Perhaps, it would not be an exaggeration if one were to state that Mira established through her *padas* a tradition of her own, a new cult in the field of devotion that appealed not only to a woman's heart but also to the feminine sensibility of all those who follow the path of devotion in the *madhurabhava*. In fact, according to Mira the only male existing is Krishna the *paramapurusha* and the rest are gopis, different manifestations of *prakriti* who hunger for Him.

Mira's *padavali* disclose that Mira is both a *sagunopasaka* and a *nirgunopasaka*. As a *sagunopasaka*, she has passed through the stages of *sravana, manana, dhyana, dharana* and *samadhi*. Among the nine modes of bhakti (*navavidha bhakti*) Mira has chosen *madhurabhakti*. In her *padavali* we find different modes, different stages and approaches that a lover would adopt to woo and win the heart of the beloved. In the first stage of "divine discontent" (Underhill) Mira renounces not only the extraneous worldly material possessions, but also the very concepts of "I-ness" and "mine-ness", *ahamkara* and *mamakara*. In the second stage where "the mind is kindled by contemplation to the burning love" she sings and dances in ecstasy in the streets keeping company with holy men almost in a trance. The third stage is when "the soul gazes upon Truth without any veils of creatures — not in a mirror darkly, but in its pure simplicity" (St. Victor) and Mira who knows Giridhari to be none other than the Parabrahman, not as an abstract concept, but as a manifestation in human form, recounts again and again his personal details. She is so bewitched by Giridhari that every minute detail of his physical appearance is enumerated at any opportunity that she gets. Therefore, in her *padas* we find her constantly describing the peacock plume in his crown, the gleaming *tilak* on his brow, the golden earring, *makarakundalas*, the raven locks, the necklace of gems, *tulasimala*, *peetambar*, the jingling anklets and the magic flute that casts a spell on the inanimate as well as the animate world. She beseeches the stealer of butter as well as the hearts of gopis to reside in her eyes so that she will never be deprived of his glorious sight: "*Basya mharo nainan ma.*"

Mira entreats him to favour her with a single glance for he is her only refuge and hope. Her spirit rises at once when Shyam looks at her body with his lustrous eyes. She is so deeply smitten by the piercing Cupid-like arrows of the glance, she realises that the deep gash of love made by him cannot be healed whether by herbs or pastes, *yantras* or *mantras*. Only the "impudent son of Nanda" knows the remedy. Her eyes are transfixed on the three angular poses (*tribhangi*) of Krishna and she knows the impossibility of breaking away from the spell. She drinks deep the beauty of the divine being, with the charming locks which look almost entangled in his brows, his fingers flying over the flute, creating the magic melody, his turbaned figure gently swaying under the Kadamba tree. To such a bewitcher Mira lost her body, mind and soul and set aside all worldly norms of proper etiquette, *lokamaryada*:

> My family members repeatedly try to restrain me
> But attachment to the Dancer with the peacock plume
> Has sunk deep.
> My mind is drowned in the beauty of Shyam,
> And the world says I have gone astray.

Mira's absolute surrender to the Lord makes her feel that she has become the personal property of Giridhari and henceforth all her actions will be motivated by him and for him. Even if he were to sell her as a slave she would unhesitatingly agree, for she has no will of her own. Her lord's wish is her will.

> Murari has come to dwell in my heart,
> ...
> I adorn myself to receive Shyam
> And prepare a bed for his enjoyment
> Mira's Lord is the courtly Giridhari
> Again and again she offers him her all. (15)

Now that she is dyed in the dye of Hari, that is, love for Hari is so all-absorbing that she would do anything to please him, she would even dance before him with no thought for public opinion. She admits that she has no one to call her own in the world:

> *Mereto Giridhar Gopal dusara na koi*
> *Tat mat bandhu bhraat apne nahi koi*

but she also knows that by discarding all the worldly ties and taking refuge in Giridhari she has churned the curds, taken the butter and left aside the buttermilk.

Makhan jab kad liyo chach piye koi.

When Mira walks in the woods and lanes in Giridhar's company she gains confidence and one can see her earlier subservient attitude and subdued tone of a slave change into an assured and defiant tone of a master. She asserts:

> Since I have bought Govind in the Market
> I proclaim it openly, beating a drum
> You say it was expensive,
> But I say it was cheap.
> And I measure it out on the scales. (22)

The price she pays is her love, her devotion and her very life, for she knows that it is a "prize beyond all price" and the prize is the great ocean of bliss, not small lakes or reservoirs, not even the river Ganga and Jamuna; it is a mine not of gold or silver but of diamonds.

Having realised the value of Giridhari's company she urges her friends not to be enamoured of worldly wealth, pomp and pleasure, not to get enmeshed in the world of *samsara* but to look for the indestructible principle, Giridhari, who alone can confer Satchidananda on them.

> Come with me, my companions,
> And refrain from visiting the houses of others.
> False are rubies and pearls
> False are glamour and glitter
> False is the external finery
> One's only real necklace
> Is the love of the Lord. (26)

However, Mira suspects that in spite of her supplication and servile attitude, Krishna has not taken any pity on her nor did he agree to stay with her. Like a Jogi he is constantly wandering from place to place and is very difficult to catch. She too, therefore, pretends to be indifferent.

> Let him go, let him go, my companions!
> To whom is a Jogi a friend?
> He remains ever indifferent to me
> Utterly peculiar in his behaviour
> He seems to speak sweetly

> But never gives his love.
> I thought the affair would succeed.
> But he left me half-way and went off. (57)

Despite the fact that Mira knows Shyam is a roguish imp, her love for him is so deep that she cannot exhibit even mock-anger and mock-indifference for long. Instead, she consoles herself by reassuring herself that "his lofty indifference is a sham." She entreats him not to let her down openly by behaving contrary to the glorious image she has built of him, he must show her at least a little consideration and express his love for her, for she has sold herself in slavery to him without accepting a fee (58). He should extend a helping hand and prevent her from getting drowned in the ocean of sorrow, at least to reprove that all the titles that are attributed to him like *Patitodhara, Anadha rakshaka, Deenanath* (the saviour of the destitute) are not lies.

> Without thee I shall suffer a mighty disaster
> Thou savest Thy devotees from their afflictions
> In every age,
> Appearing before them to grant them release
> Mira is grasping Thy feet
> Redeem Thy pledge, O King. (62)

The poignancy of agony caused by Krishna's indifference reaches a peak and she almost becomes mad. In her frantic search for Krishna she is like a mad cow looking for her calf in a pathless wood. She feels as if the very vital force of life is ebbing out of her body and she experiences all the symptoms of a person on the death-bed. In her frustration and desperation she even accuses Him of infidelity to her.

> For thy sake I have preserved virginity
> Birth after birth. (77)
> If you are now making love to another
> Why did you make love to me first? (80)

The thundering clouds, the songs of *papiha* and *koel* add salt to her wounds. Still her anger cannot last long. She wants to make the crow the messenger of her love, beseeching her beloved to come to her. She waits in vain for His return and she goes crazy pining for Him.

> Without Shyam I have gone crazy
> My mind is like wood attacked by weevils
> The pain of love is devouring me
> The fire of "absence" has set in. (90-91)

The pathos gets intensified when she begs him in the most touching and pitiable manner:

> Come to my house my darling, my beloved
> I will offer you my eyes
> As a carpet to walk upon
> My heart as a couch
> And will seat you ensconced upon my heart. (109)
> Come lovely Shyam, the indestructible
> I enjoy no comfort
> And my heart is sorely distressed
> For Thy sake have I given up all
> Food and drink do not please me
> Oh Lord of Mira, Mira begs for Darshan. (125)

When Mira realises that Akrura has taken Krishna to Mathura never to return she curses herself for not following him to Mathura.

> Oh my companion
> My modesty was my enemy
> Why did I not go off
> With Sri Lal Gopal! (182)

Then it dawns on her that it is not her modesty but egoism that prevented her from following Gopal and as he can see through her heart he wants to teach her a lesson in humility. He makes her realise the difference between her noisy weeping and wailing and the unostentatious, true love and devotion of Shabari "the wild woman of the woods" who offers him plums after biting into them and Sudama who gives whole-heartedly a handful of parched rice, wrapped up in a rag. Mira is made to accept the truth, "who so loves like this is saved."

Mira also discerns that though she is sore about his absence he has accepted her and he does care for her. Or else the poison sent by the Rana would not have turned into nectar/*charanamrut*, the snake into a garland of flowers/*saligram* and the bed of thorns/nails into a bed of soft flower petals. Then she feels reassured that the dream in which the Lord came to wed her with "fifty six crores of deities forming the bridal procession under the wedding arch" will certainly come true and become an actuality. And she keeps herself ever ready to receive the divine groom.

> I arrayed myself in full adornment
> And the beloved came running to meet me.
> I have chosen no miserable bridegroom
> Who will die at each rebirth
> O my companion
> I have chosen Shyam for my bridegroom,
> Who will be my crest jewel immortal
> Krishna has requited my love
> That has lasted from birth to birth. (201)

Mira the love-besotted maid falling under the spell of Ranchir Rai pleads in absolute self-surrender:

> O my Master
> O courtly Giridhari, O Nandakishore
> Deign to grasp me by the hand. (202)

References

Alston, A.J. *The Devotional Poems of Mirabai*. Delhi. Motilal Banarsidass, 1980. The English translations of all Mira's *padas* are taken from this book unless otherwise stated and the number of the *padas* are given in the text.
Behari, Bankey. *Bhakta Mira*. Bombay: Bharatiya Vidya Bhavan, 1971.
Chaturvedi, Parasuram. *Mirabai ki Padavali*. Allahabad: Hindi Sahitya Sammelan, 1898.
Jhari, Krishnadev. *Hindi Kavya: Pramukh Vad Evam Pravrittiyan*. New Delhi: Sharada Prakashan. 186-203, 1987.
Kishwar, Madhu and Ruth Vanitha. "Poison to Nectar: The Life and Work of Mirabai" in *Manushi* 50, 51, 52: 75-93, 1989.
Mukta, Parita. "Mirabai in Rajasthan" in *Manushi* 50, 51, 52: 94-99, 1989.
Nagendra. Editor. *Hindi Sahitya Ki Itihas*. New Delhi: National Publishing House. 216-254, 1976.
Showalter, Elaine. "Towards a Feminine Poetics" in *Women Writing and Writing about Women*. London: Croom Helm, 1979.
Shukla, Rambahori and Bhagirath Misra. *Hindi Sahitya Ka Udbhav Aur Vikas*. Allahabad: Hindi Bhavan. 180-87, 202-220, 1959.
Tiwari, Iswari Prasad. *Hindi Sahitya ka kramik Itihas*. Varanasi: Hindi, 1968.

Pracharak Prakashan. 136-283.
Underhill, Evylyn. *The Essentials of Mysticism and other Essays*. AMS Press, E.P. Dutton and Co., Inc., 1960.
Varma, Ramkumar, *Hindi Sahitya ka Alochnatmak Itihas*. Allahabad: Ramnarayanlal Benimadhav. 491-619, 1938.

SECTION IV

18

TYAGARAJA

M. Suryanarayana

Poet-saint is a peculiar compound word if it can be called so. In fact, there is a strange relationship between what we mean by saintliness and what we mean by poetic nature. This strangeness arises because of the fact that while any relationship between two entities is two-sided, the relationship between a saint and a poet is generally one-sided. A true saint is always a poet covertly or overtly, but a poet need not be a saint.

The present article deals with those who are basically poets but in whom the poetic nature is so sublime that it can push them to the higher planes of consciousness in which saints move. But strangely, when once the poetic nature in a person transforms him/her into a saint, that person no longer continues to be a poet in the ordinary sense. The taste of the bliss of sainthood is so enchanting that it would never allow him/her to go back to the level of a poet on the mundane plane. Another peculiarity is that unless a person has a seed of sainthood implanted in his/her very being, his/her creations in music, poetry, etc., however great they are, can never help him/her to grow into a saint. If the seed is there the creations would help in growth and radiate the flavour of sainthood and divinity around. But, by themselves they cannot create sainthood. In this essay we are talking about saints in whom poetry is incidental.

Kakarla Tyagaraja occupies a very prominent place in the galaxy of noted poet-saints of India. There is one unique feature about this poet-saint and that is, besides being a saint and a poet of the first order, he is a great musician too who became a pioneer of the new trends in the music of South India and stood as a living example of the possibility of the flowering of divinity in man through the medium of music and poetry.

After all, why do we take to the study of the life of Tyagaraja, or, as a matter of fact, the life of any other saint? It is not a pastime-folklore, story or a crime thriller. It does not even contain any significant and interesting incidents as the lives of political leaders or social reformers do. As far as his day-to-day worldly life is concerned, it is as normal as any one of ours, sometimes even falling below-normal levels with its oddities which often make him look perverted. It runs like a stream of insipid water that bends its flow according to the availability of space without offering any resistance to the obstructions it encounters.

It is evident that from the material point of view, Tyagaraja's life does not deserve any place in human history. But it has been recorded, and that too in bold and golden letters! Why? Because its impact on our conscious life is more important for us than its impact on our material life and also because he belongs to the rare category of those human beings who courageously live up to the dignity of human life on earth.

The life of saint Tyagaraja usually appears three-faceted — saint Tyagaraja, musician Tyagaraja and poet Tyagaraja. But among these three faces, his saint face always dominates and spreads its glittering light on the other two faces. Even in the remaining two, his musician face shines brighter than his poet face under the light of the first face. This is evident from the fact that he is usually ranked as one among the epoch-making musicians of South India, both qualitatively and quantitatively while his poetry falls short of the high estimation of critics and always runs as a supporting base for his music. On deeper analysis the difference can be attributed to two or three factors:

1. The immediate absorbing and transporting influence of music in general which gives a non-temporal quality to it. We can say that music is always related to the emotional aspect of an individual (heart) [apata madhuram].
2. The universality of music. The influence of music is always non-spatial, that is, it is not united to any particular region or locality, while the influence of poetry is localised and is related to the peculiarities of the language in which it is composed.
3. This is a specific factor specially applicable to Tyagaraja alone. He composed all his *kirtanas* and other works in Telugu or Sanskrit, though he was born, lived and moved

among Tamil people. So, naturally, the real content of his compositions always remained inaccessible to people in general. Even among Telugu people, his poetry did not gain much popularity due to its structural peculiarities in which it differs from the Telugu poetic tradition. It shines through the light of its music.

But whatever be the factors, they are from the point of view of the listeners and not from that of the creator, Tyagaraja, because he never accepted any responsibility for his creations.

Not only Tyagaraja but most saints never accept the creatorship for their own creations whether they are of music or of poetry. They simply say that creation flows through them, and they never create. In fact, this is the chief characteristic of a saint or of the attitude called saintliness. Though saintliness is a matter of attitude, it should have some deep connection to the basic peculiarity in a person's inner structure which always takes the form of music, poetry, dance or of any other rhythmic movement when it expresses itself.

Before we go into the details of some reverential recollections of the exemplary life of Tyagaraja it is necessary to do some analytical investigation into the relationship between man's attitude called saintliness and the poetic quality of his expression in general.

A wise man — probably a philosopher-cum-linguist — is reported to have said that "Life is a verb, but not a noun." This statement is very significant because it means that life is a dynamic movement not a static entity.

On the phenomenal plane, life-movement can be viewed as manifest in two aspects. The first and the most commonly experienced one is the horizontal aspect. The second aspect, the experience of which is very rare, is the vertical aspect.

In the horizontal aspect, life movement is always associated with and limited only to the physical and material changes. In this aspect of life the experiences progress through various phases of growth and decay, starting from the point called "birth" and ending at a point called "death". Whatever may be the intermediate nature of the changes death is the ultimate and inevitable experience on this plane of life.

The vertical aspect of life is mainly concerned with the growth in consciousness. The growth in consciousness means becoming more and more conscious of life experiences. As a person grows in consciousness, he begins to see that his life on the horizontal plane is always unconscious and mechanical. Then he strives to alienate himself from such an unconscious movement of life and as this alienation to material life becomes deeper and deeper, he realises that the "birth-death" experience of life is only an illusory concept and life, in reality, is a deathless movement.

In a way, it can be said that while the misery of death is the ultimate experience on the material dimension, the bliss of deathlessness is the ultimate on the conscious dimension of life. The difference between these two modes of life matters very much and imparts an unsurpassable superiority to the growth of consciousness. Naturally a complete withdrawal from material life and a constant abiding in conscious life become the supreme goals aimed at by all the yogas that humanity has devised for its own emancipation.

In the evolutionary scheme of manifestation, up to the animal level life experiences always remain unconscious while the possibility for conscious life starts only with the human species. It is a human prerogative and freedom to grow in consciousness. But it is a choice too. If a person so wishes he can as well remain an animal clinging to the unconscious material life with only one difference, that of having a vertical spinal cord which makes him stand and walk erect.

Life is a big paradox for a human being. It appears to be secure on the material plane where death is the ultimate experience, while it appears to be insecure on the plane of consciousness where the bliss of deathlessness is the ultimate reward. Due to this paradoxical nature of life, when the direction of life movement becomes a choice for a person he instinctively chooses to flow unconsciously on the material plane as he feels a sort of illusory sense of security due to the preprogrammed quality of life on that plane. But, if he chooses a conscious way of life, he feels that he has to venture into insecurity because consciousness means freedom of movement with no preprogramme and freedom always implies choice, uncertainty and insecurity. Because of this insecurity on the conscious plane people become basically afraid of choice and freedom of the conscious life and try to cling to the preprogrammed grooves of life, often giving an honourable guise of "tradition" to them.

This is the misery of humanity. On one side something from a person's inner core always tells him that material life is not the real life while on the other side the attraction of security keeps him stuck to material life. He oscillates between these two alternatives — one pulling him up from matter and the other pushing him down towards it. This is the real tension in human beings and is the root cause of their misery.

Though this is the general persistent dark picture of human degradation and dissipation on the screen of life, some glowing star-like individuals appear occasionally here and there on that screen who scatter away that darkness of despair with the light of their wisdom and courage. They appear to understand the real value of life on the human level because they courageously jump onto the insecure plane of conscious life. Such people are like lamp-posts shedding the light of hope and confidence in the journey towards the fulfilment of human dignity in this universe.

People whom we respectfully call sages and saints belong to this rare category of human beings who take delight in a life of widening consciousness without being lured by the apparent security of material life, without being deterred by the threats of the yawning insecurity of conscious life. Courage, perseverance, understanding and detachment become naturally the chief characteristics of such rare human beings.

Even for a person who starts his journey on the conscious plane of life, there are two apparently opposing paths available — one leading to the source of consciousness and the other spreading towards its ultimate flowering. The person who moves along the first path is the sage while the one who takes the second is the saint.

A sage directs his life movement to its source so his path naturally becomes a path of withdrawal and renunciation. The whole of his movement takes an inward turn (into himself) and it appears to be directed towards a converging point at the base which becomes the origin of all his life activity. He uses the light of discrimination and awareness as he dives deep into himself. So the path of a sage is often known as the path of *Jnana* or *Jnana Marga*.

But the path of a saint is the path of expansion and acceptance. His life movement appears to be infinitely diverging and expanding. He never sees any place for discrimination and choice in this manifested existence. Choice means a negation of the wholeness of God for him and this choiceless acceptance of everything as God's manifestation is what he means by Love. He uses this light of Love for his progress along the path of expansion which is often called the path of Love or *Bhakti Marga*.

Though the life flow appears to be quite opposite in direction the categorisation of a sage and a saint can never be rigid. It is simply conventional and is based on the focal importance of the individual's attention.

Attention and attitude are always the implicit functions of life. They may not be of much help to judge whether a person is a sage or a saint from his day-to-day (outward) life. Yet there is an important explicit feature, that enables us to distinguish them and that feature lies in their ways of communication.

A sage likes the serenity of silence while a saint delights in the exuberance of expression mainly through sound and its modulations. A saint expands himself along the path of love without any choice. Expansion and expression always go together. A saint always tries to embrace all possible media for his expression. For him this whole manifested existence is nothing but a vibratory disturbance of the absolute silence at the base and that he himself is a minute form of that disturbance. That being his attitude he finds no reason for negation and withdrawal and soon realises that there is a possibility to flow back to the origin (of silence) by harmonising his own disturbance with every other form of the manifested disturbances around him.

With this realisation a saint soon develops the art of attuning himself to and resonating with the whole existence without any choice. Such attuning is what we call his love and such resonance is what he calls his bliss.

The primary or fundamental disturbance is in the form of a celestial sound and is experienced by the saint as *aum* or *omkara*. He calls that sound *pranava* (or *anahata* nada meaning unstuck sound). This *aum* is the primary energy which in its turn becomes the source of all other disturbances that make up this phenomenal universe. It is the fundamental principle behind all sensory experiences whether they are of sound or light. In fact, *nada* and *rupa* the experiences of which are quite different for ordinary people become almost existential synonyms for a saint. That is why in the attitude of a saint *nadopasana* (meditation on sound) always means a choiceless love for both *nada* and *rupa*.

The human being is an intellectually developed animal and the significant aspect of that development lies in his capacity to use not only pure sound but also the modulated forms of sound to express himself to others. With the help of such modulations of sound he coins letters and words; fabricates language structures and uses them as symbols to connote his experiences, emotions, values, etc., calling them their meaning.

The letters and words of a language remain simply a group of dead symbols if they are not associated with meanings around them. That is why a word and its meaning always go together like inseparable twins. The peculiarity to be noted here is that in course of time through constant usage people give the status of "natural evolution" to these letters and words forgetting often that they are of their own creation.

Human ingenuity does not end there. A person soon learns that there is a sort of rhythm in every vibratory disturbance of all the phenomena around him and every vibration which produced an experience of sound or vision in him has a rhythm of its own. He realises that such rhythmic vibrations always have a deep influence on his consciousness in directing the course of its movement. Rhythm in sound, in shape and form, everywhere appears to humans as the main yarn with which the fabric of the universe is woven.

People, then, spread their artifice and begin to create their own rhythm in sound and shape and also in movement of language (which itself is their own creation). They name the rhythmic movement of pure sounds as music, a rhythmic flow of language as poetry and the rhythmic movement in a physical body as dance. If these concepts are taken as definitions of music, poetry and dance, then a person who is capable of creating such rhythms through sounds, words and through body movements becomes a musician, a poet and a dancer, respectively. Thus a person evolves into a creator of music, poetry, dance, etc., and becomes a representative of creativity. (According to the present day understanding the definitions of poetry, music and dance are not complete. Especially the concept of poetry is always related more to meanings or experiences conveyed through the composition. Yet, the rhythm of movement means also a rhythm in experiences, and so it is the only factor that plays an important role in transporting a person to different levels of consciousness and that is what we are concerned with mostly in this context.)

Why is there so much of a deep concern in people to create rhythm artificially in all possible expressive forms when all the surrounding nature itself is nothing but a field of rhythmic vibrations? Evidently it must be a matter connected with happiness or misery. A person learns by experience that what he calls as happiness is only a state of harmonisation and resonance of his inner rhythm with the outer and what he calls misery (or pain) is a state of disharmony between the inner and the outer.

Unfortunately, a person cannot easily attune himself to the outer rhythm to get the experience of happiness because he lacks the required insight to understand the outer and also lacks the art of adjusting his inner rhythm to the outer frequency. Thus, he always appears anxious to create his own rhythms in every expressive form, that is, music, poetry and dance, to suit his inner rhythm so that he may be able to resonate with it to derive the required harmony and happiness. If he is not capable of such a creation he searches for creators whom he worships as Gods. However, due to its basic artificial nature such a harmony does not sustain long and a person is soon dragged on to the misery of the original disharmony.

It is here that a saint differs from an ordinary person. The very infrastructure of a saint's physical existence is so flexible (egoless) that it can vibrate resonantly to any outside rhythm. This flexibility is what we call his acceptance and love.

Due to this in-built attuning and harmonising capacity a saint experiences the sweetness of melody from every rhythm of sound and the beauty of symmetry from every visible form that exists around him as phenomena. He need not create any artificial rhythms for his happiness. In fact, even a small sound of a river-flow or even an insignificant scene of a cloudy sky is enough to produce so much of an ecstasy in him that his fragile physical heart fails to contain it. In such a situation his expressive nature comes to his rescue and the overflowing ecstasy is expressed in the form of music or poetry or dance.

A saint's singing or composing or dancing is therefore nothing but an overflowing of his inner ecstasy; music, poetry, etc., simply happen through him; they are not his volitional acts.

At such times he also may stand helplessly as a witness to those spontaneous and effortless emanations, just as any other outsider.

That is what we mean when we say that every saint is potentially a musician or a poet or a dancer or a composite unit of these three put together. Starting from the mythological saint Narada if we look into the life of any saint like Mira, Kabir, Jayadev, Surdas, Tulsidas, Ramdas, Purandaradasa, including Tyagaraja and Ramakrishna, we find that every one of them composed enchanting poetry, sang melodious songs and presented ecstatic dances. But none of them claimed authorship or doership for them.

A point to note here is that there are certain distinguishing factors between the poetry of a saint and that of an ordinary poet which hinder the latter from rising to the level of a saint. For instance:

1. Spontaneity and effortlessness are the chief characteristics of a saint's poetry, while the poetry of an ordinary poet is always artificial and is composed with effort.
2. A saint's poetry does not always conform to the rules and regulations framed by men and it flows like a stream of water on a smooth sloping surface. But the poetry of an ordinary poet is always regulated by scientific technicalities and so it runs like a stream on a rough stony surface.
3. A saint's poetry always elevates people to the heights of divinity. The poetry of a common poet, though it uplifts temporarily, is mainly on the material plane.

In fact, the whole of this analysis is an intentional attempt to impress the greatness of Tyagaraja to emphasise the uniqueness and rarity of his place among us (as human beings) and to indicate the true import of his life to us, because every aspect of the preceding part of this essay is moulded keeping that great saint always in view.

Though the main intention in preparing this essay on Tyagaraja is not to give a detailed account of his biodata which appears to be quite unproductive on the scale of material measurements a cursory view of the most common happenings relating to his life is necessary to render this presentation more comprehensive.

Tyagaraja

Kakarla Tyagaraja who belonged to a Telugu Brahmin family was born in 1767 in Tiruvarur, a village of Tanjore district of Tamil Nadu. He later shifted to Tiruvayur, another village situated on the banks of the sacred river Cauvery due to certain domestic reasons and lived there until his death in 1847.

Tyagaraja's forefathers were originally the natives of a village Kakarla by name in Kambam Taluk of Kurnool district in Andhra Pradesh. Tyagaraja was the third son of his parents, Rama Brahman and Seetamba. His father Rama Brahmam was a great scholar of Sanskrit and Telugu and under his training Tyagaraja also became a great scholar of those two subjects.

His mother Seetamba was a pious and dutiful lady. She had a sweet voice and she used to sing traditional devotional songs of Jayadeva, Annamayya, Purandaradasa melodiously in her puja mandir everyday. Tyagaraja inherited the sweet voice and was initiated into music by her. Though later he had some formal training in music under a great musician of the day Sonti Venkata Ramanayya by name for about a year his mother remained the ideal in music for him all through his life because he always used his music only in the service of Rama like her.

Thus, Tyagaraja got initiated into literature by his learned father and acquired a good scholarship and craftsmanship in writing poetry sufficient to elevate him to the heights of the creators of great poetry. He got initiated into music by his mother, and acquired a great scholarship in the science of music sufficient to raise him to the levels of the greatest composers of music and concert performers of his times. Yet strangely enough these two talents, though of an unusually high calibre, remained quite unproductive for him on the material plane in an environment where people even with a little of such talents were able to acquire awards and aristocratic livings.

This inability of Tyagaraja to utilise his talents and faculties for material ends cannot be attributed to any external factor. It is related to the seed of his inner being which is of a different dimension of life, namely, the conscious dimension. It is the seed of saintliness which remained latent and unsprouted until he met a holy man Ramakrishananda Swami by name. This holy man who Tyagaraja believed to be that mythological Maharshi Narada himself initiated him into the field of divine consciousness by giving him the key mantra called *Rama Shadakshara mantra*.

Tyagaraja with the strength of his unwavering trust in his master (guru) and with the help of the key of the *Rama Shadakshara mantra* could open up all the closed channels of his being and allow his consciousness to expand to infinite dimensions.

With the expansion of consciousness the seed of his saintliness grew into a great tree with its innumerable branches which began to shower the flowers of love mixed with detachment into every activity of his life.

Tyagaraja became a completely transformed person. A sort of spiritual aura began to spread from every pore of his personality and that radiant halo began to separate him from his surroundings. He always liked to be transported and to be moving on higher planes of consciousness with divine intoxication. When his life story tells us that he could repeat the mantra ninety six crore times, in thirty-two years at the rate of one lakh and twenty-five thousand times a day, we can easily imagine the magnitude of his divine intoxication.

Outwardly Tyagaraja was as normal as anybody. He attended to his daily routine and to the domestic needs. He talked and moved with his family and friends. He gave lessons in music and Sanskrit to the disciples who approached him. He sang *bhajans* melodiously and composed sweet poetry. He did everything without any apparent abnormality. Only his changed attitude towards everything altered the quality of his experience. Everything he did always began to reflect his inner refulgent saintliness.

Spontaneity and selflessness became the chief characteristics of everything that flowed out from Tyagaraja in the form of music and poetry. The formal structuring according to the traditional rules swept into his compositions unconsciously due to the acquired training. The fact the he could compose thousands of *kritis* that were categorised later as Divyanama Kirtanas, Utsava Sampradaya Kirtanas, etc., by critics in addition to some bigger compositions in the form of ballads under the names Prahlada Bhakti Vijayamu and Nouka Charithamu in the short time available to him after his day's routine shows how spontaneous he was in his expression. He never stopped for metre, never searched for words and never waited for a mood. Wherever he went he used to sing a fresh composition. Even when he was moved emotionally that emotion was always expressed in the form of a song composition. In a way it can be said that whatever he spoke became a metrical composition with an inherent poetic quality of the elevating influence. That is why we say that poetry always flows from a saint but he never writes it. Along with spontaneity selflessness also became the chief quality of his compositions because every one of them is an address to God, a prayer to God with no desire to please others or for the fulfilment of material gains.

Similar is the case with his music. Spontaneity and effortlessness shine as its principal characteristics. He never waited for selecting a raga to suit the composition and occasion. He expected and encouraged such spontaneity and freedom in his disciples also. He often expressed his dislike when he found them trying to remember a composition with the help of the octave notations.

In fact, such spontaneity and unrestricted freedom of movement of his poetic compositions often create confusion and cause embarrassment to the critics. They cannot ignore or deny the elevating influence of his poetry and music on one side and they cannot apply the measuring rods available in their hands for testing their place in the fields of our poetry and our music. But in such situations critics are generally tactful enough either to relax the existing standards specially for him or to devise new standards to suit his compositions.

As already noted, Tyagaraja occupies a higher place as a musician than as a poet in the esteem of people who are concerned mostly with his outward expressions. The memories of such people are so conditioned that the very name Tyagaraja always brings to mind the picture of a veteran musician and even creates an atmosphere of music around them. Tyagaraja the poet always runs behind Tyagaraja the musician for them. All the rituals and celebrations that are fashioned around him are directed to the musician in him and not to the poet.

But it seems that Tyagaraja himself did not know any such distinction between these two faculties exhibited through him. His music and poetry always flowed together like an inseparable homogeneous admixture of milk and water. He never sang without composing and never composed without singing. This composite personality of Tyagaraja suggests the famous concept that music and poetry *(sangeeta and sahitya)* form the breasts of the goddess Saraswati who feeds us with the milk of bliss — of course with a difference — because music gives bliss immediately on contact and poetry gives bliss only on contemplation. Probably it is our incapacity to contemplate that makes us unable to see the beauty of Tyagaraja's poetry.

A saint's physical life is always arduous and testing as he moves out into the world and interacts with people in society unlike a sage. This difficulty arises for him because of the fact that his inner nature of detachment gets inevitably reflected in his outer behaviour which usually becomes unpalatable and sometimes disturbing to others. However impressive and absorbing his music and poetry were, Tyagaraja's unproductive and non-materialistic ways of living lay always beyond the intellectual grasp of the society around him.

When society is not able to understand the ways of life of an individual generally two things happen. Either society ignores his very existence and casts him out as a misfit, or attributes supernaturality to every happening related to him and weaves a ritualistic pattern of worship without trying to imbibe the spirit behind his ways. Tyagaraja tasted the experience of these two extreme polarities in his life. On one side his elder brother Japyesa with whom he shared his paternal house and his other relatives considered his dealing as defamatory. They often created trouble in his smooth life. Once his brother even stole the idols of Rama and Sita from his *puja mandir* and threw them away into the river Kaveri.

On the other side, there were devoted disciples and other well-wishers who adored him as an incarnation of saint Narada himself. But such an adoration had more of a hidden sympathy for his failure on the material plane than an understanding of the significance of the apex towards which his consciousness was always kept directed.

Such well-wishers included Sara Bhoja Maharaja, the ruler of Tanjavur in those days, who often tried to help him materially to make his physical life more comfortable. Tyagaraja never accepted such an assistance from anybody, even though it was from an emperor, he refused it with respect and humility.

In addition to such adorations and vocal comforts from devotees and well-wishers, Tyagaraja was very fortunate to have a great cooperation from his dutiful and understanding wife. Kamalamba whom he married after the death of his first wife Parvathi happened to be her own sister. Consequently even from the beginning she had an opportunity to study and understand the non-materialistic attitude of her brother-in-law. When she entered his life as a wife she came fully prepared to walk hand in hand with him under all circumstances without causing rupture.

A saint is always in a sense a true communist because he never owns anything and never stores anything. This spirit of communism touched its ideal limits in Tyagaraja. His surrender to Rama was so absolute that he believed that owning and storing meant questioning Rama's love towards him. He never believed in man-made security as it always appeared to him as a potential form of violent insecurity. He lived with no tomorrow in life and the care of even today he left in the hands of Rama. He did not inherit anything in the form of material property from his father excepting a portion of his house as a shelter to his body and *rama panchayatanam* as a shelter to his spirit. He chose *uncha vritti* collecting alms offered voluntarily for sustaining his family and himself because it suited his attitude of renunciation. Every morning he used to go round the streets of the village, Tiruvayur, accompanied by a few disciples, melodiously singing songs of prayer to Rama, composed spontaneously. True to his spirit of trust in Rama in these rounds he took care to collect only that much of alms required for the day to feed his dependents and himself.

These *uncha vritti* trips of Tyagaraja in the streets of that small village also acquired significance from another angle. The melody and sweetness of his music and songs radiated such an enchanting charm over the villagers that they used to gather at their door waiting for his arrival every morning. It became a ritual for them. Tyagaraja with his tanpura in his hands appeared to them as Narada with his *mahati* and they considered themselves blessed when they saw him thus.

From the point of view of the disciples these trips became important because they served as classrooms for them where they could gather new songs *(kirtanas)* and had opportunities to learn new things in music. Gradually his movements in the village streets created an atmosphere of sacredness charged with Rama bhakti and elevated that remote place to the level of a pilgrim centre.

After looking thus at a few incidents of Tyagaraja's life through the magnifying glass of his saintliness one marvels at the meaningfulness and suitability of the name Tyagaraja (which means the king of renunciation). Rarely is a name given by parents to their children at the time of birth so befitting to their character in later life. There is a story which tells that the parents of Tyagaraja considered the child as a boon from the deity of their village Tyagaraja Swami. He was born in answer to their fervent prayers asking for a son of his calibre. Soon their wish was granted and to show their gratitude they named the child after the deity. How happy those blessed parents would have been if they could know that their God-given child lived up to their expectations and fulfilled the promise of his name. Of course, the wish is theirs and the relish ours.

19

KRISHNAMACHARYA

M. Kulasekhara Rao

Sanskrit rhetorician Bharata has enumerated nine rasas or sentiments in his *Natya Sastra*. Though he had Sanskrit literature in view while fixing the number of *rasas* even the Telugu poets have followed the same pattern. Neither Bharata nor his followers have ever mentioned bhakti or devotion as one of the sentiments and no poet dared to implement bhakti as a *rasa* in his work.

In fact, sentiments of *sringara* and *santha* are generally enjoyed by learned poets and the kings while bhakti, though considered as *bhava*, is available to and experienced by the common folk. Whenever a difficult situation arises the common man looks to the Almighty with devotion and prays to Him for deliverance. Bhakti is supposed to be the easiest way to reach God. Saint Ramanuja of the eleventh century has given impetus to bhakti through his philosophy of Visishtadvaita.

In Telugu literature we do not come across any poetic work with bhakti as its main theme. Probably the kings who patronised the poets did not show much appreciation for bhakti as a poetic theme. Until Krishnamacharya of the fourteenth century who composed devotional *vachanas*, no one in Telugu literature has used bhakti. In the later periods others like Pothana, Annamachary, Ramadasa, Tyagaraja followed the path of bhakti shown by Krishnamacharya.

Traditionally Telugu poets have used the *champu* way of rendering poetry: the *champu marga* is the mingling of prose and poetry. Krishnamacharya has carried this tradition a step further by putting his writings mainly in devotional prose which is called *vachana*. Perhaps he was comfortable in composing in a style which did not require meter. This type of non-metrical writing is called *churnika* which is lucid in style and form. Since Krishnamacharya wanted to reach the common man through his writings this style was most suitable. He was successful in this through his devotion and light rendering of *vachanas*.

The apparent simplicity of the *vachanas* does not imply that they are not recognised by rhetoricians. Tallapaka Chinnanna not only defined *vachanas* and *churnika* but also acknowledged the signal service performed to these forms by Krishnamacharya in his *Sankeerthana Lakshana*. He described these *vachanas* as *Thalagrandhi* or light music.

There is also another tradition of composing poetic works which have a story and characters. Examples of this are the *Mahabharata* and the *Ramayana*. These works are considered as *mahakavyas*. A different type of poetry from this is the *anibaddhakavya* or poetry without a story. Though the theme is not structured in the form of a story its treatment is poetic. *Sathaka* poets have used this form extensively in Telugu.

As a pioneer of this Krishnamacharya composed his works running into lakhs which are the best illustration. Especially his *Simhagiri vachanas* have many features of *sathakas*: their ending with an address and rendering without a story. These *vachanas* start with a call to God and continue in devotional strains. These prose pieces like the poems of *Sathakas* enter the hearts of the readers and become indelibly printed there. They are thus very effective. Unlike the *Sathakas* which are composed in one hundred verses, for the *vachanas* no number is prescribed.

Now a question arises as to why Krishnamacharya composed these prose pieces instead of poetry. To answer this we have to turn to the tradition of Visishtadvaita philosophy. Saint Ramanuja in the eleventh century wrote prose pieces in Sanskrit and they became popular as *Gadyatraya*. For the followers of Vaishnava philosophy *Gadyatraya* is like the *Bible*. The lucid style and meaningful rendering of this prose work must have influenced Krishnamacharya deeply since he was a Vaishnava. Therefore, he chose similar prose in Telugu for his purpose which like that of Ramanuja was to reach the ordinary people.

Krishnamacharya's *vachanas* written in praise of Narasimha the presiding deity of Simhachalam, are called *Simhagiri vachanas* or *Simhagiri Narahari vachanas*.

The life of Krishnamacharya was not an easy one. Though the favourite child of his parents he had the handicap of blindness from birth. In addition, the *vyathipatha yoga* in which he was born was considered to be harmful to the family and the village of his birth. Therefore, the parents were forced to abandon him in a dry well. Fortunately the child was rescued by a holy man named Kuvvaru or Kumaru. The child was later taken to the pilgrim centre of Simhachalam. After sometime, by the grace of Narasimha, many dramatic changes took place in the life of Krishnamacharya. God gave him back his eyesight and the injunction to compose *vachanas* praising the divine. He was also given the necessary scholarship for this task. This extraordinary gift made Krishnamacharya the foremost writer of Telugu Sankirtana Literature. He reached this stature without the help or patronage of kings. Neither did he receive much encouragement from other scholars of his age.

A curious miracle of making a dead man alive is usually ascribed to Krishnamacharya. When this incident became known King Prataparudra of the Kakatiya dynasty honoured him with a place in court. Unfortunately, he was soon charged with mismanagement of funds and the king was displeased. When he was presented before the king Lord Narasimha came to his rescue. There was, we are told, *kanaka varsha* or the rain of gold with which to pay off the debt. The king was very impressed by his devotion and wanted to honour him. But the poet of the people, Krishnamacharya, refused all honours. Instead of continuing at the court he set off on a journey to Srirangam, the holy place for Vaishnavites. He carried with him his four lakh *vachanas* on copper plates. It is doubtful whether the saint came back after his pilgrimage to these parts. Therefore his *vachanas* are lost to us forever.

Of the four lakh about seventy-five have been preserved for posterity. These *vachanas* give glimpses of the composer's life. Apart from this they narrate some stories. One of them is as follows: a Vaishnava made a vow according to which he would eat only after he had visited a temple. On a business trip he once went to a far-off place accompanied by his Saivaite brother-in-law. There was heavy rain on the way which continued incessantly. Due to this bad weather the man could neither visit a temple nor take his food. Sensing his plight the brother-in-law erected a pillar, decorated it with symbols of Vishnu and told the Vaishnavite that he had spotted a temple. The latter bowed before this place and broke his fast. Later the other man revealed the truth and made fun of his blind faith. The Vaishnavite wanted to prove the power of his faith. He told the other man to uproot the pillar and bring it to him. The Saivaite tried in vain. As soon as he touched the pillar it disappeared. He realised the might of the other's faith and bowed to him.

Such stories are narrated by Krishnamacharya to project the greatness of the vision of Krishna. He did not use stories which glorify kings. He was a writer of the masses. He did not want to deviate from this set purpose of enlightening the common folk.

From the limited number of available pieces it is possible to determine the main features of the *vachanas*. They start with an invocation to God, usually the word being *swami*. At the end of each we come across the words *simhagiri narahari, namo namo dayaniti*. In some pieces the epithet "Kuvvuru" is also mentioned. Perhaps the Acharya wanted to express his thanks to the divine benefactor by remembering him.

Krishnamacharya had the skill of putting forward the highest philosophy in simple terms in his writings. For instance, he wrote:

> Swami, a person who is a devotee of Vishnu is greater than a scholar who has no faith in God.
> He may be an outcaste or of any other caste, he may belong to the highest caste.
> He may be a gem among scholars, practise all rituals rigorously, learn difficult sastras, but he is not great.
> If he becomes a disciple and devotee of Vishnu there is salvation for him.

Of all the principles of Visishitadvaita, the Acharya attacked the system of the four castes. This shows his progressive outlook. He also hated dry scholarship and spoke about the uselessness of knowledge unless tempered by qualities like kindness, His doctrines were not merely theoretical. He practised them in his own life. For instance, when he was getting married his maternal cousin came in the disguise of an outcaste. The bridegroom gave this lowly guest all respect, much to the anger and disgust of his father-in-law. But he tolerated all insults and was even ready to give up his bride.

Krishnamacharya

The *Simhagiri vachanas* of Krishnamacharya are characterised by the objective outlook of the writer. This helps to draw the reader or listener very close to the author's ideology. This becomes evident in the following lines:

> O Lord, I am submitting myself to you
> I am entangled in these worldly bonds
> I am attracted by Karma and its consequences
> Desire for beautiful girls has made me blind
> My knowledge has disappeared
> I have become bad
> Like the deer in the forest I am afraid of my own shadow.
> I am thirsty
> I do not want to go to my guru
> I am like an abandoned child
> I am like a bee in the oil
> I am like an animal trapped in a net
> . . . .
> O Lord, where is the way?
> Please get me out of this entanglement
> Please lead me to your feet, O Lord.

Krishnamacharya used simple language to express ideas which were also straightforward. He avoided ornamentation and high vocabulary. He believed that linguistic complexity would distract attention from the essential philosophy of his writings.

During the early part of its development, Telugu poetry made abundant use of compound words borrowed from Sanskrit. The trend altered by the twelfth and thirteenth centuries when the spoken language was the vogue even in poetry. This brought poetry closer to the common people and Krishnamacharya's writings contributed immensely to this.

This and many other factors have resulted in the fact that Krishnamacharya's *vachanas* have left a lasting impression on later writers. He was venerated as the father of *Sankirtana* literature. Tallapaka Chinnanna praises him as the one who has rendered the *Vedas* in Telugu. Tallapaka Tirumalacharya paid a tribute to him by composing about one hundred and twenty *vachanas* in praise of Lord Venkateswara called Venkateswara *vachanas*. They are so similar to *Simhagiri vachanas* that it is almost impossible to discern any difference unless one looks at the beginning and the end. Both have bhakti as their subject and the philosophy of Visishitadvaita is predominant in both.

In addition, Krishnamacharya also made a mark among writers of classics. Pothana, the writer of *Bhagavata* wrote twenty four *vachanas*. Srinath in *Bhimeswara Purana* and *Kashikhanda* introduced twelve laudatory pieces showing the impact of Krishnamacharya's style. Many writers of later ages have also composed *vachanas*: Kanikadhiswara *vachanas*, Sankara *vachanas*, Bhavani Manohara *vachanas*, Lakshmi Vallabha *vachanas* to name a few.

In conclusion one can gauge the popularity of Krishnamacharya's writings by noting that even today they are recited by devotees. Villagers living near Simhachalam temple sing these *vachanas* in chorus on special occasions.

20

ANNAMACHARYA'S SRINGARA SANKIRTANALU : SOME POETIC STRATEGIES

R.M.V. Raghavendra Rao

The name of Annamacharya, or Annamayya, occupies a unique place among the poet-saints of India for it was he who not only gave a well-defined form to the song or *Padamu* in Telugu but also elevated it to lofty poetic heights through his sublime thought and imagination. That is why his successors conferred on him the title *Padakavita Pitamaha* (creator of lyric poetry). Essentially devotional in its character, the *Padamu* is synonymous with *sankirtana*, a sacred song in praise of God or sages or saints. Annamacharya's distinction shared by few other poet-saints lies in his prolific output uninterrupted throughout his life and marked by consistent devotional intensity and poetic virtuosity. In him, thought and craftsmanship went hand in hand. The phenomenal number of 32,000 songs composed by him during his long and eventful life fall into two broad divisions : *Sringara sankirtanalu* or erotic songs, and *Adhyatma sankirtanalu* or spiritual songs, both written in the service of Lord Venkateswara, though the distinction is obliterated by the unified spiritual goal of Annamacharya—the attainment of the Lord as his ultimate refuge.

The focus of this paper is on some poetic strategies of the *Sringara Padams* with particular attention to their combination of wit and passion, the world of variegated phenomena and diverse spheres of human knowledge, all contributing to the unifying experience of the soul of the devotee with the Lord. Knowledge and experience and different sensibilities are yoked together and explored at an apparently mundane or profane level only to reaffirm the metaphysics of the *paramatman*, the sacred or the spiritual goal of the *atman*. Divine love is realised through the erotic experience of the body which is both organic and mechanistic, and instrument or *sadhanam* in its correlation with several other phenomena, *jiva* or the animate as well as the inanimate or the *jada*. Thus in these songs we find images drawn from the world of flora, fauna, elemental nature and even rocks as a means of exposing the finiteness of man, the macrocosm and upholding the infiniteness of God, the macrocosm. All this nevertheless only reiterates the deeply personal or subjective feeling in Annamacharya's erotic verse expressed through the symbolic figure of a Radha, a Gopi or a *nayika* or heroine. In this context one has to paraphrase the profound observation of Sri Rallapalli Anantakrishna Sarma. He says, "The chief subject of Annamayya's poetry is not the external world or *vishaya*, instead it is the inner experience of the self-externalised. His *padams* express his felt experience with no trace of affectation; and such a natural quality is termed as *aarjavam*" (Shetty, 1985: xix).

The poetic strategy adopted in these *padams* is unique for it achieves the objectification of the devotee's passion by means of arrestingly original analogies between objects which are apparently dissimilar, that is, through a metaphysical conceit. It is a coincidence of the universals of poetic imagination and literary criticism that the term metaphysical conceit was applied to the poets of the seventeenth century — John Donne, Andrew Marvell, Crashaw, Herbert, Vaughan, etc. Philosophical speculation implicit in the word metaphysics is blended with subjective response to natural phenomena — a trait highly pronounced and sophisticated in Annamacharya who could be the modern harbinger of such a creative strategy.

In the portrayal of an ensemble of relations of the devotee with God and the dialectic of the material and the spiritual the transient and the eternal resolved through the devotee's total surrender to God, the supreme lover, Annamacharya's poetic imagination picks on every object from every walk of life and harnesses it to a poetic construct of a variety of moods, descriptions and figures of speech. The mundane world of natural resources with all its material pomp and the several contradictions in nature are dealt with.

The songs describing the resplendence of *Alamelmanga* draw their material from the precious wealth of nature. Her ornaments which enhance the charm of her dance are made of gems; or when she fed her Lord, the pearls strung to her curls swayed sweetly and in the total involvement of her act she did not notice the displacement of the *pallav* of her saree studded with flowers of gold.

Precious metals gold and silver fill most of Annamacharya's exotic descriptions creating the setting for the erotic romance, explicit and implicit in his songs. In one song each part of the heroine's physical frame is compared to one precious stone or the other.

> Her beauty itself is the gold
> that made you
> the Lord of wealth (Lakshmipati)
> Her utterances are mines of silver
> Her toe nails are diamonds
> . . . . . .
> Her eyes are sprinkled pearls
> Her nipples are emerald mounds. (Vol 24, song 198)

Such analogies, however, are replaced by more original ones drawn from the rough and tumble of rocks and the different kinds of narrow passages caused by them.

> Your charming face is the passage of Somasila *(somasila Kanuma)*
> Your buttocks the Gadderati passage
> your face the Red Stone passage
> your heart itself the passage of Dongalasani. (12, 115)

All these rocks and the passages are chartered in Andhra Pradesh and the yoking of such objects with the human form speaks not only for the richness of Annamacharya's imagination but also for its boldness to equate the diversities of the human form with the suggestiveness of any phenomenon in nature — inanimate, dangerous and remote. Even as such, analogies are abundant in Annamacharya's erotic songs, yet another class of objects in them belong to the clumsy profane and repulsive spheres of human experience. The treatment of profanity and its significance in the journey of the soul to sacredness is not an uncommon theme in the poetry of metaphysical preoccupations. And eroticism or *Sringara* and its passionate treatment of love "transforms the apparently profane into the sacred, the powerful sex impulse into a deep spiritual urge" (Rao, 1989:51). Mircea Eliade calls the act of manifestation of the sacred as "heirophany" "through which something sacred shows itself to us." (1958:7) The sacred manifests itself in some elementary object, a stone (the *somasila* in Annamacharya) or a tree or the supreme one, the Lord Himself or His Lotus Feet. To quote Eliade, "In each case we are confronted by the same mysterious act: the manifestation of something of a wholly different order, a reality that does not belong to our world, in objects that are an integral part of our natural "profane" world (11).

In one of the songs a *madhya adhira* heroine (one who with tearful eyes taunts her lover) asks her lover:

> The sandal paste
> on your chest was
> applied to you by someone else.
> why do you smear that stale one on me?
> Similarly, your ornaments
> are full of sweat. (26, 461)

In another song the drowsy lover returning from another woman is told by the heroine that the betel leaf in his mouth is stale. In yet another song the *abhisarika* heroine (one who is drawn to her lover, or draws him to herself) on reaching him after facing several obstacles, says:

> When out of my desperation
> I tried to stay back
> My passion crept on me
> Like the row of ants. (12, 324)

The ants, contact with one's body rousing the inextinguishable passion is suggestive of the contrarieties coming together in Annamacharya's unorthodox poetic explorations for Eternity. One is reminded of Dr. Johnson's somewhat disapproving comment, "discordia corcors" about the imagery of the Metaphysical poets. According to him their poetry dealt with "heterogeneous ideas...yoked by violence together". The most memorable lines in Andrew Marvell's "The Definition of Love" reads as follows:

> Magnanimous Despair alone
> could show me so divine a Thing,
> Where feeble Hope could never have flown
> But vainly flapped in tinsel wing. (Gardner, 1972:252-3)

The impossibility of fulfilment of love begets despair which itself quite paradoxically spurs the *nayika* to run for her lover, since it is the "magnanimous despair" in Annamacharya's heroine too.

In another song, a perfect blend of passion and poetic imagery, the attendant maids of the heroine surmise the acts of erotic love behind the several tell-tale marks on the heroine:

> The dark marks on her red lips
> are the result of her kissing
> her beloved's Kasturi-smeared face.
> The redness of her eyes is, probably,
> the trace of the bloodstains caused by
> the sudden withdrawal of her
> concentrated look at her lover! (12, 82)

The description of the redness of her eyes is unique and inimitable, once again, for its poetic conceit, characterised by the yoking of contradictory acts — amorous glances, their violent withdrawal and the possible damage done to the otherwise charming eyes of the heroine.

The corpus of Annamacharya's erotic songs is replete with direct references to every aspect of appearance and acts of the human frame, as well as every object of the world of phenomena. Speculation and experience are blended by means of an effective poetic strategy of conceit, the metaphysical objective motivating the poetic craft which is the discovery of the sacred above the profane. It is realised not in terms of the rejection of the profane but by imaginatively comprehending its significance in the scheme of the four *purushardhas* — *dharma, artha, kama* and *moksha*.

Such a realisation of the sacred in and through the profane in one spell is also richly demonstrated in a *padam* which is both erotic and spiritual simultaneously:

> It is quite a surprise,
> signs of separation from you
> are not to be found

in the lady's looks.
As you appear in her vision
when she thinks of you,
she embraces empty space.
No doubt, she learnt from someone
that you pervade
even the void. (Rao, 1989: 56)

This is classified as a spiritual song. But as observed by Professor Adapa Ramakrishna Rao, "in such songs the distinction between the erotic and the spiritual disappears as does the demarcation between human love and religious fervour." (1989:57)

If *sringara* is the most poetically delineated emotive experience of Annamacharya, in Sri Rallapalli Anantakrishna Sarma's words (in translation) "the great soul who has the rarest distinction of elevating it to lofty spiritual heights is Annamacharya" (Setty, 1985:xx). And that, indeed, is the end of all "conceits".

References

Eliade, Mircea. *Patterns in Comparative Religion*, New York: Sheed and Ward, 1957.
—— *The Sacred and the Profane: The Nature of Religion*, New York: Harcourt.
Gardner, Helen (ed.) *The Metaphysical Poets*, Penguin (see Andrew Marvel, "The Definition of Love"), 1972.
Rao. Adapa Ramakrishna. *Annamacharya, Makers of Indian Literature*. New Delhi: Sahitya Akademi, 1989.
Shetty, K. Srinivasulu. *Annamacharya Sankirtanalu*, T.T.D. Publications, 1985.

21

VEMANA

G. Laxminarayana

In the Indian classical tradition, poetry has always been the handmaiden of religion. Great seers and saints spread their religious teachings through poetry. The meaning and significance of religion was explained in the verse form taking the life and achievement of great men as the subject. In this tradition stand out pre-eminently great poet-saints like Valmiki and Vyasa. Even today their works enlighten people on moral and spiritual matters. The poet-saints had the welfare of the universal man as their object. They were noble souls who were above all narrow and material considerations. They are the greatest benefactors of mankind.

This great Indian tradition of a man of religion taking poetry as a tool and working through it for the moral and spiritual welfare of the people is a continuous and unbroken tradition. After the two great poet-saints, Valmiki and Vyasa, in every age there have been many such saints who have awakened people whenever they failed to follow that great tradition and became too narrow and limited in their outlook and actions. Society needed the birth of such saints so that it did not decay completely and disappear altogether from the face of the earth.

When the great humanistic tradition in classical Sanskrit poetry became alienated from the common people due to the distortions and perversions of self-seeking priests and pundits, there arose a need to establish a similar tradition in the vernacular languages by other poet-saints with a similar vision and mission. Many such saints were born in different parts of our country who raised their voice against all forms of obscurantism, rigidity, narrowness in thought and action and helped their contemporary societies to revive and survive. To this glorious tradition belongs yogi Vemana who was born in the seventeenth century in the land of the Telugu people.

Without going into the historical details of the date, the place of birth and the genealogy of Vemana yogi I would like to deal mainly with his life and teachings.

Life

Yogi Vemana was Vema Reddy before he became a yogi. He was born in a rich family. His elder brother and his sister-in-law were very kind and indulgent to him. He led a carefree and even a reckless life. No responsibilities weighed him down. His intense enjoyment of life, perhaps, gave him a very deep and sympathetic understanding of human nature and its predicament. That is why he declared that there is no renunciation without intense enjoyment of the pleasures of life: *raagi kaani vaadu viragi kaaledu*. From a pleasure-seeker to a truth-seeker, I think, sums up the course of life of Vemana. There is a similarity between the life of Siddartha and that of Vemana. Both renounced the world and the enjoyment of worldly pleasures after a period of intense enjoyment of those pleasures. Both became seekers of truth. The Buddha too pointed out the evils in his society and showed the path of virtue to the people of his time. In the same tradition, Vemana attacked the evils in his contemporary society and cleansed it of those evils. The proof of the great influence of his teachings on the Telugu society is the extreme popularity of his poems in Telugu households even to this day. There is no Telugu child who does not know at least a few poems of Vemana.

Vemana attacked many evils in society. He attacked casteism, ignorance and superstition, formal religion, hypocrisy and exploitation.

Vemana's belief in universal brotherhood led him to attack casteism. Earlier the Buddhist poet Ashwas Ghosha had also expressed a similar view regarding the equality of all men. All men are created equal; all men are brothers. No caste or creed should divide them. Vemana says that if we look at the original Brahmanda from which all human beings took birth, then we have to say that people of all castes were born together at the same time. Hence they are brothers. Ignorant people cannot attain liberation as they talk only about differences in caste and do not understand the truth about birth. It is better to understand the secret of creation than merely talk about caste.

Because Vemana believed in the equality of all men and the family of man, the existence of the brahmin caste and its claim to superiority over others was unacceptable to him. Hence he pointed out the inherent contradiction in the birth of a brahmin. According to tradition women and shudras are not qualified to study the *Vedas*. Thus a brahmin woman becomes a shudra. It is strange that those born of such a woman call themselves brahmins. The difference between brahmin men and women is the wearing of the sacred thread. Vemana says that it is foolish to think that one can get rid of low birth (*shudrathva*) by wearing the sacred thread. It is of no avail if one cannot control one's mind. Here Vemana comes close to the concept of *Manojaya* (conquest of the mind) that is emphasised in the *Bhagavad Gita*. He sought knowledge and worked hard to spread it among all people. According to him knowledge makes a man brahmin and ignorance a shudra. He gave importance to character and not to caste: *kulamu ghanamu kaadu guname ghanambu raa*. Mere accident of birth is not important in his view. He pleaded for the uplift of shudras and other downtrodden people in society.

After the priestly class, Vemana attacked the arbitrary behaviour of the ruling class. He pointed out the unpredictable and unreliable nature of royal temper and never sought royal favours. He compared royal patronage to the shelter given by a snake's hood.

The position of women in Vemana's time was no better than that of the shudras. So he championed their cause too and raised his voice against their ill-treatment. He emphasised the importance of women. Woman is the mother and Vemana says knowing the mother is knowing God: *talli nerugu vaadu daivambu nerugunu*. He elevates the woman, who is a devoted wife, to a *devi* or *devata*. He considers the house in which she lives a temple, a *devatagriha*. No wonder that later social reformers and champions of women's cause like Veerashalingam Panthulu were inspired by his poetry. He condemned the evil practice of bride-price, *kanyashulka*.

Vemana's Ethic
Vemana gave great importance to ethical values in life. Many of his poems contain principles that should guide and govern human life and actions. He considered ethics in education and Veena in musical instruments as the best. He believed that the

necessity of moral teaching creates great poets. He explained his moral principles in simple, direct and clear language so that they could be easily understood by common people. He avoided obscurity and complexity in his poems on morals. According to him the one who has seen is greater that the one who has only heard; the one who partakes is greater than the one who has only seen. Hard work, perseverance and dynamic action are preferred and fatalism is rejected. He condemned weak and inefficient kings who could not provide for the needs of their subjects. A person should spend his life fruitfully and serve the society in which he lives. He should liberate himself not only from ignorance but also from want and wealth equally. Almost on all aspects of human life Vemana has commented and given wise counsel.

Was Vemana an iconoclast? Was he against idol-worship? I think he was not so much against these things as he was for giving more importance to the welfare of fellow human beings. A person's concern in life should be to work for the welfare of his fellow beings rather than waste his energies in useless and wasteful rituals and ceremonies. As a humanist Vemana was mainly concerned with the moral and material well-being of people but not with any abstract theories or superfluous liturgy. He was against going on pilgrimages. He says that one need not worry about one's inability to visit Kashi or other famous pilgrim centres. A sinner cannot hope for salvation by merely visiting those places. Today we know how these holy places have been converted into hideouts for terrorists.

Vemana also attacked superstition, orthodoxy, foolish customs and religious fanaticism. He laughed at people who believed in astrology and omens. He questioned how birds and lizards could foretell coming events. He pointed out how gullible people are, cheated by magicians, palmists and other tricksters. People's belief in horoscope also came in for his criticism. He accepted nothing that was irrational or illogical or unscientific.

Thus this great rationalist and humanist of the seventeenth century waged a one-man war against many evils of his time and brought harmony into the lives of those who were bewildered by the many conflicts and contradictions in their society. A man from whose mind such noble thoughts flowed and spread all over the land and inspired and elevated men and women alike is indeed a saint.

22

POTHANA

C. Muralikrishna

It is an unquestionable fact that India had a great tradition, culture and heritage. Its rich history is, to quote Swami Vivekananda, "the history of a few men who had faith in themselves." Many artists have enriched the Indian literary tradition with great literary works. These works reflect by and large the ideals, the values Indian culture stands for. They hold a mirror up to the social and cultural life. When we recollect great poets like Valmiki and Veda Vyasa, we are also reminded of Pothana who was born in Warangal in Andhra Pradesh and lived between A.D. 1400 and A.D. 1470. His native village was Bammera and he was called Bammera Pothana. He hailed from a simple, poor family of farmers and without any formal education he diligently studied different shastras on his own and evolved his principles of "Bhootha-daya" — the love for all living creatures. For him "Manava seva" was "Madhava Seva". Among his many works of poetry are:

1. *Veerabhadra Vijayam* - a poem about Siva and Parvati
2. *Narayan Shathakam* - a series of poems on the greatness of Lord Vishnu
3. *Bhogini Dandakam* - a romantic poem of divine love between a king and his beloved.
4. *Maha Bhagavatham* - a series of mythological episodes conveying spiritual and moral messages; a highly devotional and a spiritual guide to the people.

While the *Ramayana* and the *Mahabharata* are a continuous and coherent narrative projecting the process of disruption and restoration of their age-bound values and order, the *Bhagavatham* does the same through a body of complex collection of popular myths and parables drawn and derived from epics and other syllogistic works of philosophy. We can even say that the *Bhagavatham* through its simple stories provides to the people an easy and digestible form of Vedantic and Upanishadic truths.

Pothana is known in Telugu history as one of the most eminent poet-saints who followed the bhakti *marg*. He said:

Trupti ni minchina dhanamu ledu
bhakti ni minchina shakti ledu.

(There is no wealth greater than or superior to contentment; there is no strength greater than the strength of devotion.)

Bhakti can be explained as a means of worship which believes in loving devotion to and adoration of a personal deity. It is the doctrine of liberation by faith as opposed to the Vedic doctrine of liberation by work or by knowledge. It is considered to be the simplest and the most practicable form of attaining truth, realisation or salvation. It is a process in which our emotions are involved and the awareness is directed and dedicated to a higher being. When bhakti is of great intensity it is possible to feel the presence of the person to whom you are devoted. The *Bhagavatham* expresses Pothana's devotion, for both Sri Rama and Sri Krishna. Once while praying to Lord Rama in an intense, meditative mood Pothana went into raptures on the appearance of Sri Rama in front of him. (The legend goes that) Sri Rama blessed Pothana and instructed him to write the *Bhagavatham*.

Pothana's idea of poetry writing can be directly related to the theory of divine inspiration. It means that poetry or literature is the direct outcome of the divine will. Here the poet considers himself as a mere medium of poetic composition. The poet's own contribution or the socio-cultural context of writing is rejected and the divine will becomes the sole cause of literary production. In Pothana's poetry we find his unquestioned acceptance of this concept. Like the Goddess or Muse in the Greek world his object of invocation was Saraswati - the Hindu Goddess of music and poetry whom he calls upon to help him in his task. He however considers Sri Rama the cause of his inspiration to whom he dedicates this work. He says:

Palikedidi Bhagavathamata
Palikinchu Vibhbdu Ramabhadhrundata.

(The utterance is the *Bhagavatham*; the one who enables the utterance is Sri Rama.)

A remarkable fact about the works of Pothana is his simplicity of theme and style. As we have said earlier he wrote the *Bhagavatham* which in itself is an attempt to present to the common people the intricate philosophy in a simple form. He wrote it in simple Telugu verse known as the "Jaanu Telugu". His characters too are simple, natural and effective. He talks in lucid, simple language and imagery about Kamsa, Durvasa, Shishupala and Prahlad, of the Krishna-Balarama-Yashoda love, the enchanting Krishna-Gopikas play and Krishna-Kuchela's friendship which go straight into the heart of the reader, and appeal to the sentiment, imagination and emotion of the common people for whom Pothana basically composed. Not only the *Bhagavatham* but most of Pothana's works have mingled in the mainstream of life and have become proverbs, anecdotes to instruct and delight people of all age-groups.

Apart from his lucid and simple verse another remarkable fact about his works is the attempt to reduce the sharp differences between the two sects of Hinduism, the Vaishnavites and the Saivites. Pothana was basically a Saivite but he wrote about Lord Vishnu too. He saw no difference between Hari and Hara:

Chetularanga Shivuni Poojimpa badeni
Noaru novvanga Hari kirti nuduvadeni
Dayayu Satyambhu loanuga dhalupadeni
galuganeitiki Tallulla kadupu chetu

(A person who does not worship Siva and who does not utter Hari's name, who has no compassion and lacks righteousness is an insult to his mother and birth.)

Most people who are familiar with Pothana know about his conflict with the king over the dedication of his magnum opus, the *Bhagavatham*.

Apart from socio-cultural relevance, Pothana's work had another very important dimension also. This was his rejection of the king's power over the ownership of his literature which was in a way an assertion of the right of literature to exist on its own. He did not depend in any way on the king or his patronage. Pothana's cool and gritty refusal to dedicate his *Bhagavatham* to the king in spite of constant pressure and his willingness to leave the kingdom with his family for the cause reflects his strong rejection of the supremacy of the king and the assertion of the importance of the popular literature as against the literature that is associated with the royal court which reflects royal culture and is dedicated to the royal head. Pothana's attempt can be read as the rejection of the socio-cultural hierarchy with the king as its head and acceptance of the establishment of a higher cosmic order which recognises the power of only the Omnipotent, that is, God.

This is the kind of unflinching faith in and devotion to God that Pothana stood for. This kind of total attribution of his talented work to the will of Almighty is the hallmark of his life.

Pothana was not only a bhakti poet though he accepted the theory of divine inspiration, his work was socio-culturally motivated also. Not only did he attempt to reach the simplest and the most ignorant in the social order, his life was an active protest against the monopoly and supremacy of the king — the highest accepted power block in society.

23

BHAKTA RAMADAS

A. Ramakrishna Rao

The ethos of a nation or a people is hard to define. It is made up of ideas, values, feelings and attitudes that cannot easily be expressed in concrete terms. To derive or understand the ethos of a country or a region from its cultural heritage is an exercise that is fraught with risks. Hence one has to be guarded in making pronouncements about the ethos of the specially composite Indian culture which is largely dominated by the Hindu concepts.

This, in turn, brings us to the Hindu culture which has helped in the much acclaimed synthesis of the Aryan and Dravidian beliefs and has helped in generating a harmony of religious, philosophical and artistic concepts. The most interesting question emerging out of such a synthesis is about God, who is mostly described in extremes such as *anoraneeyan*, minutest of the minute, and *mahatomaheeyan*, greatest of the great. There is also much speculation about the elusive *"Adi Madhyanta Rahita"* who is everywhere and in everything *"Indu gala dandu ledani sandehamu valadu."*

Whom is He identified with? and how is He to be reached? — are the two important questions which attained prominence because of His elusive nature. Paradoxically, God is beyond proof as He is self-revealing *swayam prakasaha*. But the inquisitive and enquiring soul has not stopped the relentless search to get satisfying answers to these eternal questions and has been constantly in search of various ways and means to reach Him.

It is a well-known fact that Hinduism talks of two streams of traditions to reach the goal. The *rishi* tradition which represents learning, ritual, philosophy, poetry, science, etc., and the *muni* tradition which represents renunciation, contemplation and yoga. The two are not mutually exclusive — the first one is outward and the second one is inward. On similar lines even the great divine sage Narada advocates "*Karma Jnana Yogebhyo Bhaktireva gareeyasi*" in his *Bhakti Sutras* thus implying that *karma*, *jnana*, *yoga* and *bhakti* are the various supreme means to reach God.

Of these, *bhakti* and *jnana* run parallel to each other. While *jnana* can be taken as a means to voicing the inquisitive spirit, *bhakti* involves unquestioning devotion in the emotional way. The synthesis of *bhakti* and *jnana* could be said to be one of the greatest contributions of the South and its consequences have been particularly rich in the medieval and subsequent centuries. This divine reconciliation of *bhakti* and *jnana* has led to the much-enjoyed cultural and musical heritage of the South which has resulted in the flowering of the great "*vaggeyakaras*" (the term means much more than composers). The compositions of the great poet-saints such as Annamacharya, Purandaradasa, Bhadrachala Ramadas, Tyagaraja and a host of others are the products of this synthesis.

Among these poet-saints, Bhakta Ramadas belongs to Andhra Pradesh which has a rich spiritual heritage. Spirituality dwells in the hearts of the people of this state in variegated forms. While some are mystical others burst into spontaneous music and poetry.

Interestingly, Andhra Pradesh is rated as the second home of *Ramayana*. The valley of Godavari was consecrated by the long stay of Sri Rama in exile. It is a strange coincidence that this religious sacredness synchronises with a breathtaking scenic beauty all along the river. It is the home of Sri Rama as well — the home away from home. The association of this area with the *Ramayana* has resulted in the embodiment of a rich cultural heritage in the mind of the people.

Against this background we realise that the poet-saint of Bhadrachalam is bound to be a devotee of the highest order whose songs are the autobiographical records of his initiation into the *Jnana-Bhakti* cult. His original name was Gopanna and he lived during the reign of Abul Hasan Tana Shah, the king of Golconda. Being a great devotee of Rama, he proposed to construct a temple to Sri Rama on the banks of the sacred Godavari at Bhadrachalam where he was appointed as Tahsildar.

Bhakta Ramadas

In anticipation of the people's donation he diverted huge amounts of government money for the construction of the temple and was promptly arrested for misappropriation and sent to jail. While in jail, he composed several songs praising Rama. With the composition of these songs Ramadas has brought literary beauty, devotional ecstasy and musical mastery together to create what may be called the highest and most lasting confluence of the True, the Good and the Beautiful.

These compositions record his evolution as a devotee, hardships he endured on that path of thorns and finally his total surrender to his Lord. What impresses even casual readers most is the sincerity of his self-surrender to his Lord expressed in his songs. Unlike some Telugu poets who have exhibited their scholarship and command of poetical embellishments in their works, Ramadas uses a simple and natural language a language of the common people. His compositions can be understood and appreciated by one and all regardless of their command over the language and its intricacies. His songs are expressions of his innermost and intense thoughts of pain, pleasure and ecstasy he has experienced as a devotee in the service of his Lord.

Apart from the simple and lucid language what draws the common people to his song is the conversational style of his compositions. In his songs Ramadas not only praises his Lord, but talks to Him, cajoles Him, complains to Him, admonishes Him and sometimes, although verbally, thrashes Him. He immediately regrets his actions and gives an explanation for his rude remarks against his Lord. The unbearable hardships and the cruel torture he has faced at the hands of Tana Shah's men have in fact sharpened his devotion towards his Lord which ultimately helped him in attaining salvation.

As a true bhakta Ramadas is intensely emotional. To him Sri Rama is a living personality and not merely *Brahman* in the abstract. Hence his intense personal address to Sri Rama. Ramadas cries like a child asking for Sri Rama's favour. At other times, he is petulant and even rebukes God. He weeps in anguish when he thinks Sri Rama has not answered his call.

Thus, we find that his compositions are the outcome of the felt experience, an experience in which Ramadas is emotionally involved. His compositions are rich in *sabda* and *artha alankaras*. His idioms spring from the native language of his surroundings.

They rise from the soil and hence are natural without the artificial embellishments that abound in the compositions of scholar-poets.

Ramadas firmly believes that one who is an initiate into Bhakti will be released from the cycle of births and deaths: *enni janamamula nundi chesina papamu ee janmamuta vidunanna - annitikidi kadasari janmamu.*

In the song ae *teeruga nanu daya chuchitiro* Ramadas invokes Rama as *Inavamsothama*, a very apt expression because the act of looking needs some source of illumination — therefore, he reminds his Lord that he is the Lord of the solar race, the source of all illumination.

His compositions are full of accurate expressions filled with deep meanings. He pleads with the Lord's spouse Seethamma when he feels the he has been neglected by his Lord in his song "*Nanubrovamani Cheppave*". Here he invokes Sita as Janaka's daughter, Janaki, reminding her of her father, a great *stitaprajna* and *Rajayogi* and hence of nobler parentage than Rama whose father Dasaratha was a *kamuka* who yielded to Kaikeyi.

Similarly his composition *Pahi Rama prabho* abounds in excellent and catching *sabdalankara* with apt meanings. He asks the Lord to shoot arrows at his (Ramadas's) enemies. But he says that he has no foes in the external world and hence does not need the physical elimination of his foes. Here in this song he implies that the Lord is called upon to eliminate the inner enemies like *kama, krodha, moha,* etc.

Kalikiroopu is another interesting expression. *Kaliki* implies not just a woman but an attractive form. The contemporary saints have attained their sainthood merely by looking at this attractive form of Sri Rama at Bhadradri.

Ramadas's snides against the Lord — "*Ikshawku kula tilaka*" — are at once the helpless outbursts and piteous cries of a *satvika* subjected to unbearable tortures by Tana Shah's men, and immediately pleads for absolution for his improper remarks — *ee debbala korvaleka tittiti nayya:* "I cursed you, stung by the blows" of Tana Shah.

Bhavasagarameedanu is counterpoised by *Nalinadalekshana*. *Nalinadala* is a lotus which floats in water. Hence, he invokes the Lord to help his devotees while crossing the ocean of life by bestowing His "*Veekshana*" on them.

He reminds Rama that the beautiful crown adorning his imperial head was his contribution — crafted with meticulous care. Satirically he also tells Him that it was given to Him neither by his emperor father Dasaratha — who, instead, had Him exiled for fourteen years — nor by His father-in-law who never appeared on the scene after giving away his daughter Sita to Rama. He asks impertinently how can the Lord flaunt this crown and be indifferent to his sufferings. This prompts him to use expressions such as *adrijavinutudu, bhadragireesudu*, both denoting a link with mountains and hence of stony hearts which lack pity and kindness.

Thus we find that Ramadas wants to drink not just the nectar of Rama mantra but the distilled essence of that nectar, which comes through unceasing and relentless chanting and repetition of the Lord's name. With this in mind he has composed a "garland" of one hundred and three poems popularly known as "*Dasarathi Satakamu*" and has chosen "*Dasarathi Karunapayonidhi*" as the vocative motto and has used it as *"mukta"* or headline for almost all the poems. This *satakam* is rated as the best among the *Bhakti Satakas*. In this *Satakam* Ramadas expresses his strong devotion to Sri Rama which can be broadly categorised into ten parts devoted to highlight *namakeetana, neeti, bhakti, vairagya, sujana, durjana* and other *gunas*.

Thus we find Ramadas is at times a *karma yogi*, at other times a *jnana yogi* and almost always a *bhakti yogi*.

SECTION V

24
HARIDASA LITERATURE IN KANNADA

K.G. Narayana Prasad

Karnataka is the birthplace of the dualistic philosophy of Madhavacharya. This philosophy though centred in Karnataka has also spread its arms outside the state and obtained many followers throughout the country. But the hard-core was in Karnataka. According to this philosophy, Sri Hari is the God Supreme. All others are his servants. The word Haridasa means "servant of God Sri Hari". In the lifestyle of these Haridasas much importance was given to bhakti (devotion to God) and it was considered as the main path to self-realisation and salvation. Almost all Haridasas were the followers of Madhavacharya. Most of them were scholars in Madhava philosophy. Some of them, such as Sri Padaraja, Vyasaraya, and Vadiraja were *mathadhipatis*. They were sound scholars in Sanskrit too. They have produced many works in Sanskrit on Madhava philosophy. But the progress made by them in the field of Sanskrit literature is beyond the scope of the present essay. Hence only that literature which is produced in Kannada by the Haridasas is taken into consideration here. Thus, the Haridasa literature under consideration is, in a way, the literature produced in Kannada by the followers of dualism, the Dvaita of philosophy.

This literature has developed through three main stages: the first one is up to the age of Vyasaraya; the age of Vyasaraya is the second one; the third one starts from Bijayadasa. According to the available sources, Naraharitirtha of the last part of the thirteenth century is considered to be the first Haridasa to write in Kannada. He was a direct disciple of Madhavacharya and was the chief of the Madhavamatha at Udupi, in Karnataka. He was the third in succession from Madhavacharya. He hailed from Srikakulam of

Kalingadesa (now in Andhra Pradesh) and Madhavacharya brought him to Udupi. He composed some songs in Kannada with Raghupati or Raghukulatilaka as *ankita* (special name given by the guru) But, unfortunately, only two or three of them are available to us.

After him, up to Sripadaraja of the fifteenth century for nearly the period of over a century we cannot find any name belonging to this group. Sripadaraja (1406-1504) was the chief of the Madhavamatha at Mulabagal in Kolar district of Karnataka. He composed many songs in Kannada with Rangavithala as *ankita* and a good number of them are available. Some of them like *Bhramaragite* are very long. Besides these, he wrote in Sanskrit too.

The second stage starts with Vyasaraya (1447-1539), the disciple of Sripadaraja. He was the chief of the Madhavamatha at Sosale in Mysore district. Later on he moved to Vijayanagar and played a great role in the development of Haridasa movement. At one stage, he helped Krishnadevaraya, the great emperor of Vijayanagar, and was honoured by him. He has composed many songs with Sri Krishna as his *ankita*. but only a few of them survive. Just like his peer he was also a good scholar of Sanskrit. Besides this, he had a group of disciples full of zeal to work, like Purandaradasa and Kanakadasa. The patronage of the emperor was also an incentive. Thus, in his period the Haridasa movement reached its zenith. Up to this stage, knowledge flowed only in one direction, that is, from the peer to the common people of the upper class. But this stage changes the direction of knowledge which now flowed towards the common people of all classes. Purandara and Kanaka worked as the leaders in this mission. The two terms Vyasakuta and Dasakuta came into vogue during this stage. Vyasakuta means that group of scholars who used Sanskrit as their medium of expression while the other group which wrote in Kannada got the name Dasakuta. The former propagated the Madhava philosophy mostly among scholars whereas the latter propagated it among the common people. Vyasaraya acted as a bridge between the two. He was the guiding force for both the groups. Thus he is the root cause for the quick development of the Haridasa movement. This invested him with a distinct place in the history of the Kannada Haridasa literature.

Next to be considered in chronology is Vadiraja. He was the chief of the Madhavamatha at Sode in Karnataka. He composed many songs in Kannada with Hayavadana as *ankita*. Some of them like *Vaikunthavarnane, swapnapada*, etc., are lengthy poems. Besides these he wrote many scholarly works in Sanskrit. "The numerous songs composed by him in Kannada are the precious treasures of high philosophic thought in elegant classical and dialectic idiom" (Panchamukhi, 1952: xxvii).

The next person, contemporary of Vadiraja and also a disciple of Vyasaraya is Purandaradasa (1484-1564). He was neither a *sannyasi* nor a chief of any *matha* like his peers. According to tradition initially he was very rich and close-fisted; but later he gave away all his possessions, due to a traumatic experience in which his wife played a significant role and lived as a mendicant. All his songs end with the name Purandara Vithala, which was his *ankita*. It is said that he composed more than four lakh songs but only few are available at present. Purandara was considered as the ideal Haridasa by his guru Vyasaraya. His works are also very simple and attractive. Through them he carried the religious message to the common people of all classes. He blended literature with music and dance to make it more effective. He himself sang them and danced to their tune with great devotion. "He is acknowledged to be the father of karnatic music" (Rao, 1983 :77). He taught the *bhakti marga*, spoke about dedicating oneself to God, and also exhorted one to lead a pure and simple life. "He himself was a radiant example of total surrender to the Lord and the joy of this surrender" (ibid.). He converted all his sons to Haridasas. They joined their hands in the mission of their father. They also composed many songs in Kannada and enriched the Haridasa literature.

Contemporary to Purandaradasa and also belonging to the same school is Kanakadasa (1508-1606). He was of the hunter caste or, as some say, a shepherd. He composed many songs in Kannada with *Kagineleyadikesava* or *Badadadikesava* as *ankita*. Besides he wrote four different *Kavyas: Mohanatarangini* in *Sangatya* metre; *Nalacaritre, Haribhaktisara* and *Ramadhanya carite* in *satpadi* metre. In this respect his is a distinct place among the Haridasas which was shared by only a few like Jagannathadasa, the author of *Harikathamrtasara,* and others belonging to the modern period. Kanakadasa's songs are full of strong feelings and are more poetic in effect. Just like Purandaradasa he also carried them to the door-step of all people.

With the decline of the Vijayanagar empire, the Haridasa movement also faced a decline. In the seventeenth century Sri Raghavendra Tirtha once again brought it to the limelight. He was mainly a sound scholar in Sanskrit and wrote many works in it. It is believed that he composed many songs in Kannada too. But among them only on *Indu enage Govinda* has come down to us. According to that *Dhiravenugopala* is his *ankita*. Being a *mathadipati* he did a great service to Madhava religion:

> For the Dasakuta he was a guide and help and inspired several promising aspirants into devout Dasas by his wholesome tuition and guidance. From his seat at Mantralaya he radiated his influence in the surrounding region which produced the saints Byagavatti, Narasimhadasa, Panganama, Timmannadasa, the forerunners of the group of Vijayadasa and his disciples. Thus the future glory of the Dasakuta under Vijayadasa, etc., owed its rise to the seeds of an all-round renaissance sown by Sri Raghavendra Tirtha in the spiritual and intellectual lanes. (Panchamukhi, 1952: xxxiii)

Thus started the third stage under the leadership of Vijayadasa. Vijayadasa (1687-1755) belongs to Chikalaparivi in Raichur district. Being a very poor Brahmin he suffered much in his early life. Afterwards he got *diksha* from Purandaradasa in a dream and dedicated his life to the religious uplift of society. It is said that he composed nearly twenty-five thousand songs (including *suladis*) in Kannada. But now only a small portion of those are available. Vijaya Vitthala is his *ankita*. During his period religion was completely neglected. Hence his main task was to revive it. Therefore he wrote mainly to explain religious principles to the common people of the upper class. That is why he selected the *suladi* form as the major medium for his compositions. Afterwards he became famous as "the suladi dasa". He also built a strong group of disciples who could propagate the Madhavamatha effectively. Gopaladasa, Jagannathadasa and others belonged to this group. Helavanankatte, Giriyamma, Harapana Halli Bhimavva and other women also belonged to this tradition and joined their hands in the propagation of Vishnu bhakti. The tradition continues to this day.

Thus the Haridasa literature in Kannada has a history of over six hundred years. Regionally the first stage belongs to the south and south-west of Karnataka, the second to the banks of Tungabhadra and the third to the northern parts. Thus it spread all over Karnataka.

As mentioned earlier, Sri Hari is the God Supreme for the Haridasas. According to them He is independent from the world different from man and far superior to him. He is the efficient cause of the universe and everything moves according to His will and wish. He dwells in all beings and everything is found in Him. Hence the devotees must not entertain any fear in their hearts. The chanting of His divine names is so powerful that it can remove all sins and give salvation. Hence the Haridasas frequently pray to Him for his kindness, grace and protection. Therefore, the chief object of their compositions "is to extol Vishnu above all other gods and exhort men to worship Him" (Rice, 1921: 81).

In order to get salvation the individual has to surrender himself to God. For this, first of all he has to give up his vanity and think of his mortality. He should think that death is approaching very fast. At the time of death no worldly matter such as wife, children, relatives, his own house, wealth, kingdom, etc., will come to his rescue. Hence he should not be much attached to them, instead he should always have the divine names of Sri Hari on his tongue and in his mind.

While achieving this one has to abide by some ethical codes which will prevent him from bad deeds and guide him towards the correct path. This is the summary of the teachings of the Haridasas. According to the subject mater we can classify their compositions as follows:

1. Prayers of different kinds.
2. Biographical songs.
3. Narrative songs.
4. Philosophical songs
5. Ethical and ritualistic songs
6. Songs with the aim of social reform.
7. Songs for religious reform.

Many of the Haridasas, as said before, are not *sannyasis*. They had family and children and lived among common people. Their aim was to convey their feelings and knowledge to the common man. Hence their mode of expression was also very simple. They used a special form of Kannada language which was a blend of the literary and colloquial forms. Thus it was very simple and comprehensive to the common people.

Poetry is the main form of their expression and it is mainly of three kinds: *Kirtana, Suladi* and *Ugabhoga*. The first one starts with a *pallavi* (refrain) followed in some cases by an *anupallavi* and stretches to some odd number of stanzas. *Pallavi* contains the gist and the *anupallavi* supports it whereas the stanzas describe the same in detail often with examples.

In a *suladi, pallavi* and *anupallavi* are not there. It contains many stanzas, each in different *talas*. At the end there is a couplet called *jati*. *Ugabhoga* is a single stanza composition. In the case of *kirtana*, the *ankita* appears only once that too usually in the last line of the last stanza. In *ugabhoga* the same feature prevails. But in the case of *suladi* it is not so; it appears in each stanza including the end couplet. As far as the distribution of the content is concerned in a *suladi* each stanza explains one aspect of the central theme mostly with the help of appropriate examples and the end couplet contains the gist of the central theme of the whole poem. *Kirtana* follows both *raga* and *tala* whereas *suladi* gives prominence to *tala* and *ugabhoga* to *raga*. In a way *suladi* are tough and used mostly to explain the philosophical details. They are very vast and hence appropriate for that purpose. The *ugabhogas* are very brief in form and hence are used to narrate the theme in a nutshell without going in for elaborate description. Unlike these two the *kirtanas* are very simple to understand and also to sing. That is why the famous Haridasas like Purandara and Kanaka used mainly these.

Now we can summarise the main services done by the Haridasas as follows:

1. They propagated the bhakti cult and hence the Madhavamatha.
2. They corrected the way of life of the people.
3. They brought literature to the doorstep of the common man.
4. They produced a considerable amount of literature of good quality
5. They introduced and popularised the special literary forms like *kirtana, suladi* and *ugabhoga* in the field of literature and music.

Thus the Haridasa literature in Kannada is a literature of social, religious, philosophical, musical and literary importance.

References

Panchamukhi, R.S. "Introduction" in *Karnataka Haridasa Sahitya*, Bangalore: Kannada Sahitya Parisattu, 1952.

Rao, L.S. Sheshagiri. *A History of Kannada Literature*, Bangalore: Viswa Kannada Sammelan, 1983.

Rice, Edward P. *A History of Kanarese Literature*, Calcutta, 1921.

25
PURANDARADASA

B. Ramachandra Rao

It is a rare instance in history that a millionaire carrying on a flourishing business turns into a mendicant and philosopher-poet of a very high order.

Among Kannada poets, perhaps more popularly known than any other poet in Karnataka and outside the state is the poet-saint Purandaradasa. He is an exemplary personality among the devotees of Sri Hari: *"Dasarendare Purandara Dasarayya"*. This tribute was paid by no less a person than Vyasaraya who was his guru as well as the Rajaguru of the Vijayanagar emperors. The same guru acclaimed the literature produced by Purandaradasa in Kannada as *Purandaropanishat*. Purandaradasa is supposed to have written four lakh and seventy-five thousand songs or *Kirtanas*. They are musical compositions in literary style embodying philosophical and religious truths. They are given the status of *Upanishads* by his guru Vyasaraya.

The two important socio-religious movements in the twelfth and fourteenth centuries in Karnataka which moulded the culture of the people were intended to carry Vaishnavism and Dvaita philosophy propounded by Basaveswara and Madhavacharya respectively to the masses. Both the Vaishnava and the Dasa movements employed the mother-tongue of the people, that is, Kannada, to educate the masses on the lines of their thinking. The illuminating thoughts, spiritual experiences and religious messages were expressed in the form of *vachanas* and *kirtanas* by Sivasaranas and Dasa which attained the status of the highest type of literature. *Vachanas* are rhythmic prose compositions in the medieval Kannada which are very effective in reaching the heart of the common man. Haridasas blended music with literature and went on singing psalms of wisdom and taking their message from place to place.

Basaveswara spoke for Sivanubhava Pantha. Ramanujacharya (A.D. 1100) of Tamil Nadu and Madhavacharya (A.D. 1249) of Karnataka (Udupi) established two different kinds of Vaishnava movements in the south. The two acharyas made their teachings less abstract than the Metaphysics of Sankarites. The common people needed something tangible to love and be loyal and devoted to, something which they could live with in their daily lives and feel human. They could not accept Nirguna Brahmavada of Sankara nor the identity of Atman and Brahman. The bhakti movement made a direct appeal to the heart of these men and women. The worship of young Krishna at Udupi naturally cherished and propagated all the legends current about Krishna. Billions of disciples of Madhavacharya spread the Madhava movement all over Karnataka. Narahari Tirtha (A.D. 1281), Vyasaraya (A.D. 1520), Jayatirtha, Sripadaraya (A.D. 1451), Purandaradasa (A.D. 1520), Kanakadasa (A.D. 1509-1607), Vadiraja (A.D. 1550), Vijayadasa, Gopaladasa, Jannathadasa (A.D. 1727), Raghavendra Swami of Mantralaya are some of the important figures of the movement who have contributed immensely to the spread of the Dvaita philosophy and the bhakti movement. With the advent of Purandaradasa on the scene of the bhakti movement Vitthala bhakti which was already prevalent in Pandarpur in the north of Maharashtra came into the fold of Krishna bhakti at Udupi. Vitthala was equated with Vishnu and Krishna. Many devoted saints and singers of Maharashtra were fond of Vitthala or Vithoba of Pandarpur (also known as Pandange in Kannada inscriptions) and the people of Karnataka called him Kandi God. Hence Vithoba bhakti was added to Krishna bhakti of Dvaita philosophy and extended its horizon outside Karnataka.

Contemporary saints of Maharashtra, especially Eknath, tried to bring about a beautiful combination of Dvaita and Advaita. But Haridasas of Karnataka introduced the Dvaita elements throughout their work.

Traditional accounts about Purandaradasa say that he belonged to Purandaragadh near Poona. Recent evidence is of the opinion that he belonged to Purandaralaya Ghatta on the Sahadri ranges of the Western Ghats and hailed from a royal family. His father Veradappa Nayak was ruling that region (Jagirdar, 1984:1-25). Whatever it may be, the following accounts about his early life are popular. A legend about his early life says that he was carrying on business as a jeweller and moneylender. He became known at Hampi as Navakoti Narayana and was a byword for miserliness. It so happened that once an old Brahmin approached him with his boy begging aid from him for the boy's Upanayanam (thread ceremony). For six months the old man went to him daily but could not get anything. Realising the futility of this the old man went to Purandara Nayak's house and got a nose-ring from his wife, a pious, generous and noble lady. The old man took this and went to Purandara Nayak's shop and asked for a price for the same jewel. The Nayak was surprised and intrigued. He wanted to ascertain the truth and went home. When he demanded that the wife should show him the nose-ring she was helpless. She had no other way of escape except to commit suicide. But as soon as she took up a cup of poison the ring dropped into it from above. She was overjoyed and rushed to show it to the husband. The Nayak was puzzled. When he went to the shop he found that the nose-ring had disappeared from the safe and the old man was nowhere to be found.

This miracle was the turning point in the life of the rich man, Purandara Nayak. He renounced everything he had. He distributed his wealth among the pious people and dedicated himself to the service of Lord Vitthala. He went in search of a guru along with his wife and four sons. In Vijayanagar Sri Vijayaraja bestowed on him the *ankita* (signature) — Purandara Vitthala — and initiated him to the Haridasa *diksha*. Thereafter Purandara Nayak became known as Purandaradasa. A decisive moment came into his life when he took a vow of poverty and left his house. From that day he begged for alms enough for the day's sustenance and go about singing the praise of the Lord.

Purandaradasa had seen the pinnacle of glory and the decline of the Vijayanagar empire. After Vyasaraya passed away in 1539, times became hard in Vijayanagar. The entire moral tone of the capital suffered badly. Purandara was aware of the social evils of the period: decline of moral standards and deterioration of culture of the people and havoc played by casteism. Hence social reform and moulding the culture of the people was the aim of the Haridasa movement. This meant that there was great need for a person like Purandaradasa to speak his mind about goodness and virtue and cleanliness of body, mind and deed. He observed that bhakti had become a farce. People were going after several gods one after the other for selfish reasons, immersed in blind beliefs, and valued women, gold and land more than human life. Purandaradasa travelled extensively and wherever he went he worked for a religious awakening. He made people lead a pious life. He allayed the fears in the anxious minds of people about the uncertainty of their existence. He advocated unflinching faith in Sri Hari and his wondrous qualities. The plea of a literature of the people received further impetus at the hands of the Dasas. The exposition of philosophy in simple language, reflections on life, social criticism, satire, lyrical songs enriched Kannada literature to a large extent. The exposition of the tenets of the Dvaita philosophy in simple language was the chief aim of the Dasas of the Dasa Kuta led by Vyasaraya. The tenets of Dvaita philosophy preached by Madhavacharya is beautifully summarised in an oft-quoted Sanskrit verse composed by Vyasaraya as follows:

Srimanmdhvamata Harih paratarah satyman jagat tatvoto
Bhedo jivagana Hareranucarah nicocca bhavam gatah
Muktirnijasukhanubhutiramata bhaktisca tatsadhanam
Hyksaditritayam pramanamakhitamnayaika vedyo Harih.

This verse is known as the garland of nine jewels of the Madhavamatha (*navaratnamalika*):

1. Hari is supreme
2. the world is real
3. the intrinsic difference in every object is true
4. the individual souls are infinitely graded as superior and inferior
5. individual souls are dependent on God
6. liberation is self-realisation consisting of such bliss as has remained latent in the soul
7. pure bhakti is the means to this end
8. perception, inference, testimony are the sources of knowledge, mundane and heavenly
9. Hari is knowable in the entirety of the *Vedas* and by *Vedas* alone.

Purandaradasa proclaimed the supremacy of Vishnu who is Vitthala and Hari but there is nothing derogatory to the dignity of Siva in his songs. In fact he praised Siva, too.

Purandaradasa went through trials, tribulations and agony in life, its doubts and uncertainties and how in the end he achieved realisation through faith and single-minded devotion to his God are revealed in his songs. He was an excellent example of total surrender to the Lord and exemplified the joy of this surrender. Admission of human weakness and complete surrender to God are beautifully brought out in the following songs:

> I have no face to ask for any favours from you when
> I have countless faults in me, says Purandaradasa.
> I am arrogant, caught in the vanity of wife and children,
> I am swayed by desire, I am attached to this life, which
> I am bound to lose some day.
> How can I ask for any favour from you?
> I have approached your feet, you are my refuge, etc.
> Knowing all and aware of all, may you forsake me thus?
> I have no friends, you are father and mother ...
> I have trust in you as competent to save, etc.

The state of mind of the devotee when he has given up the way of the world as no way for him, and has not felt the assurance of realisation is pathetic. When he could not realise God or the chance of realisation seems remote his apathy towards God is expressed in the following song:

> What happened to your devotees like Brigu, etc.
> Who has trusted and prospered, my God? Listen!
> If a man accepts you he cannot get even a handful of grain as alms.

Then comes realisation. First he sees God in dreams. In a song he gives a vivid description of Krishna from his feet to the crown with all his decorative attire. Then he sees God approaching him. He sings all his attributes and gets enchanted. Then he sees Krishna standing before him eyes. He depicts in the *lila* songs of child Krishna which make the devotees enchanted. Now Purandaradasa assures that there is no need to doubt His presence. He confirms that there is no one who trusted in God and lost. If anyone did not believe and is lost, it was his fault. Those who do not trust or have firm faith in Hari may be lost, not the genuine ones.

> In a song Purandaradasa says:
> Are there outcastes only outside the village?
> Is there no outcast within?

Suggesting that there are men who are outcastes by their character. According to him an outcaste is one who has learnt but does not impart learning, who owns but does not give in charity. There are people who call themselves clean and refuse to touch others:

> Will the dirt of Karma go if you wash the skin?
> Why do you not understand the true meaning of things?
> No dirt can be washed off till the mind gets washed.
> Of what use is the dipping of one's body in the waters
> When devotion is not firm in the mind?
> Dasa asks who among the three wishes well of you,
> Woman, land or plenitude of wealth?

Finally he says that it is only fame and disgrace earned in this world that take shape and go with you. One comes to grief by trusting the body alone.

> Meditate upon the feet of God with peace of mind and think of Purandara Vitthala with a pure heart, and gain freedom from bondage by this constant thought. Do not give room for regrets at the end of your life. Dasa has experience at the hands of uncharitable people. He has seen a shrew closing the doors of her house when she sighted Dasa from a distance.

He also says that a man must be on the right path, otherwise what is the use of showy business? There is no meaning in religious observances if one is always engaged in evil deeds:

> What is the good of putting neem in sugar or
> pouring milk ceaselessly to a venomous snake?
> What is the good of thinking of Vitthal
> When one does not give up speaking untruth?
> What is the use of the wicked uttering mantras, etc.

Dasa warns that the messengers of death have no pity whatsoever, so remove worldly thoughts and think of Sri Hari.

> You may say, I married but the day before yesterday,
> I have one or two buffaloes to milk,
> I bought a piece of land but yesterday
> and I am expecting its yield.
> I have money and gold,
> I simply cannot die.
> But do you think, O vain one, that death will relent?

Purandaradasa says that he cannot see any greater glory or beauty in any other God than Purandara Vitthala:

> He is the Lord of the earth,
> He is the Lord of the Goddess of prosperity,
> In God-heads he the master of gods
> Which God other than Purandara Vitthala
> Who can be known only by the Vedas,
> Has this glory?

Talking about the magical effect of the Lord's name Purandaradasa says that the strength of His name is sufficient. Even the substantive help of the Lord is not necessary if one can get the aid of His name. He says it is a mark of good fortune to be born as a human being and one is a fool to spoil it. He desires people not to waste the opportunity on trivial satisfactions. The mind should be taken away from temptations. Show of orthodoxy and ceremonial purity are worthless. Those who do not give up desire but are orthodox and showy and worship, do it for food. Theirs is saintliness of the stomach. He criticises pretenders, hypocrites, showy orthodoxy and worship elaborately.

Purandaradasa offers some practical advice to the devotees:

> One should swim across, live and win.
> True, samsara is dirty and disgusting
> Your attachment must be no more than a drop of water on the lotus leaf
> Your involvement in family life must be no more than
> the connection of the seed of the cashewnut with the fruit,
> not contained within but attached without.

He says that one should be like a stone in the harsh life at the same time flexible in the company of learned people:

> You must stand like a rock in this sea of life,
> hard and unmoved by happiness and misery
> you must be humble before the learned
> bending before them like the bow.

Purandaradasa is of the opinion that *dharma* alone triumphs. He preaches patience to fault-finders and kindness in return for unkindness. He suggests the giving of sweet and tasty food to the person who gives poison and serving the one who hates us. He often startles with a pun. The one message that comes through all his writings is that the devotees should live the life of a hero and fight ignorance with courage, have unflinching faith in Sri Hari and be detached from selfish worldly pleasures.

References

Jagirdar, Sitaram. *Purandaradasaru Caritrika Sangatigalu*, Kannada *Sahitya Parisatpatrika*, Vol.69, No.1, 1848.

26

KANAKADASA

N. R. Shastri

The historic movement of Vaishnava religious devotionalism which made its indelible impact on the masses during the Middle Ages, had its origin in what is called *Dasa Kuta* or the order of Vaishnava saints of Karnataka. This order of *Dasas* (servants of God) was built by a regular band of saintly souls who dedicated themselves to the service of God, and, singing the glories of Hari, they wandered from one end of the country to the other. Devotional literature of Haridasas was pioneered by Narahari Teertha towards the close of the 13th century and developed further by Sripadaraya of the 15th century. It reached its zenith in the 16th century when Purandaradasa and Kanakadasa led by their guru, Vyasaraya, composed a large number of devotional songs and popularised them by going from house to house with these haunting tunes on their lips. As in the *Vachana* literature of Veerasaiva saints, so also in the Kirtana literature of Vaishnava saints, the *raison de etre* is a flowering of personality as a devotee of God. As R.S. Mugali puts it, "Such literature can never be produced by mere erudition or by sheer imagination." It attempts to render the mystic experience of the highest truth.

These saints of the Dasa order, however, centred their affection on Vithala of Pandharpur as the patron deity. According to Dr. B.N. K. Sharma, "Karnataka had cultural sway over Pandharpur and its neighbourhood... and Pandharpur itself was looked upon as the holy city of Maharashtra mysticism. Even as late as the time of the great Maharashtra saint Jnanesvara, Vitthala of Pandharpur was still spoken of as 'the deity' beloved of the Karnataka, enshrined in Karnataka." Indeed, the saints of Karnataka were the first to develop the cult of devotion to

Vithala, and make it a living faith and a powerful instrument of mass upliftment with the aid of their soul-stirring music and *kirtanas* in the language of their province. Their example was subsequently emulated and popularised by the saints, Ramadas, Tukaram and others, of the neighbouring province of Maharashtra. But the essential feature of their cult, besides the emphasis laid on true devotion to Vitthala, was the comparative unimportance of social and caste barriers in the spiritual realm and these are to be found in the songs of the early Dasas of Karnataka. The *Dasa Kuta* may therefore be regarded as the earliest movement of religious devotionalism in the South and from here it spread to other parts of upper India and produced kindred movements.

These saints of Karnataka, it is obvious, exercised a powerful religious influence on the mass consciousness and on the average Kannadiga, including women and people of the lower strata of society who were not acquainted with Sanskrit. The saints composed songs in easy colloquial language — the language really used by men — which captured the heart and imagination of the people. Singing praises of Krishna and Vitthala, they moved through the length and breadth of the country, extolling the merits of *jnana* and *bhakti*, giving wholesome advice to the people on ethics and religion. This was done by conveying their teachings in the form of melodious songs based on various *ragas* (tunes). Proficient in philosophy and Sanskrit, they simplified the most difficult doctrines and put them in easily intelligible verses. They viewed the world as full of misery and pain and counselled men and women to turn to God for their emancipation. They were also advocates of reform and condemned sham and cant in most scathing terms. Ardent followers of Madhava faith, they exhorted their followers to be truthful in thought, word and deed. The Haridasa movement strove to place a complete scheme of religion and morality before the people. It condemned fanaticism and ritualism and preached the philosophy of *naiskarmya*, that is, enlightened action in a spirit of devotion and dedication to God, as interpreted by Madhava.

Kanakadasa, a contemporary of Purandaradasa, belonged to this order. He was a great devotee with a distinct individuality of his own. When we examine the sources both internal and external, we are able to gather that he was born in a shepherd (beda) family and rose to the position of an army chief by sheer merit. It seems that he renounced worldly life in response to a higher call which he received during a battle. There is also a story about his exemplary devotion. It is said that Kanakadasa was not allowed to enter the temple of Krishna at Udupi. Kanaka, however, went behind the temple and stood there praying to God. The image of Krishna in the temple is supposed to have turned round and stood facing Kanaka. The idol remains in this position even to this day. There is a little window through which people get the *darshan* of Lord Krishna. The window still continues to be known as *Kanakana khindi*, Kanaka's window.

Like Purandaradasa, Kanakadasa went to Vijayanagar and became a beloved disciple of Vyasaraya. However, there is an essential difference in his approach and that of Purandaradasa with respect to religion. Purandaradasa accepted the Madhava doctrine in *toto* and cultivated such liberalism and courage as he could muster within its framework. Kanakadasa was brought up in the Ramanuja tradition in his early days but he kept himself open to all benign influences of religion and culture. The most potent influence was that of Madhava faith, which he followed under the guidance of his guru. He was, in other words, more Catholic but less committed than Purandaradasa.

Kanakadasa wrote some long poems in popular metres besides devotional songs *(kirtanas)*. Among them, *Ramadhanya Charite* is one of the few poems in Kannada with an original theme relating to a debate between rice and *ragi*, each trying to establish its supremacy. Ultimately *ragi*, which is the staple food of the poor, is adjudged superior by Rama who has been asked to arbitrate. The poem is not just fanciful, but is symbolic as well. It suggests that God is a champion of the poor, a votary of the common man. Another poem of his is a narrative based on the popular story of Nala and Damayanti in simple, flowing Kannada. The narrative is gripping, not vague or halting. The noble characters of the hero and the heroine stand out against the background of their trials and tribulations, The third work, *Mohanatarangini*, is longer than the others. The subject of this work is the love between Usha and Aniruddha as recounted in the *Bhagavata*. The work abounds in descriptions, some of which seem to portray the contemporary life and glory of the Vijayanagar Empire. The poem ends with an emphasis on the fact that there is no difference between the two gods, Hara and Hari, thus revealing a Catholic attitude in matters of religion.

It is in his devotional songs that Kanakadasa has given us the outpouring of his heart. The stream of his devotion to God has flowed full to the brim in these spiritual lyrics. He does not show much zeal in spreading the tenets of any particular doctrine as Purandaradasa does. He is mainly interested in single-minded devotion and is concerned with human values. His songs are not as numerous as those of Purandaradasa, but, like him, Kanakadasa has some evocative songs to his credit and some others which may be called exhortary. In one of his songs he asks the people to rest assured that God is looking after all of us and that there is no cause for anxiety. Kanakadasa has at times played the role of a preacher like Purandaradasa but he shows great freedom of thought and universality of outlook. His understanding of the life of the people and of their idiom is deep. He has exposed social evils in a frank and forthright manner. He goes to the root of the matter in his analysis of society. For instance, his song on the question of *kula*, that is, caste is in the form of powerful argument. He says:

> They talk of kula
> times without number.
> Pray, tell me
> what is the *kula* of men
> who have felt real bliss?
>
> When a lotus is born in mire,
> do they not bring it
> and offer it to the Almighty!
> Do not the gods of the earth
> drink the milk
> which comes from the flesh of the cow?
>
> Do they not besmear
> their bodies with deer musk?
>
> What is the caste of God Narayana?
> and Siva?
> What is the caste of Atman?
> and of Jiva?
> Why talk of *kula*
> when God has blessed you?

Kanakadasa

The painful aspects of worldly life take Kanakadasa to the regions of higher thought and intellect. He feels the agonies of *samsara* very intensely and eventually depicts the tragic aspects of worldly life in gloomy hues. He describes the nature of this perishable body as "having appeared just like a bubble on the surface of water, disappears. And in this big forest of samsara, I am lost." In one of his verses he exposes the hypocrisy of mankind:

> What is the use of practising meditation and penance when people are possessed of deceit, sin and wickedness?
> Having struggled without realising the first preceptor (Adi Guru) and having dried up the tongue by reading the Vedas and Sastras, they remain without realising the Primeval Being (Adi Manu).
> If the supporters of the doctrine of the Bhedas, who are engrossed in argumentation, remain without doing any charity whenever possible, just like a tank in the forest which is filled up and dries up also — what is the use of practising meditation and penance?
> Having stored up ornaments for wife and children, they are caught in the net of servants of Yama (God of Death).
> Having got up in the cold, rain and extreme darkness, having meditated after taking a full bath in the river and having struggled hard, do not perish. But, Oh, mind! Remember Adikesava soon!

Indeed, nothing belongs to man in this world. The only thing that man possesses or should possess is his true devotion to God. Kanakadasa says:

> Wicked man! do not say myself and thyself. But consider within yourself through knowledge who you are.
> Are woman, land and wealth yours?
> Is desire accrued from food yours?
> Is the sound accrued from the ears yours?
> Is the body that is once leaving you away yours?
> Are you the one who has come
> through these several births and
> are you the one that resides in the womb full of dirt?

> Are you the one who has come
> through the canal of urine, or
> are you the one who has got
> caste, creed and clan *(gotra)*?
> Do the time, working, purity
> and method belong to you?
> Does the idol (body) of nerves
> fastened to plugs of bones
> belong to you?
> Yes, you become the devotee of
> the joyous Adikesava.

In his devotional poems Kanakadasa sings of his surrender to the divine and the joy which he has experienced.

Kanakadasa is, above all, a great *bhakta* and *anubhavi*, a mystic who sings of his wholehearted commitment to and faith in the divine which is the fount of his experience of bliss.

The term 'mysticism' can serve as an equivalent of *anubhava*. It is used in certain contexts in the sense of something mysterious, exclusively esoteric, too vague or recondite to realise and justify by logic or discursive reasoning, not specific but charged with emotion (William James). Besides, it is also used to express a term synonymous with the word hypnotism, or to denote a queer state of a day-dreamers mind. The *Encyclopaedia Britannica* defines mysticism as that which "... appears in connection with the endeavour of the human mind to grasp the divine essence or the ultimate reality of things, and to enjoy the blessedness of actual communion with the Highest." The first is the philosophic side of mysticism, the second its religious aspect. The first is theoretical or speculative, the second practical. Both of these aspects are considered here. If the former aims at an investigation into truth, the latter points to its actual realisation and experience. It is not a name to be applied to a specific path but is a synthesis of different paths which have attempted to realise the one Truth.

Man, in his attempt to discover the mystery of nature, looks at the world in three ways. An attempt to discover the mystery of the world through mere intellect is one way. The intellect alone is adequate enough for knowledge and the knowledge gained through the intellect determines man's experience. This is the essence of Rationalism which insists upon the intellect as the only basis of knowledge.

The second method goes a step further and believes that it is not possible to find out the entire nature of truth through the intellect alone. It may be possible to have a thorough knowledge only through experience derived through tests and experiments. Hence experience itself is the basis of knowledge. This is what is called Empiricism.

The third way believes that it is not possible to find out the whole truth through mere intellect or experiments. At some point or the other intellect is bound to fail and find itself baffled and helpless. The truth that pervades the entire universe is beyond the grasp of logic or reason or of test or experiment. To know that which is transcendent one needs the eye that is transcendent too. It means that the individual in quest of truth must turn his eye within. A new world unfolds itself within his ken. Some unseen spirit inaccessible to mere intellectual pursuits or experiments wakes up the heart. The seeker then realises that this spirit can offer genuine solutions to the serious problems of life. This may be called mysticism.

Meditating upon this spirit that is within the heart maybe, in a sense, called *anubhava* or experience of the divine, or the mystic experience. This concept of *anubhava* is a gift presented by the Haridasas and Saranas to the spiritual heritage. The Haridasas have used it in a special sense to denote an experience derived from their consciousness and their way of life lived in loyalty to it. It is the realisation of the Godhead and the resulting bliss therefrom. It is in this sense that mysticism is the immediate feeling of the unity of the self with God, and the mystic engrossed in the Almighty rises to a higher level and finds it impossible to remain without Him. As Kanakadasa describes in one of his devotional songs:

> O Hari! Is it possible to remain having forsaken thee?
> It is possible to observe penance having forsaken parents,
> It is possible to forsake the nearer relatives,
> It is possible to quit the kingdom, if the king gets angry,
> O, Father of Cupid, it is not possible to remain separated from thine feet.
> It is possible to forsake food, even when the belly is empty,
> It is possible to get away from the place of birth,
> It is possible to forsake wife and children for ever,
> But it is not possible even for a moment to forsake thine feet.

> It is possible to give way the life to others,
> It is possible to shed egoism and honour,
> But, O Adikesava, the bestower of my life,
> It is not possible to forsake thine feet.

The soul is fundamentally dynamic and blissful in its essence. But as long as it is confined and cabined within the body, its conscious force manifests itself in different forms and different measures. The same current of electricity flowing through wires made of different metals takes different forms like heat and light. Similarly, the soul reveals itself in varied functions. Mysticism constitutes progressive ascent of the individual, step by step, from matter or the food-sheath, through the vital, mental and intuitional sheaths to the ultimate stage of bliss, which is its real nature. In other words, it is a journey from the *annamaya kosa* (food sheath) to the *anandamaya kosa* (bliss sheath). This is the supreme height that mystical experience attains to and the devotee feels the presence of God everywhere. Kanakadasa describes this omnipresence in one of his songs:

> This body is thine
> and this life is also thine.
> All the joys and sorrows
> that I experience day after day
> are thine.
> The ear that listens to sweet words
> and Vedic lore is thine;
> the eye that looks at the beauty
> of bewitching women
> is thine.
> The five senses that get enmeshed
> in the web of *maya*
> are thine.
> O Lord, how are men free
> as you are.

This is reminiscent of the mystic outlook expounded by the Upanishadic sages where we see how the mind turns within and absorbs itself in quest of truth:

> *om kenesitam patati, presitam manah*
> *kena prathamah praitiyuktah*

Kanakadasa

kenesitam vacmimam vadati
caksuh srotam ca devoyunakti

"At whose behest, at whose instance does the mind engage itself in itself? At whose fiat does vital breath begin its function for the first time? At whose wish do people talk? Who is the god that commands the eye and the ear?" For all our physical movements some unseen power must be responsible. What is the power that governs this world of diverse forms and names? One must see the omnipresent God in this Atman.

This mystic experience in its ultimate state is indeed ineffable. As Sri Ramakrishna Paramahamsa says, it is, as it were, a doll of salt trying to fathom the depth of an ocean. Speech stills into silence. It is a height which transcends the reach of thought and speech. Nevertheless, the seeker has to express, in terms of words and symbols, his experience of the divine and the nature of the path that leads to it, for the benefit of others. These words, however, cannot reveal the perfect state of the experience, but at least, they serve as pointers to the seeker to ponder over the apparent duality. Kanakadasa in one of his oft-quoted devotional songs presents the dialectic of duality with ease and lucidity. If God is omnipotent and omnipresent, what must be His exact nature?

> O God, art thou within the illusion, or
> is the illusion within thee?
> Art thou within the body, or
> is it within thee?
>
> Is the building in the open space, or
> the open space within the building? Or
> are both the building and the open space
> within the eye?
>
> Is the eye within the mind, or
> the mind within the eye? Or
> are these both within thee?
>
> Is the sweetness in sugar, or
> sugar in the sweetness? Or
> are they both in the tongue (itself)?

Is the tongue within the mind, or
the mind within the tongue? Or
are both of them within thee?

Is the flower within the fragrance, or
the fragrance within the flower? Or
are these both in the nose?

O Adikesava! Is it possible to say exactly,
what is what?
But it is certain that
everything is within thee.

Kanakadasa was one of the most sublime thinkers of his age. In his poetry one finds the boldness of thought and expression, and the aptness of imagery. The intensity of devotion and the liberality of attitude exalt him to the level of a poet-saint of a very high order.

References

D. Javaregowda, ed. *Kanaka Sahitya Darshana*, Bangalore, Kannada and Culture Directorate, 1990.

A.P. Kamarkar and N.B. Kalamdani, *Mystic Teachings of the Haridasas of Karnataka*, Dharwar, 1939.

H.S. Krishnaswamy, ed. *Dasasahitya Darshana*, Mysore, Mangala Bharati Prakashana, 1984.

R.S. Mugali, *History of Kannada Literature*, New Delhi, Sahitya Akademi, 1975.

B.N.K. Sharma, *Philosophy of Sri Madhavacharya*, Bombay, Bharatiya Vidya Bhavan, 1962.

27

BILWAMANGAL

A.V. Suresh Kumar

This great poet-savant of Deccan — Bilwamangal — is mostly unknown though he is one of the foremost devotees, singer of the praises of Lord Krishna. He is the singer of *Krishna Kathamrita*. The superb trait in Bilwamangal is that which depicts the cream of *saguna* (with form) worship of Lord Krishna and the climax of *bhav* (feeling) known as Braj *bhav* is shown at the outset. When Sri Krishna, once after holding Bilwamangal by the arm, later tears Himself away and eludes his grasp, then follow the memorable words of the great saint and poet:

> What bravado is thus wrenching off Thine hands from my grasp? Deservedly shalt Thou be praised if Ye can slip off my heart.

This fascinating aspect of addressing the Lord as the body present in front of him marks the songs of Bilwamangal. Usually it is the *nirguna* (formless) *bhav* that dominates Krishna worship but Bilwamangal saw Krishna not far off, far above us, but hand in hand with us, as a beloved, a friend, a brother and a father. He sings the glory of this intimate relationship.

A Shiva worshipper, a paramour of the courtesan Chintamani, a composer of songs for unworthy clients, a hankerer after sensual enjoyment — such are some of the activities that mark the early life of this great poet-saint of Deccan — Bilwamangal.

The great saint Bilwamangal was so infatuated by the charms of the dancer, courtesan, Chintamani, that even on sacred days, when for instance he was observing a fast on the death of his father, on a stormy night he crossed the river on a dead body mistaking it for a plank sent by his beloved, Chintamani and in climbing on to the roof to reach her he caught hold of a cobra hanging there. The noise created by his jump from the roof into the courtyard aroused the sleeping Chintamani who observing her paramour's infatuation was suddenly fired by the latent memories in the recesses of her heart covered over with impious *prarabdha-karma phala* which was responsible for this unholy love. She exhorted Bilwamangal in a very plain way. She asked him to behold the picture of Gopal hanging on the wall in her room and told him if he conferred such devotion on Him, he would cross the ocean of metempsychosis and forever dwell in the realm of Eternal Beatitude. Struck by these simple but soul-stirring words Bilwamangal woke up, as if from a reverie. Impelled by a Divine power he proceeded immediately to Brindaban - with the ecstatic song "Govind, Damodar, Madhav" on his lips.

The sheen that transferred him into the effulgent abode of Lord Sri Krishna saw him emerging into a great devotee of the Lord. Obviously Bilwamangal saw in Chintamani the root of his transformation. Hence, he consecrated himself at her feet, enshrining her as his first guru. True to her words Chintamani followed Bilwamangal to Brindaban and implored the Lord Himself to redeem her from this world. She commenced a fast unto death determined to have food only from the hands of Lord Krishna. Her determination moved Sri Krishna and He Himself appeared and fed and blessed her. Thus began a saga of brilliant Sanskrit poetry of the duo.

The passionate outpouring of Bilwamangal accompanied by the music of Chintamani's trinkets transformed into exquisite garlands of verses marked by melody, devotion, thrilling in rhythm, replete with mystic love.

28
ANDAL'S *TIRUPAVAI*

Mohan Ramanan

This paper proposes a consideration of the eighth century Vaishnava bhakti text, Andal's *Tirupavai*, from a historical perspective. The exploration relies on a translation I have done of the work. A translation is a kind of reading in itself and is conditioned by the pressure of culture. I use the term culture in its widest sense to include factors like politics, social mores, economics and religion. We cannot read an eighth century text without bringing ourselves into the reading, without seeing history as in a dynamic relation to ourselves. Therefore a translation-reading compels one sharply to focus on not only historical sameness but also historical difference. A contextualised reading of this sort is apt to be bristling with creative possibilities.

Some years ago I happened to listen to a series of discourses on bhakti and on the *Tirupavai*. The speaker was not a Tamil but a Maharashtrian whose ancestors had settled in the Tanjavur region of Tamil Nadu. Professor A.S.V. Pant was a philosopher by training, a scholar in Sanskrit and Indian aesthetics. He had, in the course of his studies, learnt Tamil. That he knew his *Nalayira Divya Prabandhams* (the four thousand sacred hymns of the Vaishnava Azhwars, also called the Tamil Vedas), of which the thirty verses of the *Tirupavai* are a small part, was amply clear from his discourse replete with telling examples and allusions to a whole range of scriptural and philosophical works. I used to catch him on mornings expounding the *Prabandhams* to an elderly and eager Vaishnava, who was only then educating himself in his religious traditions From an outsider, as it were, like Professor Pant, I felt drawn to the Tamil devotional tradition, and to the

Tirupavai in particular. Because of certain particular personal circumstances I was not literate in Tamil, though I could converse in what after all was my mother tongue. The only language I knew was English and so I determined to render the Tamil *Tirupavai* into English. This would be my humble tribute to a glorious tradition of musical recitation I was familiar with. During the month of Margazhi (December-January) Tamil women take a vow and devote themselves to the chanting of the *Tirupavai*, one *pavai* or verse for each day. This and other spiritual practices during the month are supposed to bring rewards, the most important being the reward of getting a good husband. Tamil women in traditional homes sing these hymns and I had admired this, as I had the rendering of these hymns in Karnatak Kutcheris by stalwarts like Ariyakudi Ramanuja Iyangar and others like K.V. Narayanaswami and M.L. Vasanthakumari. When I approached Professor Pant with the idea of a translation into English he agreed to help. So on a wintry December we sat together day by day piecing together the text.

He would recite the hymn and I would take in the spirit of the verse. He would then give me word for word meanings and explanations and I would then paraphrase the text into English. Eventually I began revising the paraphrase and to put it into free verse. My aim was to suggest the speaking voice of the author — Andal or Goda, as she is known. I had come across versions of the *Tirupavai* in English which suffered from the blight of pomposity. Many translators of our scriptural texts are loyal to a Romantic-Victorian idiom and in their English translation attempt the sonorities of that tradition, producing consequently flat translations. Here is an example of what I mean. It is a translation of the first *pavai* of the Andal text:

> In this month of Margazhi, of waxing mooned good day;
> Ye maids for bath prepared! Come on, O maids of jewels gay!
> O, devoted maids of Aaipaadi of wealth divine!
> He's the son of Nadagopan of mortal dart so fine.
> A lion's cub of Yasoddhai of beauteous eyes is He!
> He's of cloud-hue, red eyes and of face of bright moon, see!
> E'en that Narayana himself will enthrall us with joy!
> May we have our baths, while all the worlds praise Embaavai!

The version is circumlocutory as one can see. It is not in the language of conversational speech which incidentally is one of the most important elements of Andal's style. The adjectival excess —" waxing mooned good day", "jewels gay", "Yasoddhai of beauteous eyes", the stylised Victorian inversions — "bath prepared", "wealth divine", the stilted rhyme scheme — all testify to a lack of verbal energy, a loss of vitality. A Victorian translation of the sort I have quoted attempts to cover up the humanity of the text with a formidable facade — a facade of gentility. It does disservice to Andal's idiom, which is a varied mix of homeliness, earthiness, exuberance and which has the jouissance of a complex literary effort.

Let us go back to Andal's verse. It opens with a personal poem by invoking the month of Margazhi, the occasion for the song; it addresses the Sakhis or companions in a direct manner — a feature of the natural and vigorous style of Andal; it alludes to the relation the bhakta must have with Krishna, and it introduces the symbolism of the bath. With this in mind I attempted the following version:

> O my dear, the auspicious Margazhi full-moon day has come.
> O my friends, desirous of bathing, O Sakhis,
> beautiful with ornaments, come.
> O girls, wealthy and prosperous,
> inhabitants of the hamlet of cowherds, come.
> Let us gather together,
> for heroic and mighty Nandagopa's son,
> Wide-eyes, beautiful Yashoda's lion-cub,
> with body like a full cloud,
> eyes of royal red and a face
> grand as the sun and the moon,
> no less than Narayana Himself,
> Will fulfil our wishes so that the world may praise Him.
> (Verse 1)

I do not wish to claim too much for my version, imperfect as it must be. Vaishnavas I have consulted feel that my translation captures the spirit of the original. That is no doubt gratifying but I want to claim here some kind of an autonomy for the translated effort. This, in turn, is the result of a historical perspective. The patristic text must take variable shapes in its encounter with history. The individual talent, while tackling a traditional text, must nevertheless be prepared to alter it. When Dr. Johnson imitated Juvenal in "London" and "Vanity of Human Wishes" he was producing his own version or reading of a classical poem. Johnson's reading of a classical author was determined by the pressures of contemporary culture, particularly his own relation to society and to the London of the eighteenth century. His work is Juvenal, surely, but it is Juvenal with a difference. Something like this happens in my translation or reading of Andal. There is a complex interplay of the present with the medieval past while my reading is Andal, it is also Andal with a difference.

The difference lies in a different conception of history. My reading sees it as a complex pattern of contradictions, dominant and subordinate elements and currents, declining and emergent energies, not as unified or monolithic. An older historicism assumed a somewhat mechanical relationship. Thus E.M.W. Tillyard would speak of the Elizabethan world picture and read Sidney, Spenser or Shakespeare as reflectors of that worldview. Lovejoy explained literary expression in terms of the units of thought prevalent at different points of time. His concern with the development of Ideas, for example, explained Romanticism. The Frenchman Taine spoke of the relation between Man, the moment and the milieu and explained literature as an expression of the soul of the race. Something like this informs the historical thought of Jayakar or Mazumdar. These approaches see history as something unified and in some way determining the character of literature. Their view is monological.

My approach is dialogic and attempts to relate the present to the past dynamically. It sees history as problematic and not as simple or unified in the least. A literary text has to be necessarily contextualised. This can be done in two ways — first by relating the text to its complex age, second by relating it dynamically to ourselves. The Victorian translation of Andal quoted earlier does neither. It treats Andal as an occasion for an exercise in a language game. In other words Andal's vibrant text loses it humanity and gets appropriated by an arid formalism which throws a cover of gentility over the text. This prison-house of language will not allow the word to relate to the world, the text to history or Andal to anything beyond herself. The *Tirupavai* gets valorised and suspended in an aesthetic realm which resists and denies the gravitational pull of history. This kills the text because history alone can transform it to life.

Medieval India was hardly monolithic. It was a period of great ferment, of intense conflict of class and caste. It witnessed the emergence of a protestant individualism and questioning. Bhakti was the new element which catalysed progressive thinking in a variety of ways. It questioned at one level Brahminical elitism and the intellectual and cerebral tradition of commentary and exegesis. It was a force which had its origins as a developed philosophical concept in the *Gita* related to notions of *Karma* and *Jnana*. But from a philosophical concept it became a centre for the reaction against the intellectualism of Vedic culture and the philosophical splitting of hairs. It promoted the individual's need to speak, as it were, directly with God, without the intervention of ritual, priest or institutions. For intellectualism it substituted emotionalism, something akin to the "enthusiasm" and exuberance of the dissenting tradition of England of the eighteenth and nineteenth centuries. Bhakti was an affair of the heart and as such a subversive force in a strict, formal, patriarchal and hierarchical society. It released certain kinds of energy which may be broadly termed Dianysiac. Profoundly questioning established authority it was a major element in the democratisation of Hindu society. The Azhwars and Nayanmars came from various castes and asserted the oneness of Man before God. Also bhakti provided gender justice. It was during the medieval period that women bhakti poets like Mira flourished in the North and Andal in the South. The dominant patriarchy had now to contend with the feminine mystique and its potential for subversion.

Bhakti thus is a concept which dramatically binds the present with the past and makes for an exciting historical reading. It has an appeal for us when we ourselves are concerned with the meaning and content of democracy. A reader of Andal has necessarily to be a *sahrdaya* if he is to justice to her. The *sahrdaya* cannot be in a confrontationist relation to his/her author. If the author has *Karayitri Pratibha* (creative imagination) the reader should have *Bhavayitri Pratibha* (responsive imagination). Bhakti in Andal is fused with bhakti in the reader who must humble himself/herself before Andal's devotional intensity and her superior spiritual claims. Such a relation between the original author and contemporary reader produces a vibrant exchange, making for the proper internalisation of the eighth century text and amalgamating it with our contemporary notions of femininity, the radical questioning of the mores of patriarchal society, the democratic aspirations for a new social order based on the reorientation of human relations devoid of manipulation, exploitation and tyranny.

With this context in mind I would assert that Andal's *Tirupavai* is a subversive document particularly in its eroticism. I would further argue that eroticism is a central motif in the text and that, though it is perhaps not as intense as the dream in section 6 of Andal's *Nachiyar Tirumozhi*, it is nevertheless so widely dispersed in the text as to be an enabling agent in the breaking down of hierarchy and authority. A response to patriarchal repression is what Andal's poem represents at one level. Andal introduces into her bridal mysticism the element of dream with explicit sexual connotations as an answer to brute reality. She is recounting to her Sakhi her dream of being wedded to Krishna and the overt sexual symbolism is unignorable. The latent meaning of the bath in the first *pavai* quoted at the outset and the imagery of water and rain in the fourth *pavai* where Andal evokes the state of beatitude are strong examples:

> Release your continuous shower of rain,
>   as does He His arrows,
> Your beneficent rain,
>   that we may bathe in joy
> and prosper.

It is tempting to allegorise such passages and make Andal look like someone superhuman and sexless. Andal's greatness is not in need of allegorisation and in frankly recognising the sexual overtones of the bath we do not diminish Andal one jot; rather her humanity is foregrounded. The bath, quite clearly, is not a mere religious observance, but suggests union with the beloved. But then the transference of her affections to Krishna has behind it one other stage. Freud's formulation regarding the child's relation to water in dream and mythology is helpful in understanding it. The delivery of a child from the uterine waters, according to Freud is frequently presented by distortion as the child's entry *into* water. Andal's fondness for the bath and the dominance of the rain/water image in the *Tirupavai* can be explained in terms of Andal's sense of insecurity. She was a foundling after all and her repressed resentment against an absent mother finds expression in her transferring her loyalty to Krishna who is seen both as father and lover. Indeed Nappinnai, Krishna's wife, mother of the world, comes in for scolding at her hands. Andal cheekily ticks her off:

> O Nappinnai, expansive eyes one, tinged with collyrium,
> how long will you keep Him from us?
> Will you not permit Him to get up?
> Can you not be separated from him, even for a while?
> I tell you this is not proper, and
> alas, that is the truth.

This could very well be Andal's way of getting back her own on a mother who abandoned her in a tulasi grove and allowed her to be raised by Periazhwar. Andal hits where it will hurt most, at Nappinnai's possessive love for Krishna. Andal is telling her that Krishna belongs to the whole world and in so saying cocks a snook at decorum, propriety and established morality.

Andal is the perpetual child in the poem. Her childlike angle of vision is basic to the poem. Andal and her Sakhis are children looking up to Krishna for succour. A kind of paradise of the child is repeatedly suggested in the poem. The opening of verse 6 reads as follows:

> See for yourself the birds chirping;
>   Did you not hear the
>   loud white conch of the temple
>   of the Lord Garuda?
> O my child arise;

And here in verse 8 evoking a pastoral scene:

> O see, the Eastern horizon has grown white,
>   and the buffaloes have rushed out
>   to graze in the backyard pastures

The house of Andal's Sakhi in verse 9 is "bedecked, and beautiful lamps burn all around." Her Sakhi sleeps

> On a beautiful bed,
>> with joss-sticks fumes,
> fragrantly seeping in from all directions.

The juvenile world is bounteous and plentiful:

> The buffaloes out of love for their young ones
>> ooze milk through their udders,
>>> and wetting the courtyard make it miry.

And there can be no question that the children's paradise they have entered is the epitome of all desire. Andal tells her Sakhi in verse 14:

> We have entered your backyard garden.
> The red-lily has blossomed,
> The blue-lotus has shut itself up,
> in your well.

The childlike vision modulates into childlike sensuousness. Andal and her Sakhi have a kind of female bonding or togetherness. A good part of the poem is taken up with this dalliance. There is banter and a kind of sexual foreplay in the following exchange with the Sakhi:

> Did you not hear the shrill noise
>> of the sparrows chirping?
> O perverse girl, the milkmaids
>> with fragrant locks of hair,
> Churn,
>> and their gold necklaces and bangles
> tinkle, when they churn.
> Do you not hear the sound?
> O you leader among us,
>> the sacred names of Narayana and Keshava are uttered.
> Can you still sleep?
>> O lustrous girl, please open the door.

The Sakhis form an important part of Andal's dreams of the erotic encounter with Krishna. She will not go to see Krishna by herself. She requires their company and the bath in fact has to be performed together. In their aspect of bonding Andal already had a readymade image of the Gopis and their common love for Krishna popularised in Vaishnava discourse. The image of the

Gopis yearning for Krishna here becomes transformed into the Sakhi dreaming and sleeping inordinately. Andal projects on to her Sakhi her own erotic desire and no doubt the Sakhi reciprocates because she too is dreaming erotic dreams.

Andal's earthiness and homely style comes to the fore in the following exchange she has with the Sakhi (verse 15) where the loving banter is at its best:

> "O, you parrot like girl, do you still sleep?"
> "Please don't talk so coldly to me, O my friends,
>   I come".
> "O you can talk well; we knew how well,
>   much earlier"
> "It is you who are good at talking. Anyway,
>   let it be that it is I who am to blame."
> "Please come quickly. What other work do you have?"
> "Has everyone come?"
> "Yes, all have come. Count if you like.
> Let us sing of the man of powerful deeds, who
> killed the mighty elephant and destroyed the
>   respect of his enemies."

Female bonding of this kind is recognisable as a response to the repressions of patriarchy. In Andal's case we know from tradition that she was found by Periazhwar in a grove and brought up with great love. Andal too evidently reciprocated the love of her foster father but for a foundling, parental abandonment is a cruel fact and while a foster father might provide a certain degree of security, the fears and anxieties cannot be shut off permanently. Freud's theory of neuroses and its expression in Art, while it has had it opponents, has not been seriously challenged, and is serviceable here as an explanation of the erotic motif in Andal's work. Andal's poem is constantly foregrounding her transference of affection. At first it is the Sakhi and then it is Krishna. In any case it is certainly not Periazhwar her foster father who is the object of her affection. He is present, of course, but present in his absence. In her biography the complete extinction of her mother and the presence of only a foster father in Periazhwar, I submit, would have resulted in peculiar psychological pressures. The resultant neuroses found sublimation and expression in her poem. The *Tirupavai* after all is the supreme example in Vaishnava literature of bridal mysticism. Transporting herself in dream to the abode of Krishna, yearning for him as a bride, giving full play to the erotic motif, was Andal's powerful answer to her psychological condition under patriarchy.

Andal's work is informed by a broad democratic spirit. She will no doubt aspire for Krishna but will want that joy to be spread to the widest commonalty. The *parai* or drum she asks for from Krishna is the wealth (spiritual certainly, but also material) she wants all to share. The Sakhis, she insists, must join her in the bath and in the way of the spirit:

> O Sakhis, having decided to observe our rite,
>   We must bathe early
> and sing the glory of Utthama,
>   the world-traversing.
> If we do this,
>   there will be properly dispersed rain,
> unattended by natural calamity,
>   three times a month,
> throughout the year, throughout the land;
> The fish will frisk about the tall stalks of red paddy;
>   the dotted bee,
> intoxicated with honey,
>   will sleep on the Lotus.
> The milkman will untiringly milk the plump udders
>   of the highly benevolent cow;
> And the cow giving abundantly
>   will offer us inexhaustible wealth.

A common sharing is what Andal is suggesting here and this aspect of her hymn squares with her response to her abandonment we have noted earlier. Abandonment on one hand, community-spirit on the other — Andal's balance is certainly noteworthy.

The quality, then, which these extremely tentative probings of mine into Andal's poem, suggest is jouissance — a unifying quality because it does not distinguish between Man and God, the individual and the community, the private and the public, the body and the soul, the sensuous and the spiritual. This unified sensibility, achieved after much struggle with the restrictions of necessity, make Andal a superior human being. She is *not super-*

human, only perfectly human. Andal's bridal mysticism leading to beatific grace, perhaps, offers a way out of our present troubles. reading her in historical terms, perhaps, allows for a fuller and more complete view of a person whose path we could well follow. Seeing her, as I do, in profoundly human terms, my reverence for her intensifies, and I see quite clearly my own inferiority of spirit in relation to her. In a paradoxical way, then, the intellectual and other issues of our times might be properly tackled if we confront them with the unified sensibility of an Andal. Her *sringara bhava* might possibly be an antidote to our sick and divided aims. Her work suggests the possibility of a more genuine humanism. In her dreams lies our responsibility.

SECTION VI

29

THE BHAKTI TRADITION AND RAMPRASAD

Tutun Mukherjee

I

The bhakti movement, with its fundamental emphasis on total surrender of the self as an important element of worship, expressed itself in two streams: one quiet and meditative and the other emotional and ecstatic. The latter type of emotional religiosity was more potently felt in the atmosphere of the country everywhere from the thirteenth century onward and, in fact, nourished the innate flexibility of Hinduism for it to survive the disastrous onslaught of the Muhammedan conquest of northern India during 1193-1203 and the sweep of Islam that dealt the death-blow to Buddhism (Farquhar and Grisworld, 1920:220).

The bhakti movement inspired powerful spiritual leaders who not only stimulated cultural expression of a high order but also led to social changes which profoundly affected the course of Indian history. Richard Lannoy (1971:205) describes bhakti as "historically one of the main agencies of social fusion developed in India...(and) still very much a living force."

The basic features characterising the movement were the idea of spiritual grace and love quite alien to Vedic culture, the attitude of personal inadequacy and consequential self-effacement of the worshipper and the use of regional languages and dialects rather than esoteric Sanskrit as the mode of expression thus registering the challenge of the vernacular against the class. In the centuries of its greatest vitality it played a role of primary importance encouraging new forms of social cohesion based on classless, casteless ethico-social ideal of harmonious equilibrium, though eventually it remained mostly confined to the religious and literary plane. Some of the greatest saints of this period (1300-1800) were pre-eminently the masters of bhakti and the attempt to label them according to the familiar theological taxonomy of *sants* and *bhakts, nirgunis* or *sagunis,* Vedantists or Vaishnavas, means running the risk of obscuring the shared emphases that related them to one another and made them participants of the same movement. They are best understood as arrayed in a spectrum transcending the narrowly defined loyalties to convey in rapturous language explicitly their faith in God and the *satguru* and implicitly a social protest (Bryant 1979: 65-74; Thiel-Horstmann 1983 : Introduction).

Another distinctive quality of the bhakti saint was that either they were exceptional poet-singers themselves or inspired such devotional literature which constitutes not only the most powerful and pervasive literary heritage but also that which provided the architectonics of the Indian poetic tradition. In the words of Vatsyayan and Mishra (1983: 11) the Indian poetic tradition is "a fabric woven around three strands and one cannot understand the special textual quality of the fabric without appreciating their sustaining strength." The first strand represents the concept of *vak* or speech as the embodiment of creative energy. For this reason, oral poetry, recitation and incantation were considered amongst the highest achievements in life. The unmanifest word was the seed of creation. *Kalyani vak,* benign speech or the rightly-spoken word became the efficient instrument of communion between man and his deity and between man and his fellowmen. *Kavi* or the seer-poet became the analogue of the creator: autonomous, comprehending, all-encompassing. Language and revelation became identical. The second strand reflects the mythological, ahistorical, non-chronological bases of poetry; for instance, the changing and the transpositional figures of Siva, Durga, Rama, Krishna from myth to myth, poem to poem, as perceiving the incarnations of the changeless Absolute, the playground of the One becoming many. The third strand in the poetic fabric constitutes a worldview which rejects the dichotomy between matter and spirit, man and nature. In this holistic view, all life is one and inner and external reality are mutually dependent (Mishra, Nathan, Vatsyayan 1983:11-36).

The large body of bhakti *strotra* or prayer literature composed by Saiva, Vaishnava, Sakta, Buddhist, Jaina devotees and sants reveal these ideational bases. Each poetic effusion either dramatises "the devotee's longing for the Deity, the finite's hunger of the Infinite, the soul's yearning for the Oversoul" (Swami Budhananda 1982: Preface), and/or invokes a poetic image of man's participating in the *lila* or the eternal play of creation and/or celebrates the most profound and mystical refractions of companion and love (Schomer and Macleod, 1986).

Through continuing popularity and widespread diffusion, the devotional poems and songs moulded folk consciousness in a way that is rare for any literature. Had the bhakti movement confined itself to metaphysical discussions and the writing of learned commentaries, its influence would have been limited and its purpose defeated. Herein lies the tremendous relevance of the poet-saints as the propagators of bhakti. They secularised not the message as much as the mode.

II

A theme common to all devotional poetry is that of the poet (and through him, the devotee) importuning his deity as a child addressing his parent, seeking forgiveness and grace. The distinction of bhakti poetry lies in its exploring and interpreting the relationship between the worshipper and the worshipped in every *rasa* and *bhava*, emotion and mood, the most recurrent being that of the lover and the beloved or of the child with the parent. This latter type is indeed unique, says Sudhir Kakar, because in this "recreated utopia of childhood" the Divine is conceived as a maternal rather than a paternal matrix or as a playful child with the poet as the mother/witness (Kakar 1989:201-4).

One of the deep-rooted Hindu ideas somewhat alien to Western minds is the worship of God as Mother, that is, the worship of Sakti. However, the logic of this theology is inseparable, being based on the dualistic principle of Brahman as impersonal, inactive, and His energy or emanation — Sakti as the matrix of creation and sustenance, and the agent of change and destruction. Without Sakti, Siva is merely a corpse, *Sava;* yet the distinction between them does not mean a difference. In the words of Sri Ramakrishna, "the suprapersonal and the personal are the same thing, like milk and its whiteness, the diamond and its lustre, the snake and its wriggling motion....The Divine Mother and Brahman are one" (cited Mayorga 1966:44). Together they represent the unitary cosmic principle, the imbalance of which disturbs the macrocosmic equilibrium.

Mother figures are not uncommon in religious hierarchies (example, Mary, Demeter, Isis, Kwangin, Kwanon, Coatlicue), but they are not totally identified with and worshipped as God. In his feminine theology, C.M. Brown says, Hinduism "preserves and constantly reaffirms one of man's earliest religious orientations to the universe, an orientation that particularly in the West seems to have been largely forgotten" (1974:115).

Kakar writes that in an "adult-centred world" that "over-values abstractions, prudence and reason" (1989: 203), it is refreshing to find this "surrender of adulthood" (Kakar 1986: 147) and the celebration of childlike virtues as innocence, delight, vivaciousness, mercurial anger and quick reconciliation—all evoked as dimensions of the devotee's yearning for the infinite and unconditional love of his God, the Mother, Sakti, is known by the general name *devi*, from the Sanskrit root *div*, to shine; so she is Tara, the Shining One, who is given different names in different manifestations in different places as the matrix of the life-giving powers of the Universe. Sometimes she may not even have an icon but be represented as a mound of stone or a *yantra*.

The principal seat of Sakti worship is the Bengal-Assam-Bihar belt (Mookerjee, 1988); and one of the most famous, prolific and inspired worshippers of the Divine Mother was the "melodious mystic of Bengal," Ramprasad Sen (1718-1775) (Budhananda 1982: vii). He belonged to that wonderful galaxy of Indian mystics whose approach to the Divine found expression and consummation in the songs and melodies which form a part of the spiritual heritage of India.

Edward J. Thompson (1923:9-30) points out that the great period of Sakta poetry in Bengal was the eighteenth century when the country's fortunes reached the lowest ebb. Thompson suggests the example of Ramprasad's predecessor, Mukundarama, known as *kavikankan*, or "gem among poets", who composed his epic *Chandi* in 1589. The poem lives today mainly for its picture of the village life in Bengal: dismal and oppressed. The poet evoked Chandi (Kail/Devi/Sakti) for the irruption of the sudden dreadful power to "fling down the highest and exalt the lowest" (Thompson 1923:14).

The cult of Kali had a great revival also in the days of the *swadeshi* struggle and became identified with nation worship (as represented, for instance, in Bankimchandra Chattopadhyaya's *Anandamath*).

But it is not only political distress that makes one despair. Calcutta is a different world; it was in the villages that Ramprasad and the poet of Chandi lived, where the sorrow seems deeper and more permanent as the peasant struggles against the caprice of Nature. There are years when Nature seems caressing, bountiful; the fields are filled and the mud huts stand. Another year the heavens are shut and there is drought. Famine follows bringing incalculable misery in the form of death and disease. Another year there is excessive rain and the water courses swell in flood. A village two miles from the main river living in security beside its "blind river" wakes at midnight to find a shoreless sea heaving and thrusting at the mud walls. It is not surprising that villagers should worship *prakriti*, Nature and Earth Spirits or God as Mother. As Ramprasad frequently sings: there is little hope of succour from Bholanatha, the forgetful one, Kali has all his power and her energy is unsleeping.

Ramprasad was born into a Vaidya family in Kumarhati (Halisahar). He was a good student and when he was disinclined to become a physician like his father, he was encouraged to study languages. But it soon became apparent that he yearned only for religious life. After his father's sudden death, the responsibility of the family fell on him. He managed to get a job as an accountant and bookkeeper at Sri Vakulchandra Ghosal's in Calcutta. A breadwinner's task was painful for Ramprasad. He longed for freedom and filled his ledgers with pleas to the Mother:

> Give me your treasuryship, Mother
> I'll be your servant without pay
> I seek only the dust of your feet...

His employer recognised the poignant cry of the great soul. He encouraged Ramprasad to seek his Mother and assured him an allowance for the rest of his life. In relieving Ramprasad of the burden of earning a livelihood his patron gave the world the priceless gift of unforgettable songs whose devotion and lyricism live in the heart of the people. More than two centuries have passed since crowds listened to Ramprasad on the banks of Ganga, yet, as E.J. Thompson describes, Ramprasad is heard everywhere. His songs are sung by "coolies on the road, or workers in the paddy fields... by broad rivers at sunset when the village folk throng from the market to the ferry.... The peasants and the pundits enjoy his songs equally. They draw solace from them in the hour of despair and even at the moment of death" (1923:19).

Ramprasad wrote a few other longer poems like *Bidyasundar*, (which brought him the title of *Kaviranjan* from the Raja of Krishnagar) *Kalikitana, Sivakirtana* and *Krishnakirtana;* all of which show erudition and craftsmanship. However, they lack the qualities in which his lyrics excel: spontaneity, melody, the richness and depth of emotions. These songs comprise the major part of the body of Sakta lyrics called *Shyamasangeet*. Swami Prajnananda traces the development of this branch of devotional music that is based on classical music and classifies them as belonging to the folk tradition of *padagitis, padavali kirtana dhruvapada* (1973:12,302). Dilip K. Roy (1975:5-10) finds *kirtana synonymous* with *bhajans* — both deriving from Vedic hymnology (example, Narada's *Bhaktisutras*). The noteworthy quality of this "Little Tradition" is that though the lyrics and songs may repeat themselves and ideas may not always excel in poetry, they achieve the purpose they have been composed for: to serve as the prime vehicle of a *rasa*.

The best edition of Ramprasad, issued by *Basumati* (Calcutta) contains 226 songs. This collection is neither complete nor authoritative. Some undoubtedly authentic songs exist without his name and it is likely that sometimes his name is added by other hands. However, for the *aficionado*, the poet's signature and the poems setting to the "Ramprasadi" tune is sufficient.

III

According to Swami Vivekananda:

> The greatest aid to (the) practice of keeping God in memory is, perhaps, music. The Lord says to Narada, the great teacher of Bhakti, "I do not live in heaven, nor do I live in the heart of the Yogi, but where My devotees sing My praise there I am." Music has such tremendous

power over the human mind; it brings it to concentration in a moment. (1973:V, 125)

Indian musicology is based on Patanjali's concept of the supreme Sound: *sphota* or *Sabda Bhrama*. The causal sound or *anahata nada* is the unmanifested sound effecting the *ahata*, the gross sound, through the friction of the vital air (*prana* with *agni*). Blissfully churning the ocean of beauty (*satchidananda*), the bhakta finds the universe full of *rasa* and from this fountainhead of experience, poetry flows in his speech, *vak* "like a stream of clear water — uninterrupted," wherein the subjective transforms itself into the objective (Johari 1984:21).

Ramprasad was a *sadhaka* of Tantrayoga which teaches the ways of practical realisation of the soul's conquest for *moksha* by arousing the inner energy, the *Kundalini Sakti* to reach the *sahasrara*, the eternal state of cosmic consciousness (Avalon 1922).

A fugitive from the material world, Ramprasad immersed himself in his *hridaya ganga* in devoted supplication to Tara, the Blissful Mother. The tidal wave of his yearning for god-realisation bursts forth in his ecstatic songs (Masson and Patwardhan 1970).

Edward Gerow explains that the devotional song is "a perfect finished offering to God which alone suffices" (cited in Dimmock 1989:14). Coming to expression in God's name is the reason for the song's being. Bhakti remains an abstract concept without its song or performative utterance (that is, doing *bhajan karna*). The song becomes, therefore, a mode of worship, an integral part of bhakti and functions on several planes for the poet-devotee as well as for the hearer, suggesting also the different levels of appropriation of the song's content.

A song is a thing of inherent purity establishing an intrinsic link between singing and the life of faith. For the poet as quester, it is a sacrificial ritual of bonding. The song offers comfort even as a lament because the act of voicing and directing it to its source contains a taste of deliverance and brings a measure of fulfilment.

A song has a yogic core that can steady the mind by calling to the mind the reality that is unaffected by change or circumstances.

The mnemonic quality of reiteration of God's name acquires the power of *mul-mantra* to invoke the salvific power of the deity. The inveterate discipline of the song makes God palpably present, thus working its own salvation by calling up in the mind of the poet and of the hearer, the reality of the absent-present God.

The song is a way to harness aural energy in the service of greater humanity. The element of devotion present in the artistic expression thrusts upon it an empirical duty and ties it down to the positive spiritual aims of life.

The anthologies (in Bengali and in translation) of Ramprasad's hymns to Kali are arranged either thematically or in alphabetical order and not according to the evolution of his devotional life. Some translations are questionable because though the translator has applauded the literary value of songs, the religious content has been questioned or belittled (e.g., Thompson and Spenser, 1923:20). Few of the songs are placed in the context of certain incidents in his life but largely they express the praise of Kali's multiple forms, the invocation of her dreaded power or the lament of separation.

Ramprasad's range of themes, ideas and illustrations may be limited, often repetitive, but within that range he is a master. The songs range from the simplest to the most complex expression of Tantric practice but the hallmark is poignancy and sincere appeal. The simplest lyrics often have the quality of a rhythmic jingle and sing themselves into the memory of the illiterate folk by a riot of punning sound, alliteration, a musical toss and play of similar syllables and the use of colloquial expressions (often lost in translation). He was especially fond of playing with the name of Kali or "inky-black". Ramprasad took childlike pleasure in these and the untrained literary instinct out of which folklore and folksong are born responded with the same pleasure and heard him with rapture:

> Taking the name of Kali, dive deep down, O mind,
> Into the heart's fathomless depths,
> Where many a precious gem lies his . . .
> Dive deep and make your way to Mother Kali's realm...

Ramprasad's verses ring with vitality and enthusiasm:

> Jagadamba's watchmen go out into the dread, black night
> Jagadamba's watchmen!

His illustrations are racy, from the soil and of the soil, drawn from the agrarian ethos. The "local habitation" of the poet's mind enriched the songs with narrative contexts of folktales (example, about Uma's family of Siva, Ganesha, Nandi; the *agomoni* and *vijoya* songs), stories (example, "the flower in the undergrowth"), superstitions (example, the ominous throbbing of the eyelids), humour (example the Lord of Anxiety-Chintaram), and games (example, "in the world's marketplace, O Shyama, thou are flying kites").

The wealth of metaphor drawn from simple life fills every song. Every villager recalls the poet's reproof to his soul: "thou, a snake, fearing frogs!" His personalised and experiential images acquire a more generalised rural ambience, "his mind had been a bad farmer," "he is tied to the Round of Existence like the blindfold ox at the oilpress," "his load of firewood has become heavy," "the Six Passions are like crocodiles lying in wait for his at the bathing ghat," or they are "like robbers leaping over the mudwalls of his courtyard." The senses are like "cowardly boatman who forsake the soul when the tempest sweeps" or "ruffians kept by Zamindars." Very often his thought turns to death when his friends will abandon his bones and ashes on the burning ground.

Sister Nivedita compared Ramprasad with Blake. E.J. Thompson finds his "self consciousness" and "the habit of looking at himself from outside" like Herrick (1923:19). Indeed, he can be compared with the poets of the Western tradition of meditative poetry traced by Louis Martz (1954).

It is often found that the simple faith of the illiterate folk contradicts arguments of philosophers. For example, Indian philosophy and religion may be epitomised in the Vedanta yet the *nirguna* worship is considered the more ratified form. Ramprasad too, aware as he was of Sankara's monism and sympathetic to pantheistic teaching, was emphatically theistic and relied on the interchange between a personal goddess and a supplicant devotee. What is the use of salvation if it means absorption. Ramprasad sings, "I like eating sugar but I have no desire to become sugar." However, he does not much care for religious conventions; he scoffs at pilgrimages and the bargain offering to the deity:

> What have I to do with Kasi?
> The lotus feet of Kali are pilgrimage enough for me...

Ramprasad is sturdily ethical and does not believe that good and evil are the same thing, philosophically considered.

The most poignant and emotive of Ramprasad's songs are those invoking the power of Kali and his poetry touches ecstatic heights. The cruel and horrific image of the goddess with her lolling red tongue and garland of severed heads was his Mother, Mahamaya, the mistress of *maya* and the *gunas*. He saw her in the red flames of the pyre, in the dancing breeze, in the flash of lightning, in the matted cloud-locks of the storm. She played hide-and-seek with the world and her bhakta called out to her by many names. Ramprasad admonished her for standing on her lord and asked her to come to her senses and step down. Such songs of intimate personalisation transform the *mrinmayee* stone image into *chinmayee* Dynamic Presence.

As a *sakta yogi* Ramprasad often referred to the misunderstood and maligned Sakta practices. These poems are strongly allegorical. For example, he referred to live sacrifices associated with Sakti worship. He condemned the practice by offering the better alternative of sacrificing the passions of the flesh instead of living creatures:

> ...Fashion her image with the stuff of your mind
> Set it upon the lotus-throne of your heart
> Parched rice and plantains—how vainly you offer these
> Feed her with the nectar of your devotion...
> Why do you bring sheep, goats and buffaloes for sacrifice
> Saying "Victory to Kali" sacrifice the six passions.

About the occult physiological powers he often used the metaphors of the sun, moon, lotus; he sang that his heart had acquired the tint of the lotus.

Another noteworthy contribution of Ramprasad was blurring the distinction between sectarian modes of worship. He saw Kali as inseparable from Siva, the forceful aspect of Durga, synonymous with Shyam (Krishna) the manifest *(saguna)* form of the Abstract *(nirguna)*.

Very often his thoughts turned to death. Then invariably would he appeal to Kali:

> O Mother, in the world's play
> What was to be has been
> Now at eventide, call your child to your bosom and
> Let us go home.

Just as there are several legends associated with his life (that Parvati asked him to sing to her; Kali assisted him as his daughter to repair a fence), legendary is the way he died. Carrying on his head the ritual pot for immersion after Kali puja, Ramprasad stepped into the Ganga in a trance and sang three songs. At the end of the final song, as he sang "...all is finished — I have offered my gift," his life-breath left him through the top of his head—*brahmarandhra* — and he sank into the river with the image of his beloved Mother. Ramprasad had conquered ignorance and was forever awake:

> From the land where there is no night
> Has come One unto me . . .
> My sleep is broken. Shall I ever sleep more?
> I have given sleep unto Him whose it was
> Sleep have I put to sleep forever.
> The music has entered the instrument
> And of that mode I have learned a song.
> Ah! that music is playing ever before me
> For concentration is the great teacher thereof.
> Prasad says, understand, O soul, these words of wisdom.

Such is a typical Ramprasad song exhibiting the mnemonic, localised, picturesque language that conveys philosophical truths of life. Typical also is the signature (often also used by pretenders) at the end of each poem. Besides identifying the poet and providing an aesthetic closure, the signature also dramatises a poetic valency. Added to the personal singular voice of the poet is the syntax creating space for another generalised overtone. This is an exceptional feature of all bhakti poetry distinguishing it from the anonymity of Vedic hymns. A neutral poetic voice would have vitiated the effect.

Ramprasad strengthened the tradition of Sakta poetry. The more well-known among these poets who made their contributions after him were Kamalakanta Bhattacharya, Nilakanta Mukhopadhyaya, Maharaja Ramkrishna of Nator, Bharatchandra Ray and Ramnidhi Babu. The themes were usual:

Kali's neglect of her votary, Siva's carelessness, the poet's threatened law-suit or desertion of the Mother, the Mother's absorption in her wild destructive dance over the Lord of Death. The *kirtana* style melodic quality established the particular school (*gayaki*) of Ramprasadi Shyamasangeet. These songs became immensely popular. The Calcutta theatre troupes and itinerant singers contributed to the wide permeation of these offerings.

Ramprasad songs received their deserved acclamation when they echoed in every heart in every corner of Bengal thus validating the rich oral tradition of Bengal as an effective mode to actualise the inherent spiritual potentialities. When Sri Ramakrishna sang or even heard a Ramprasadi hymn he would be transported into a *samadhi*.

References

Avalon, Arthur. *The Serpent Power*, New York: Dover Publications, Inc., 1922.

Brown, C. Mackenzie. *God as Mother: A Feminine Theology in India*, Hartford, IV: Claude Stork, 1974.

Bryant, Kenneth E. "*Sant* and *Vaishnava Poetry*: Some observations on Method," *Skin Studies: Comparative Perspectives on a Changing Tradition*. ed. Juergensmeyer and Barrier, Berkeley, Calif.: Berkeley Religious Studies Series, Univ. Press, 1979.

Dimock Jr. Edward J. *The Sound of the Silent Guns*, Delhi: Oxford Univ. Press, 1989.

Farquhar, J.N. and H.D. Griswold. *The Religious Quest of India*, London: Oxford Univ. Press, 1920.

Johari, Harish. *Leela: Game of Knowledge*, Calcutta: Rupa and Co., 1984.

Kakar, Sudhir. *Shamans, Mystics and Doctors*, Delhi: Oxford Univ. Press, 1986, 1982.

—— *The Inner World*, Delhi: Oxford Univ. Press, 1989, 1978.

Lannoy, Richard. *The Speaking Tree*, London: Oxford Univ. Press, 1971.

Martz, Louis. *The Poetry of Meditation*, New Haven: Yale Univ. Press, 1954.

Masson, J.L. and M.V. Patwardhan. *Aesthetic Rapture* 2 volumes, Poona: Deccan College, 1970.

Mayorga, Nancy Pope. "Ramprasad," *Vedanta and the West* 180. Vedanta Society of South California: Vedanta Press, 1986.

Mishra, Nathan, Vatsyayan (eds). "Introduction," *Indian Poetic Tradition*, Agra: Y.K. Publishers, 1983.

Mookerjee, Ajit. *Kali: The Feminine Force*, London, New York: Thames and Hudson, 1988.

Roy, Dilip K. "Introduction," *Sangeet Sangraha*, eds. Swamis Gorishwarananda and Vedananda, Santhal Parganas, Bihar: R.K. Vidyapeeth, 1977.

Swami Prajnananda. *A Historical Study of Indian Music*, Calcutta: Firma K.L. Mukherjee, 1973.

Swami Vivekananda. *Complete Works*. Vol V, Calcutta: Advaita Ashrama, 1973.

Schomer, Karine and W.H. Macleod. *The Sants: Studies in Devotional Traditions in India*, Berkeley, Calif.: Berkeley Religious Studies Series, Univ. Press, 1986.

Thiel-Horstmann, Monika (ed). *Bhakti in Current Research, 1972-1982*, Berlin: Dietrich Reiner Verlag, 1983.

Thompson, Edward J. and Arthur M. Spenser. *Bengali Religious Lyrics: Sakta*, London: Oxford Univ. Press, 1923.

30

BAULS: THE SINGING *SADHAKAS* OF BENGAL

Sumita Roy

I

In his usual inimitable way Sri Ramakrishna Paramahamsa of Dakshineswar has given the injunction : *jata mat, tata path*, as many faiths so many paths. This simple yet irrefutable logic has been repeatedly acknowledged and variously expressed by thinkers all over the world, more so in India — a country renowned for the harmonious coexistence of the greatest diversity and variety of faiths and paths leading to the "goal supreme".

One of the various paths leading to this ultimate stage of evolution of the spirit is the path of devotion or bhakti which gained currency throughout the country during the Middle Ages. Though the concept of bhakti does find adequate exposition in the Vedic texts, with the passage of time it was superseded by the cult of sacrifice. Dissatisfaction with the excesses resulting from the sacrificial leanings of the Aryan practices gave precedence to the conception of divine love as a mode of religious experience at a more personal level. Although bhakti was not totally alien to the Aryan tenets of spirituality it is believed to have become a part of the popular attitude by borrowing heavily from the non-Aryan tradition. Ramanuja's teachings of bhakti as intense love for a personal God considering Him as a friend and refuge found an instant echo in many hearts which had long felt the need to revolt against the oppressive ritualistic approach to the divine prescribed by the religious leaders of society. The remoteness of the latter could conveniently be replaced by a sense of intimate contact with the hitherto unapproachable Being. Every individual aspirant had direct access to this feeling because the path of bhakti prescribes dedication to and involvement with the divine through the emotion of love and rewards each with a sense of security and satisfaction. So the unprecedented popularity of this movement of devotion became a powerful and widespread phenomenon bringing about a totally new ethos of cultural, literary and spiritual development into being. It reached almost every corner of the country and found some startlingly original expression in a variety of modes and languages.

II

The *baul* songs of Bengal are an example of one such expression of spiritual rejuvenation. Though these songs have not, until fairly recently, been given their due recognition in and outside the state, they are rich compositions containing a veritable treasure of material fostering the Bhakti Movement and the tradition rooted in this movement. Combining the framework of bhakti with the rich folk heritage of Bengal arose this order of singers, poets and composers collectively called the Bauls. In the past they formed a part of an oral tradition which handed down its verse from generations to generation. But in the twentieth century much effort has gone into making a systematic study of these songs. They have been transcribed into writing, translated and extensively discussed in order to discover the principles involved in their composition and the philosophy behind them.

A virtual explosion of scholarly interest has made the songs of the Bauls an inseparable part of the culture of modern Bengal. This can be judged by taking an inventory of the deep influence the songs have had not only on the average person but also a poet of the stature of Rabindranath Tagore. A Nobel laureate of international fame, Tagore has acknowledged without reservation his debt to the Bauls by using their tunes and images in his own compositions.

A very popular baul song — *"khachar bhitar achin pakhi"* — finds its way almost without noticeable alternation in Tagore *Gitabitan*. This song not only has a melodious and captivating tune but its lyrics have a pattern of complex symbolic connotations startling in their depth and sophistication. The word *khacha* (cage) is used to imply a great variety of different fetters binding the human spirit; this is brought out with such subtlety that it is no wonder a creative genius of Tagore's eminence found its fascination irresistible and effectively translated it into his unforgettable "Rabindra Sangeet".

III

The origin of the term *baul* is not very easy to discern and its meaning has thus been variously interpreted. Some say that it signifies a state of spiritual intoxication akin to madness and may have been derived from the Sanskrit word *vatula*. There are others who trace its roots to the word *vyakula* because of the extreme eagerness and anxiety for union with the divine that is displayed in the lyrics of the *baul* songs. It is also probable that the term is a colloquial derivation of the word *vayu* in both its senses — that of "wind" associating the *baul* movement with its yogic practices of breath control or the wind-like freedom to which the members of the group aspire; and the second instance is that of its use as "nerve currents" linking the whole process of composition, singing, dancing and ecstatic fervour to the workings of the central nervous system. Various other possible implications can be added to this catalogue and since these singing minstrels display all the above qualities to a greater or lesser extent, it is rather difficult to assert the efficacy of any one of them in comparison to the others.

In a similar manner, there is much speculation about the origin and history of the Baul sect. As a religious organisation they have a long history which is obscured by time. They are said to have originated in North Bengal almost simultaneously with the Natha and Sahajiya branches of the Tantras deriving inspiration from both. For instance:

> The Baul cult of Bengal is indeed a transformed form of the Natha cult. The Bauls have adopted the yogic practices of the Nathas and have inherited their mystic poetry and talking in riddles. But they outwardly admit God and call him Krishna and Chaitanya, as the Vaishnavas do. The Natha yogis had no concern with God; each of then was God in the universe of his own body. (Bhattacharyya, 1956:280)

The Bauls too follow this tradition of giving due respect to the individual human being and the physical body is considered by them as an important tool for carrying out spiritual activity effectively; but in their affinity to Vaishnava strains they come closer to the Sahajiya doctrine than to the Nathas. An analysis of many of the songs of these wandering minstrels suggests that it is apt to conclude "the Baul derives inspiration from the Vaishnava Sahajiya" (224). To suit their requirements the Bauls have borrowed or adapted many of the typical Sahajiya injunctions like:

> ... *raga marga* (the path of spontaneous love) which they profess to follow...A Sahajiya requires a woman other than his married wife as a companion of his sadhana... A Sahajiya is not a vegetarian, nor does he observe... austerities... he does not bother himself much with any course of self-discipline. (199-200)

Scholars have traced several other possible sources which may have contributed to the growth and development of the Baul sect. According to Reese:

> ... the most complete dedication to Bhakti and the most complete divorce from ritual knowledge is to be found in the Bauls of Bengal, a cult which grew out of the destruction of Buddhism, Tantra and Vaishnavism, forming itself from the lowest strata of Indian society. Believing that one's body is the temple of God, and something like conscience is the scriptures, they allow no external form of worship whatever, keep no records, and sustain no visible form of organisation other than the informal guru pupil relationship. Their goal is simplicity, freedom and avoidance of man-made distinctions and the inward practice to direct relation to God. (1980: 223-4)

All these characteristics abound in the lives and works of the Bauls; in addition, the unconventionality and spontaneity of their mystical verse establish some affinities with the tradition of Sufism. The Bauls may also be defined in the same terms used for Sufis — "those who loved a simple life and were intoxicated with Truth, in any form." (Bhattacharyya, 1956: 593)

Another interesting parallel between the Sufis and the Bauls lies in the fact that in both "importance is attached more to the activities of the inner self than to the observance of outward religious practices and rituals" (594). This point of similarity also highlights the deeply mystical leanings of the Sufis and the Bauls alike. William James, in his attempt to distinguish the ordinary, everyday experience from the mystical, has identified four marks of the latter — ineffability, noetic quality, transiency and passivity (1902: 370). A discussion of the baul songs *vis-a-vis* these four distinguishing features is sure to yield rich dividends. It will also establish the link between the *baul* song and the mystical tradition extant all over the world and place these songs alongside the works of well-known mystics the world over such as St. Augustine, St. John of the Cross, St. Theresa of Avil, St. Francis of Assissi. Julian of Norwich and such others.

In spite of identifiable resemblances with other branches of spiritual endeavour, the Bauls have constantly displayed an admirable originality in their philosophy and their verse. It is possible that this is the result of integrating the various influences they have absorbed with the authenticity of their own experience and realisation. The product of the unique integration — the baul song — can be described as a novel mode of fulfilment of the material aspirations of the common masses. The reaching out towards truth and enlightenment, the effort to put into words the ineffable, the indomitable urge to give permanence to the transitory nature of a mystic vision, to unravel the mystery of human existence—these are some of the crucial ideas that invigorate the songs of the Bauls.

A pervasive point of originality which underlies the Baul Movement is the powerful strain of unconventionality of the life and works of the group. The Bauls have scant regard for the established norms of social and spiritual behaviour. Their major contention down the ages has been that the so-called profane or "baser instincts" associated with physical urges can be redirected towards sacred channels and converted into aids to spiritual evolution. These men and women have never believed in or practised any kind of "restrictions"—frames which determine orthodox behaviour — because they feared that these might hinder their progress towards their ideal, that it, the Perfect One, the deity of the heart, their *maner manush*. The depth and sincerity which characterise the Baul singers' pursuit of their ideal adds that extra dimension to their melodious renderings which make them akin to the verse of other representative poet-saints from other parts of the country.

IV

The songs of the Bauls — simple in language, sometimes colloquial, impure, too, sensitive in touching a deep chord within the human heart, concise and direct in outlining the purpose of human life — have endeared themselves to a wide cross-section of people and helped to inculcate an enduring core of values in them. These compositions can be studies keeping some important aspects in mind — such as their spiritual significance sketching the path leading to the ultimate reality, their literary merit in adding to and enriching the literature extant in the country through the centuries, and their socio-cultural contribution in criticising the ills of society or offering correctives to them with a view to establishing a commendable standard for cultural evolution.

One of the important injunctions brought forth through these songs constantly is the need for realising the infinite potential inherent in the human being. Lalan Shah Fakir, one of the well-known Bauls, has stated this with incomparable simplicity and clarity in a song — "*Amon manab janam aar ki hobe....*" In it he says:

> Since you may never again get
> A human birth like the present one
> Why not follow the dictates
> Of your mind
> And strive for perfection?

Throughout this composition Lalan continues to extol the merits of human birth by explaining how even the gods are eager to be born in the human form. The human being is the last word in creation because the "Shain" has made this being as the ultimate of perfection. Since human birth is so precious every individual should make the most of it by attempting to manifest the hidden perfection.

It is worthy of note that the first step in this direction is the acquisition of self-knowledge. At this stage the aspirant becomes aware of the voice within but is also baffled by its elusive quality. He feels that:

Bauls: The Singing Sadhakas of Bengal

> It speaks but is invisible,
> It moves about but cannot be found
> Even after a life-long search.

Thus begins the game of hide-and-seek which compels the outward directed sense perceptions to look within. Gradually it becomes clear that without diving deep inside and analysing the self, the aspirant can never reach his/her chosen goal. This fact is memorably enshrined in a verse entitles *"Aaponare aapni chini ne"* in which the individual despairs of ever gaining self-knowledge and laments his ignorance in these words:

> I do not even know myself.
> Then how will I know the One
> Whose name is Manhar?

and visualises an escape from this unhappy plight by seeking to know the self:

> If I knew myself
> It would bring me
> Untold treasure,
> And fulfil my destiny
> As a human being.

The inwardness which arises from self-analysis and soul-searching form the subject of constant preoccupation in the *baul* songs. It has found a fine evocative expression through the use of the symbol of a mirror in a song which mourns:

> I haven't yet seen him once —
> That neighbour of mine
> Who lives near my house
> In mirror town...

The reference to the human conscience as the neighbour finding reflection in *"mirror town"* is only one of the abundant symbolic portrayals occurring in the *baul* songs adding to their beauty and sublimity.

As in various schools of mysticism, the use of mirror as a symbol acquires various levels of complexity in this and other songs where it is used. The mirror symbol fulfils many functions: in its mythological overtones it denotes the narsissistic trait of humanity; in its modern psychoanalytic context it brings to mind the Lacanian concept of the child's self-absorption; while in its mystical implications it can signify the many-faceted, incomprehensible mystery of the human personality. The mirror in mystic language may denote the self which reflects the vision of God when it is "polished" and pure, or it may be the frame for accurate interpretation of worldly experience.

Apart from this, many concrete images of everyday use are invoked to illustrate the abstract, ineffable nature of the knowledge and experience which the Bauls have tried to immortalise through their songs. One such illustration is that of the earthen pot as metaphor for the mind in which the water of divine love can be stored. The song, *"Kancha handi te"*, visualises a situation where the mind is not yet adequately prepared to experience the ecstatic upheaval of divine love. It demonstrates this by portraying the impossibility of filling the water of divine love in a pitcher unbaked by the heat-like austerities of *sadhana*.

This brings to mind the next stage in the path of spiritual progress prescribed by the Bauls — the need for divine love and grace to actualise and aid individual effort. Sometimes the yearning for the Beloved takes the form of the gopis' call to Krishna:

> The day has ended, O Lalita,
> But Krishna has not come . . .

The divine is often the friend, as in the song *"Tomar moto dayal bandhu..."* which says:

> Never again will I get
> A benevolent friend like you.
> Having revealed yourself once
> O, Rasool!
> Do not leave me, please.

Such a pathetic cry is heard repeatedly in many songs. For instance, in a haunting melody rendered by Purnadas Baul, rich in its alliterative cadence, the human heart is the child who implores the Divine in its aspect of mother not to be forsaken. It says:

> *Moro na moro na Mago,*
> *Dhori tomar sricharane;*
> *Ma mole ma mele na ma,*
> *Khujile ma tribhubane.*

(Do not die mother/I beg of you/If the mother dies/It is impossible to find another/Even after searching in the three worlds.)

One thing becomes apparent from the tone of these entreaties: there should be total emotional involvement with the divine on the part of the devotee. A song which enunciated this truth states:

Hari bolte kyano
Nayan jhare na?

making it imperative that unless the eyes shed profuse tears on uttering the name of Hari the vision of God will not be afforded to them.

From this it is self-evident that before pleading for mercy and support one should understand and/or relate to the divine. This we are told in a poignant verse, *"Shamanye ki taar marmo jana jai."* The song cautions the aspirant that it is not easy to know the essence of the Supreme Being. Here the word *"shamanya"* has two distinct connotations: one indicating the difficult process of acquiring inwardness and the other referring to the maturity requires by the human spirit before it can approach the divine.

Such sophisticated word-play can serve as the beginning of a discussion on the literary merit of the *baul* songs. Many of them are structured in the form of puzzles whose solution — or even mere repetition like that of the Japanese Koan — has the capacity of imparting liberation. In addition, almost all the songs have an engrossing lyrical intensity which draws the mind away from the outer realms.

An important literary achievement of the Bauls is the wide range of tonal variations they have used with the greatest felicity in their songs. The tones vary from intensely serious to playful and frivolous, from pathos to joy and suppressed laughter, from child-like innocence to an excitement of sexual awareness, from superior irony to downright mockery. An instance of the last is depicted in the following lines:

> You want to become
> The salve of Huzoor?
> But your mind is full of confusion
> You neither know worship
> Through service,

> Nor through love.
> Your meanness is always evident.
> Then, in what manner
> Will you please Prabhu?

The *baul* songs employ some of the most refined and complex literary techniques with a flourish. For example: their metaphoric dexterity is admirable. In the song *"Mor maina buli dhare na"*, the mind is compared to the bird, maina — well-known for its capacity to imitate human speech fluently. But in this case the bird refuses to take lessons and only evinces interest in flying away to the forest. The long-drawn comparison portrayed in the song depicts the effort needed to control the agile and straying mind which is constantly fluttering towards the temptations of the material world.

Inseparable from the literary, spiritual and musical virtuosity of the *baul* songs is their function as the awakeners of social consciousness. Much of the effort of the Movement has been spent in fighting against the evils pervasive in society.

Inequalities perpetuated by caste or religious distinctions supply the thematic construct for many of these songs. For instance, the laudable aim of unity of religions or a quest for this is sketched in the following couplet:

> *Ami morchi ghure shei dukaner shahaj thikanay,*
> *Jethay Allah, Hari, Ram, Kali, God ek thala te khay khana.*

Discrimination on the basis of caste has been one among the worst of social evils confronting the nation. Most of the poet-saints have something to say about this. Lalan's notable contribution for its eradication takes the form of a song — *"shab loke koy Lalan ki jat shanshare"* — everyone asks Lalan what caste he belongs to. The Fakir's reply to this is powerful and effective: he says that he has never seen/perceived these distinctions because they are artificially imposed by a *japa mala* or *Tasbih*. During birth or death a person has neither any sign of caste nor any awareness of it.

In the same song Lalan furnishes another important testimony towards a better social order by posing a crucial question: "A Musalman is identified by sunnat and a Brahmin by his sacred thread, but what about the women of these sects?"

Such illustrations are innumerable and citing them would mean an unending exercise. So these few examples should suffice as an introduction to gauge the immense possibilities hidden in the *baul* songs. While ar one level they have the capacity of offering intellectual challenges for scholarly deliberations, at another level they may serve as tools to activate the intuitive core of the inner being thus making available higher levels of consciousness. They may afford interesting areas for research or help the striving human mind to attain absolute concentration. Whatever be the approach, the contribution of the music and philosophy of the Bauls to the bhakti tradition is unique and undeniable.

References

Bandopadhyay, S.M. *Baul Songs of Bengal*, Calcutta: United Writers, 1976.
Bhattacharyya, Haridas (ed). *The Cultural Heritage of India*, Vol. IV. *The Religions*. Calcutta: Ramakrishna Mission Institute of Culture, 1955.
James William. *The Varieties of Religious Experience*. New York: Oxford University Press, 1902.
Katz, Steven T. (ed). *Mysticism and Religious Tradition*, New York: Oxford University Press, 1983.
Reese, W.L. *Dictionary of Philosophy and Religion: Eastern and Western Thought*, New Jersey: Humanities Press, 1980.
Sarkar, Sir J. *History of Bengal*. Dacca: Dacca University Press.
Tagore, Rabindranath. "The Baul Singers of Bengal" in *The Religion of Man*. Hibbert Lectures.

SECTION VII

31
ASHTACHAP AND TALLAPAKA POETS

R. Suman Lata

In the history of India, the medieval period has its own importance. By this time, that is, around A.D. 1300-1600 the Muslim invaders stayed back in India and became the rulers of most of North India. These alien rulers were not particularly considerate to their native Hindu subjects. Naturally, this period witnessed a religious, political, sociological and cultural struggle of the Indian people to retain their identity. It was during this period of confrontation that a great religious movement spread throughout India. This is popularly known as the bhakti movement.

The bhakti movement has its origin and roots in Sankaracharya, Ramanujacharya, Alwars, Nayanmars, Vira Saiva or Lingayats, Haridasas, Siddhas and Nathas. Hitherto the literary works and commentaries which were written in Sanskrit were accessible to the educated few. But "in post Sankara period, there arose in different parts of the country a line of saints and mystics who brought the wisdom of the ancients to the common man. They adopted the local language and used the medium of song for their mission" (V. Raghavan). For example, Kabir, Sur, Tulsi, Rahim and Raskhan from North India, Guru Nanak and other Sikh gurus from Punjab, Lalla Devi from Kashmir, Jnaneshwar, Namdev, Tukaram from Maharashtra, Narasi Mehta from Gujarat, Mira from Rajasthan, Aruna Giri Natha from Tamil Nadu, Purandaradasa and other Dasakuta poets from Karnataka, Tallapaka Annamacharya, Bhadrachala Ramadasa, Tyagaraja, Kshetayya from Andhra Pradesh, Vidyapati and Shankara Deva from Mithila and Assam, Chandidas from Bengal — are just to mention a few names known throughout India.

Their songs are enthusiastically sung by the musicians, the lyrics are read by the common people, studied and analysed by scholars and chanted with great faith by the devotees. Hence, we can say that the contribution of these saints was like a "Triveni Sangam" where music and art, literature and culture are happily blended with bhakti or devotion.

A study of the life of these poet-saints reveals the fact that they came from different classes of society since the gates of the kingdom of bhakti were open to one and all. This in itself is a symbol of the unity of humankind.

All of them equally emphasised fundamental truth and eternal values. They revitalised the devotion and faith of the classes and masses. In coming together of cultures confrontation was not the only result, there was also a synthesis, which gave rise to poet-saints who bridged the gulf and spoke the same voice of integration.

With this general background of bhakti literature and bhakti movement I would now like to draw your attention to the Ashtachap poets of Hindi or, to be more specific, of braj bhasha and the Tallapaka poets of Telugu.

The four disciples of Vallabhacharya, that is, Surdas, Krishnadas, Paramanand Das and Kumbhan Das, along with four disciples of Vittalnath (son of Vallabhacharya), that is, Chaturbhujdas, Cheet Swamy, Nand Das and Govind Das were together called "Ashtachap" or the eight seals or dye stamps, because they were the eight acknowledged masters of the dialect in which Krishna bhakti poetry has been written. They were supposed to be the eight friends of Lord Krishna. They came from different places of North India, but settled in Vraj Pradesh, the birthplace of their beloved deity, and chose to write in the local dialect of Vraj. All of them were given *diksha* in *Suddhadvaita* or *Pushti Sampradaya*. Surdas is regarded as "Sur" or the sun not only of Krishna bhakti literature but also of the entire Hindi literature. It is widely accepted that he was blind by birth, left the house at an early age and came under the influence of Vallabhacharya. The latter showed him the eternal path of bhakti. After this Surdas spent the rest of his life in the temple, as a singer. He was not willing to leave Krishna even for a fraction of a second. His fame as a singer spread to far-off places. He always remained an introvert — so the subjective style of lyrics or *pada sahitya* was most suitable for him. He was greatly influenced by *Bhagavata Purana*. Some of his works are *Sursagar, Sur Saravali* and *Sahitya Lahari*, among which *Sursagar* is the most significant because in it his poetic art has reached its peak. Lord Krishna's life was depicted along with aspects like the incarnations of God Vishnu, divine worship, rituals and other aspects. In *Sursagar* the poet has depicted Krishna as one "who delights his mother in the garb of a son, his friends, the cowherds, in the garb of a comrade, the gopis and Radha in the garb of an aesthete. The whole Vraj is delighted with and blessed by the various relationships he had established and is wrenched in pain and insufferable agony when Krishna decided to leave the place. *Sursagar* is the epitome of the entire Vraj life" (J.R. Verma). *Sahitya Lahari* is a collection of Sur's verses remarkable for their emotional content and ornate expression. He could visualise Lord Krishna's mischief, his nobility of gesture towards the people of Vraj, his love and tender romance with Radha, his eternal *ras leela* with the gopis and his *jnana chaksus*. Sur is supposed to be the emperor of Vatsalya, Sringara. "*Bhavargeet prasang*" is the innovation of Surdas in *Sakhya Rasas Viraha*. Alongwith the story of Krishna, Surdas has systematically defined the *shuddhadvaita* aspects of *moksha, jeeva, brahma, maya,* etc. He was very grateful to his guru Vallabhacharya and says that— "If there was no moon called Vallabhacharya, the whole world might have been in the utmost darkness." At another place he feels that he cannot express his gratitude towards his teacher in a proper way and feels that the experience is like the dumb person enjoying the taste of jaggery.

The other Ashtachap poets also sang with great devotion to Lord Krishna. Nandadas holds a pride of place among the Ashtachap poets. He was an ardent worshipper of beauty which is reflected in his works. His works are *Bhasha Dasham Skanda, Raspanchadhyayi, Siddhant Panchadhyayi, Shyam Sagayi, Anekarthmanjari, Man Manjari, Virah Manjari* and *Bhavargeet*. *Bhramargeet Prasang* has been a favourite subject of Krishna bhakta poets. In this the poets have dealt with *saguna* and *nirguna* aspects of bhakti where the gopis represent the *saguna* and Uddhava, the scholar friend of Krishna, represents the *nirguna*. In Surdas's *Bhavargeet*, in addition to this discussion, an unending sorrow of the gopis is described where the heart of the reader melts with sympathy and they feel for the gopis — "*Nisi din barasat nain hamare"* — meaning that we have only rainy season in Vraj after the departure of Krishna. Verse after verse describes the same plight of the gopis but each with new similes. Nandadas did not concern himself so much with the heart-burning of the gopis. He took the gopis and Uddhav as great instruments in dealing with *saguna* and *nirguna* with the *tarka* where the brain plays a more vital role than the heart. In the end Uddhav, of course, bows himself before the gopis' tender love which indicates the victory of *saguna* over *nirguna*. Nandadas, unlike the other poets of Ashtachap group, was a scholar. Each verse of this poet depicts his skill as a poet and perfection as a scholar. A popular saying expresses this — *"Aur sab gadai, Nandadas jadia,"* meaning that other poets are mere smiths before Nandadas, the stone-setter. Not a single word is superfluous in his poetry and each word is so arranged as to embellish the other. Nandadas is a master of alliteration" (K.B. Jindal). His poetry is musical with a charm of variety. He gave birth to a polished style in bhakti cult.

Krishnadas hails from Gujarat and was made in-charge of the land and temple of Lord Krishna.

Paramananda Das hailed from Kannauj. He wrote *Paramananda Sagar*. His verses on *bal leela* of Krishna are next only to those of Surdas in their greatness. Whatever he wrote flowed from his heart. It is said that he was an artist and an art lover to. He loved music and poetry alike and had perfection in both. He was a true devotee and his humility was such that he was satisfied to call himself the servant of God's servants. He cannot imagine a life without the stories of Krishna, without chanting Krishna's name and without being devoted to Krishna. Without this the days drag meaninglessly. He is surprised at the fact that such people are alive.

Kumbhandas has not given any account of his life. It is said that he hails from Jamunavatho, a village near Govardhan. His miscellaneous poems are filled with devotion. Though he was not highly educated he was a good singer which gave him a place in the Ashtachap group. He was a true follower of *Suddhadvaita* and tried to follow the path with great concentration all his life. He looked after the maintenance of the temple, too. It is said that the emperor was so impressed by his poems that he invited him to his court and he refused saying — *"Santan ko Seekari so kya kaam"* — meaning that what would a holy man do in the capital. He would not use his muse except in the service of God.

Chaturbhuj Das, Cheet Swamy and Govind Swamy are also the authors of miscellaneous verses praising Lord Krishna. All these eight poets were great singers and each was in-charge of singing at different hours of the day and night. They believed strongly that *nadamarga* or music was capable of uniting the devotee with his supreme Lord.

The famous Tallapaka poets hail from the Tallapaka village of Rajampet Taluk in Cuddapah district of Andhra Pradesh. Tallapaka Annamacharya was the first poet in their family also known as the *padakavitapitamaha* of the Telugu language. It is widely accepted that he lived around A.D. 1425 and 1503. He was aware of the selfishness of people and disgusted with worldly relations left his home at an early age and went to Tirupati. He was an ardent devotee of the Lord of the Seven Hills, Lord Venkateswara. While climbing the hills verses came to him spontaneously which took him to the peak of spiritual experience. In Tirupati Acharya Ghanavishnu made Annamacharya his disciple and gave him *diksha* in Ramanuja's *Vishishtadvaita* or *Sree Sampradaya*. From his sixteenth year to the last day of his life, Annamacharya dedicated at least one verse every day to the Lord. He was the author of 32 thousand verses among which only 14 thousand are available. He felt that only one *pada* or *sankirtana* was enough for *moksha* or salvation. He was not only a profound scholar and a natural poet of rare distinction in both Telugu and Sanskrit but was also a great musician. All the *padas* were set to *ragas* and *talas*. He was also the author of *Sringara Manjari, Duripada Ramayana, Venkateswara Satakam, Venkatachala Mahatmya* and *Sankeerthana Lakshana*. He flatly refused to sing the praises of the king and was consequently arrested. The *Adhyatma Sankeertana* deals with philosophical aspects while the *Sringara Sankeertana* depicts the eternal love and romance of Lord Venkateswara and Alavelumanga. These are the examples of *madhura bhakti* in philosophical aspect where the Atman, the soul, is the *Nayika* and Paramatman is the *Nayaka*. Their union is *moksha* or salvation. The bhakti poets always connected themselves with the Atman which they felt was trying to unite with the Paramatman.

The greatness of the Tallapaka poets lies in the fact that generation after generation they gave birth to poet-saints and singer devotees. Annamacharya's wife Timmakka, the author of

Subhadra Kalyanamu, is regarded as the first lady poet of Telugu literature.

Annamacharya's eldest son, Tallapaka Peda Tirumalacharya, was a worthy son of his father. He also followed the footsteps of his father and continued to offer one *Sankeertana* a day to Lord Venkateswara. In addition to the *Adhyatma* and *Sringara Sankeertanalu*, Peda Tirumalacharya was also the author of *Suprabhata Sthvamu, Vairagyavachana, Malika Geethalu, Sringara Dandakamu, Chakravalamanjari, Sudarshana* and many more. He has the rare distinction of not only creating poetry in all the styles of Telugu language but also in Tamil. Thus he was the emperor of wide literary territory. There is another important factor worth mentioning: that is the pain he took to preserve this literature and spread Vaishnavism in far-off places. He made copper plates to preserve his songs in Tirupati and made copies of these to send to different places which had great Vaishnava shrines like Srirangam and Ahobilam. Even today the Tallapaka poets' shelf can be seen in front of the temple of Tirupati. Hundreds of acres of land, villages, cash and gold given to him by kings and people were in turn donated by him to the Lord. He regularised the worship of the Lord by introducing many innovations in *puja*. For all these occasions songs were written by him. Singers were appointed on salary basis to sing these songs. In the season of summer *Sankeertana Alaruppadu* was organised which means asking the Almighty to shower his grace and blessings on his devotees. The audience present there would be entertained with rose water and sandal paste.

Peda Tirumalacharya was a poet, singer scholar and great saint. Hence it is not surprising that his fame reached to far-off places and earned him many titles — Kavitharkika Kesari, Sharanagatha Vajrapanjara, Vedantacharya, Vedamarga Prathishtapanacharya, etc. He was always in search of new methods of expression and made literature and music an instrument to spread the Vaishnava cult. He enjoyed total affection of God, reverence of the king and respect of the people. But never did he bow to any king or any worldly pleasures. His pen and his voice were only for the praise of God.

China Tirumalacharya was the son of Peda Tirumalacharya and grandson of Annamacharya. He was also the author of *Adhyatma and Sringara Sankeertananlu, Ashtachasha Dandakamu,*

Sankeertana Lakshanamu. He defined the *sankeertana* in simple Telugu and made the rules and regulations available to the common reader from the original Sanskrit. Even today these guidelines are followed by students. He expressed his gratitude to his grandfather for showing the path to bhakti and enjoining on the family the benevolence of Lord Venkateswara. He regarded Annamacharya as his guru and felt that his grandfather was the incarnation of Hari himself. He installed the idols of Annamacharya along with Alwars, Bhashyakaras and Desikas. He travelled throughout the state to popularise Vaishnavism through their *sankeetanas*. He got the title of Ashta Bhasha Chakravarthy.

China Tiruvengalanatha is popularly known as Chinnanna to the Telugu people. He is often remembered in the context of Dwipada Chanda. He was such an ardent admirer of this Dwipada, that all his four works *Usha Kalyanamu, Ashtamahishi Kalynamu, Parama Yogi Vilasamu* and *Annamacharya Sankeertanalu* are written in Dwipada. It is a landmark in the history of Telugu literature and language but scholars were not in favour of this style. It was restricted to folklore. But it was Chinnanna who popularised this style among scholars in addition to giving in detail the theory of Dwipada. Among the works of Chinnanna, *Annamacharya Charitra* has historical significance. Since it is the biography by a grandson it is very authentic.

Annamacharya's great-grandson Tiru Vengalappa, was a scholar and poet, too. In addition to creative poetry Tiruvengalappa interpreted Sanskrit works like *Amaruka, Mammata Kavya Prakash* and *Ramachandropakhyanam*. These Sanskrit works were made available in the Telugu language to the people.

Thus the Tallapaka poets contributed to literature, music and poetry for nearly one and a half centuries. All of them took great interest in music, poetry, religion, temple festivals with zeal and enthusiasm.

After this study of the life and works of the Ashtachap and Tallapaka poets we come to the conclusion that whatever be the language, style or means of expression all of them were great devotees. They had certain common factors such as rejecting wealth offered to them, not having interest in worldly desires, never bowing before or praising any mortal soul to gain earthly pleasures, etc. All the aspects of bhakti are found in them. Their heart, minds and souls were fully devoted to God Himself. They did not even desire *moksha* or eternal salvation but prayed to the Almighty that they may be given an opportunity to serve the other devotees and called themselves their servants. They attached great importance to Vraj and Tirupati which for them was superior to Vaikuntha. These poets also sang about the rivers, ponds, lakes, mountains, hills, cattle, birds, trees and plants — that is to say, every inch of the place of their Lord.

This gave rise to a vast body of literature. They declared that bhakti is the only and the greatest aspect of life. To them it was a democratic doctrine which consolidates all people without distinction of caste, community, nationality or sex. For example, Sur says, "*Hari ka bhaje so Hari ka hoyee*", meaning that a person who worships Hari belongs to Him without any distinction of caste or creed.

Annamacharya also says that in this world there are no great or small people. All are equal because a Brahmin or an untouchable or a king has the same Hari in them. So who is greater? They have declared that the guru or the teacher is Hari Himself without whom they would not have known the eternal path. They hold the Lord's name as fundamental to their approach to salvation. Repeatedly they emphasise the unity of all paths. The writings of these poets are true examples of the Navadha bhakti — *smaran, sravan, sakhyam, dasyam, padasevanam, archana, atmanivedana, vandanam, keertanam*. They worshipped and related themselves to God as Dasa, Santha, Vatsa, Sakha and these give birth to various types of bhakti and *rasas*.

When we turn our attention towards the literary aspect of their works, we can mention their sustained metaphors, employment of popular images embodying their popular saying, wit and wisdom. Rhymes are used to facilitate memorising them. These poets in order to describe the beauty of their hero and heroines always searched for new similes. Language was like wax in their hands. They could mould it in every way they liked. Sri Puttaparthi Narayanacharyulu says that Annamacharya's language was like a *chakkera bomma* — a sugar toy, wherever you taste it, it is full of sweetness. This remark is apt for both the Hindi and Telugu poets. After a deep study of their language it is felt that all the *sastras* just bow themselves before these poets. Such was their command of the languages they used. Justice Ranade says, "It may be safely said that the growth of the modern vernaculars in India is solely the result of the labours of these saints." They chose the language and the poetry always nearest to the hearts and minds of the people. Aurobindo's general remark about poet-saints is applicable to the Ashtachap and Tallapaka poets, "In abundance, in poetic excellence, in the union of spontaneous beauty of motive and lyrical skill this poetry has no parallel in its own field in any other literature."

To conclude, we can say that these poet-saints had one ultimate end and that was bhakti for which they chose the medium of poetry and song. Temples were their base. Epics were their source. A beautiful combination of all these aspects gave rise to a great literature and music in all the Indian languages.

32

MIRABAI AND MAHADEVI VERMA

Moutushi Chakravartee

A connection between poetry and religion is as old as human civilisation. The incarnations and hymns uttered during ceremonies and rituals are in verse. Since there is no definitive record it is difficult to conclude that the writers of these verses were saints, although there is little doubt that they were poets. Saintliness is not only piety but a religious connotation is also instinct in it. In India, however, one has a long and sustained tradition of singer-saints; in fact, one of the four *Vedas* — the *Sama* — consists of songs. As the authorship of the *Vedas* is unknown, what can be said with some amount of certainty is that there is a philosophic-religious inspiration behind the writings.

The cut-off line between medieval time and modern period, according to the *Shorter Oxford Dictionary* is the fifteenth century. With the resurgence of humanism, man's position in the universe got a new meaning and significance not very distant from divinity as the Bengali poet, Chandidasa's couplet indicates:

> Above all other truths is man
> Beyond which there is none.

It also stresses man's stature in the scheme of things. Whether one reaches the ultimate consciousness, or realises the Self, or has a God-vision, it is the one and the same thing. Man's quest for the self has no fixed prescriptions. One may attain it by penance, another by renunciation, yet another by offering devotional and ritualistic prayers. Or, one may sing in praise of the Lord through lyrics and poems which may culminate in the realisation—all roads leading to Rome.

Devotional poetry in India has a long tradition irrespective of the beliefs and creeds. Saints, according to common belief, are supposed to be such people who have assiduously followed the path of truth in the face of myriad temptations with which life is beset. Moreover, sainthood is neither anybody's privilege nor anybody's birthright. An uneducated person of questionable birth like Kabir or the Baul singer like Lalan Fakir or a sophisticated person like Tagore are in more senses than one poet-saints for poetry and devotion are rolled into one unified consciousness in their *oeuvre*.

Since the decline of Sanskrit and the rise of vernaculars the Vedic songs were handed down to generations in the modern period. It is well-known how Tulsidas popularised Valmiki's *Ramayana* in Hindi. This influenced North and North-east India pervasively and still enthrals millions. The idea of incarnation is inherent in the bhakti cult (bhakti strictly speaking is untranslatable as it combines love, respect and devotion without a desire for any return in material terms). This desirelessness is a characteristic feature of the poetry of such poet-saints as Kabir, Mirabai, Tukaram, *et al*. Ram and Krishna are the two incarnations most commonly referred to in the poetry of Indian poet-saints. They provide the ideal concept of manhood and both of them are on the side of the eternal values of truth and goodness. Their struggle is against the hydra-headed material temptations symbolised by Ravana and a vile possessiveness and blind filial attachment symbolised by Duryodhana and Dhritarashtra respectively. The *Ramayana* and *Mahabharata* are the two fountainheads of almost all devotional poetry of the poet-saints. As poetry is primarily communication the poet must needs have a scaffolding of popular culture. The question of "difficulty" or "obscurity" is not a problem as love of the infinite finds a metaphoric representation in the finite. A rapport, therefore, is immediately established between the poet and the reader. Poet-saints offer prayer through their poems which are intelligible (as they ought to be) to the common people.

By definition, the, poet-saints are the ones who intend to speak of eternal values in a fast changing world. *Bhakti* is one of the nine *rasas* (humours according to the medievals) described in detail in Indian poetics. When Tulsidas re-wrote the *Ramayana* he turned Rama into an ideal and Hanuman into the very embodiment of bhakti. Hanuman is endowed with supernatural powers, yet he believes that all his powers emanate from his deep devotion to Rama; he can achieve anything just by chanting the name of Rama. Hanuman or Mahavira (as he is popularly called) is a metaphoric representation of the idea that faith can move mountains. The apparent dichotomy in Hanuman reaching Lanka in one leap and his Lord needing a bridge to be built on the same can be explained thus: Rama being an incarnation in the human form has to act as a human being (otherwise his wife, Sita could not have been kidnapped), whereas as the supreme Lord of the universe, He is capable of bestowing boons on His devotees. What actually distinguishes the modern trend from the old philosophic concept of divinity is the emphasis on fervent devotion (bhakti) to God. It is evident from the works of poet-saints that they know that "all charms fly at the touch of cold philosophy" (apologies to Keats), and so they take recourse to devotion. In fine, it is a sort of revolt against mere intellectualisation:

> The movement as a whole was a revolt against the cold intellectualism of Brahmanic philosophy and the lifeless formalism of mere ceremonial. (F.E. Keay, 1920:19)

If devotional poetry of modern times is a liberal force that liberalism has its roots in the notion of brotherhood of men. Now, poet-saints are not ascetics in the common sense of the term. Legend has it that Tulsidas turned to devotional poetry having been rebuked by his wife for sexuality. Even Mirabai was a married woman, although she had embraced Krishna as her husband in childhood. These acknowledged poet-saints were not ascetics, but their poetry records a sense of surrender not easily available among the serious poets. Mirabai's poetry reveals her love for Krishna as a spouse. As she had become in her real life a widow, such an open admiration for Krishna as a lover was anti-establishment, non-conformist and an anathema. But it is on record that she cared neither for criticism nor for persecution both of which she suffered ungrudgingly. Finally, she left the house of her in-laws never to return.

It is noteworthy that a complete surrender to God (whatever form is given to God by the devotee) is of paramount importance to the poet-saints, whether Tulsidas, Tukaram, Mirabai, or in our own time, Mahadevi Verma. This surrender is coupled with a passionate intensity that informs Donne's religious poems as well. In the latter, there is an argumentative, logical approach, whereas in Mirabai there is hardly any room for conscious intellection. Poetry, to Mirabai, was prayer as it is to most of the poet-saints not excluding the Baul singers of Bengal. Lalan Fakir, one of the famous Bauls, belonged to this tradition that influenced Tagore (*Gitanjali* in Tagore's translation is "song offering").

Mirabai's devotion is peculiarly amatory as a result of her personal feeling of nearness to Krishna. But at times the lover goes out of sight away from the beloved. So she expresses the pangs of separation in many of her poems but hope, not despair, is writ large in her poetry. Tragedy struck Mirabai quite early when she lost her mother, she became a widow within a very short period of her marriage, finally, the death of her father left her completely lonely in this wide and alien world. Further, her brother-in-law (husband's younger brother) began persecuting her after her husband's death. Surrounded by misfortunes and sorrow, she tried to find solace and comfort in her love for Krishna, whom she had been considering as her husband from a very young age even before her marriage. The desire for union with Krishna seems to be her only aim in life:

> Hari, I'm engulfed with sorrow and none appreciates my sorrow
> Everyone flocks in times of happiness and wealth, but none in times of adversity
> If the Lord of Mira, her lover, becomes the physician all her painful ailments will disappear.

This is devotional love at its best which finds expression in her poetry.

Because her poetry is heavily dependent on physical relationship, Mirabai's Krishna is not a myth nor an ideal concept, he is a three-dimensional God. Perhaps it will not be inapposite to suggest here that mysticism of the later religious poetry or, philosophic intellectualism of the Vedic and Upanishadic verses is not to be found in her songs (*bhajans*). But they are genuine song offerings. In actuality, she did not practise any ritual worship; perhaps, she was ignorant of them. Yet masochism, the innate feminine virtue (particularly of Indian womanhood), finds a telltale description in her poetry. She would suffer persecution and indignities, but that would not deter her from her chosen path of love for Krishna. In the face of opposition and severe criticisms, she would, and she did, cling to her faith.

Labelling in literary studies is fraught with inadvertent slips. Yet one may venture to add that the bhakti movement went into some sort of eclipse although religiousness never deserted Indian poets. Spirituality and/or mysticism appears to be peculiar to the Indian literary ethos. Even in recent times, we have such poets as Tagore and Mahadevi Verma, who are inheritors as well as exponents of the spiritual tradition of Indian poetry. However, being an inheritor of a particular tradition is not limited to one's individual talent. Neither Tulsidas nor Mirabai was a saint in the strict sense of the term as they were both worldly persons having married. But our concern here is with the intrinsic connotation of "saint" rather than with its peripheral attributes. A formal saint is supposed to renounce the world, not so the poet-saints. Tagore is quite forthright in one of his lyrics:

> Deliverance through renunciation is not for me...
> My infatuation will light up in emancipation
> My love will ripen into fervent devotion

Being deeply influenced by Kabir (he translated a large number of poems of Kabir into English), he incorporates religious mysticism in his poetry. Two different streams of Upanishadic intellectualism and fervent devotion merge in him. Thus, he has been rightly described as a poet-saint of modern India.

In her turn, Mahadevi Verma was influenced by Tagore. The streams of devotional (bhakti) poetry never went dry. Like the Phalgu, it ran as an undercurrent invisible to the naked eye. True, one does not find the single-minded devotion and submission of Mirabai's songs either in Tagore or Mahadevi, but they are not at variance with the tradition set by the early poet-saints. Without being fastidious about nomenclature, both Tagore and Mahadevi can be designated poet-saints. The latter tries to establish a relationship with her invisible lover in contradistinction to Mirabai's palpable Krishna. Confident of a bondage, Mahadevi asserts in one of her poems of *Jeevan Drishti* (Life's vision):

> When the relationship even of stars with
> Tender grass has been severed (Parikrama, 1980:40)

Metaphorically, a person's relationship with God is eternal, and whatever the circumstances, the tie is never broken. Mahadevi's poetry is not only a remembrance, but also a celebration of that relationship.

The nearness Mahadevi feels with God is reminiscent of Mirabai's although the former has never described Him as a palpable reality:

> What use worship and ritual?
> My tiniest life is a temple of that infinity
> My breath constantly sings in praise of my lover (p.39)

She, too, like Mirabai, considers God, the infinite as her lover. But there is a note of intellectualism also: the reflection of the macrocosm in the microcosm. It is a union of the differentiated with the undifferentiated. Further, the repetition of the lover's name works as the telling of beads in formal prayer. She prays (without naming, unlike Mirabai):

> Give me strength to efface myself wholly by effacing bit by bit (p.40)

What she says in one of her poems is perhaps a fitting description of her poetry:

> By sacrificing my diamond necklace, I've decorated my heart with drops of tears (p.44)

These tear-drops are small pieces of invaluable stone. She exhorts Buddha in this poem and at the same time remembers Krishna. The various incarnations are manifestations of the Supreme, the Infinite. In another poem she refers to the breaking of the mirror that used to reflect "I" and "You". The subject-object relationship has come to an end which is the highest point of realisation where all qualifications cease, where God and His devotee become one. It obviously points to the supreme realisation: "I am He".

It appears that the poet feels embalmed with a passionate sense of unification with the divine, otherwise her poetry would ring false. This passion results in the expression of an ecstasy rarely to be achieved in the present day. As Tagore sees God as his life's deity *(jeevandevata)*, and addresses Him as "My innermost one" and the whole poem is surcharged with an atmosphere of conjugal love and nuptial fulfilment, so Mahadevi also feels drawn towards her lover. Right from Mirabai to Mahadevi, poet-saints have actually tried to have a personal union with God expressed in terms of conjugal love—a love that is physical and yet is capable of transcending into a singular spiritual experience. In this context one easily remembers Donne's *Extasie*, where one notes the quality of transcendence of sensual love into a spiritual one.

The poet-saint finds an inexplicable cohesion and relationship between the finite and the infinite, between the differentiated and the undifferentiated, between emotion and intellect. Integrity, not divisiveness, is the unifying principle of the universe. Realisation of this integral force makes one a saint, and communicating that idea through poetry makes one a poet. Perhaps the fact of renunciation does not enunciate a saint, but even an emotional involvement and union with God in any form bestows saintliness on an individual. In her anthology *Parikrama*, Mahadevi rightly distinguishes between reality and truth:

> Truth and reality are essentially different.
> Reality is knowable through sense perception,
> but truth is beyond sense-knowledge, and it
> can be achieved only through man's super-consciousness (p.7)

What Sri Aurobindo calls "supra-mental", becomes super-consciousness in Mahadevi. She further clarifies that what the common people dismiss as "fancy" or "imagination" may be, in actuality, the perception and/or achievement of truth by the poet who by virtue of his intuition and intensity of passionate devotion reaches a point of consciousness not easily attainable by the average man. No wonder the poet represents the focal point of the civilisation in his time. Both her belief and her work are indicative of the possession of super-consciousness, which to my mind, qualifies her to be a poet-saint. The firm conviction that comes out in one of her poems illustrates her sense of oneness with God:

> I am one with you like light and its ray. (p.60)

That in both Mirabai and Mahadevi divinity is intelligible, graspable through human love is because love leads to happiness and God is Happiness (He has been called Ananda). And a human being is in constant quest of happiness. The sense of oneness with God and the profundity of love that their poetry shows corroborates Lawrence's statement: "Love is the happiness of the world" (1954:24). Hence, the eroticism noticeable in their poetry has to be understood in the light of a quest for sacred happiness in oneness with God. Let us listen to Lawrence again: "Sacred love is selfless, seeking not its own. The lover serves his beloved and seeks perfect communion of oneness with her" (ibid.:27).

This defines perfectly the poetic urge of the two women poet-saints only the root words "lover" and "beloved" need to be interchanged as Mirabai and Mahadevi are women, and then everything falls into place.

In their poetry, one finds a covert presence of the question of identity. They are seekers of truth with an innate faith in the scripture; saying "Seek, and ye shall find". Both Mirabai and Mahadevi fervently seek a union with their Lord. For, He is whole and perfect whereas a human being is partial and imperfect. It is, indeed, impossible to define the parameters of devotional love. Yet self-effacement, as noted above, distinguishes the devotional poems of Mirabai and Mahadevi. As a river effacing its old identity finds a new one at its mouth by becoming one with the sea so the fervent devotional love in the poetry of these two women poet-saints proves that they can establish their identity only after a union with God, by merging their individualities in the infinite. That is true identity where wholeness becomes holiness.

References

(All English renderings of poems are mine)

Keay, F.E. *A History of Hindi Literature*, Calcutta: The Heritage of India Series, 1920.

Lawrence, D.H. *Selected Essays*, Harmondsworth: Penguin Books, 1954.

Verma, Mahadevi. *Parikrama*, Allahabad: Sahitya Bhawan Private Limited, 1988.